Navigating Difficult Moments
in **Teaching Diversity** and **Social Justice**

Navigating Difficult Moments in Teaching Diversity and Social Justice

EDITED BY
Mary E. Kite | Kim A. Case | Wendy R. Williams

AMERICAN PSYCHOLOGICAL ASSOCIATION

Copyright © 2021 by the American Psychological Association. All rights reserved. Except as permitted under the United States Copyright Act of 1976, no part of this publication may be reproduced or distributed in any form or by any means, including, but not limited to, the process of scanning and digitization, or stored in a database or retrieval system, without the prior written permission of the publisher.

The opinions and statements published are the responsibility of the authors, and such opinions and statements do not necessarily represent the policies of the American Psychological Association.

Published by
American Psychological Association
750 First Street, NE
Washington, DC 20002
https://www.apa.org

Order Department
https://www.apa.org/pubs/books
order@apa.org

In the U.K., Europe, Africa, and the Middle East, copies may be ordered from Eurospan
https://www.eurospanbookstore.com/apa
info@eurospangroup.com

Typeset in Charter and Interstate by Circle Graphics, Inc., Reisterstown, MD

Printer: Gasch Printing, Odenton, MD
Cover Designer: Mercury Publishing Services, Inc., Rockville, MD

Library of Congress Cataloging-in-Publication Data

Names: Kite, Mary E., editor. | Case, Kim A., editor. | Williams, Wendy R., editor.
Title: Navigating difficult moments in teaching diversity and social justice / edited by Mary E. Kite, Kim A. Case, and Wendy R. Williams.
Description: Washington, DC : American Psychological Association, [2021] | Includes bibliographical references and index.
Identifiers: LCCN 2020014047 (print) | LCCN 2020014048 (ebook) | ISBN 9781433832932 (paperback) | ISBN 9781433833199 (ebook)
Subjects: LCSH: Multicultural education. | Culturally relevant pedagogy. | Social justice—Study and teaching.
Classification: LCC LC1099 .N38 2021 (print) | LCC LC1099 (ebook) | DDC 370.117—dc23
LC record available at https://lccn.loc.gov/2020014047
LC ebook record available at https://lccn.loc.gov/2020014048

https://doi.org/10.1037/0000216-000

Printed in the United States of America

10 9 8 7 6 5 4 3 2 1

Contents

About the Editors   *vii*
Contributors   *ix*
Preface—Faye J. Crosby   *xvii*
Acknowledgments   *xxi*

1. **Pedagogical Humility and Peer Mentoring for Social Justice Education**   3
   Kim A. Case, Mary E. Kite, and Wendy R. Williams

2. **Ground Rules for Discussing Diversity: Complex Considerations**   17
   Susan B. Goldstein

3. **Social Justice Burnout: Engaging in Self-Care While Doing Diversity Work**   31
   Asia Eaton and Leah R. Warner

4. **Mistakes Were Made by Me: Recovering When an Instructor's Error Affects Classroom Dynamics**   45
   Mary E. Kite, Samuel M. Colbert, and Scott M. Barrera

5. **When the Professor Experiences Stereotype Threat in the Classroom**   59
   Desdamona Rios, Kim A. Case, Salena M. Brody, and David P. Rivera

6. **Becoming a Target: Anonymous Threats While Teaching Diversity Courses or Working on Social Justice Issues**   75
   Lisa S. Wagner and J. J. Garrett-Walker

7. Inclusion–Exclusion: Balancing Viewpoint Diversity and
   Harmful Speech in the Multicultural Classroom   91
   Salena M. Brody and Darren R. Bernal

8. The Efficacy Paradox: Teaching About Structural Inequality
   While Keeping Students' Hope Alive   105
   Lisa M. Brown

9. Emotionally Charged News in the Classroom   119
   Ryan M. Pickering

10. Raising the Consciousness of Students Holding Ingroup
    Stereotypes   133
    Lisa M. Brown and Wendy R. Williams

11. White Privilege in the Classroom   151
    Leah R. Warner, Lisa S. Wagner, and Patrick R. Grzanka

12. Navigating Difficult Moments Outside the Classroom   165
    Wendy R. Williams and F. Tyler Sergent

13. Contemporary Issues in Terminology: Using Gender-Inclusive
    Language to Create Affirming Spaces   179
    Amanda J. Wyrick

14. Aging as an Element of Diversity: Best Practices for
    Challenging Classroom Conversations and Avoiding Ageism   195
    Lisa S. Wagner, Tana M. Luger, and Matthew Calamia

15. Outsiders Teaching Insiders: How Instructors From
    Privileged Groups Can Effectively Teach About Diversity   211
    Susan B. Goldstein

16. When Students Frame Prejudicial Speech as "Freedom of
    Speech": Classroom and Institutional Implications   223
    Leah R. Warner

17. Student Evaluations of Teaching: Can Teaching Social
    Justice Negatively Affect One's Career?   235
    Guy A. Boysen

18. Flotsam and Jetsam: Staying the Course While Navigating
    Difficult Moments in Teaching Diversity and Social Justice   247
    Wendy R. Williams, Mary E. Kite, and Kim A. Case

Index   255

About the Editors

Mary E. Kite, PhD, is a professor of social psychology at Ball State University. She received her BA, MS, and PhD from Purdue University. She has held a number of leadership roles for the Society for the Teaching of Psychology (American Psychological Association [APA] Division 2), including past-president. Her leadership in the Midwestern Psychological Association also includes serving as past-president. She holds Fellow status in APA Divisions 2, 8, 9, 35, and 44; the Association for Psychological Science; and the Midwestern Psychological Association. She maintains an active research program in the area of stereotyping and prejudice, including coauthoring *The Psychology of Prejudice and Discrimination* (3rd ed.) with Bernard Whitley, Jr.; Kite and Whitley also coauthored *Principles of Research in Behavioral Science* (4th ed.). Her recognitions include the Charles L. Brewer Award for Distinguished Teaching in Psychology from the American Psychological Foundation (2014) and a Presidential Citation from the Society for the Teaching of Psychology (2011). Her website (breakingprejudice.org) is devoted to social justice teaching and received the Multimedia Educational Resource for Learning and Online Teaching (MERLOT) Classic Award for Exemplary Online Learning Resources, Psychology (2019).

Kim A. Case, PhD, is the director of faculty success and a professor of gender, sexuality, and women's studies at Virginia Commonwealth University. As director, she develops and implements faculty mentoring programs, supports faculty career development and scholarship productivity, and oversees the

Center for Teaching and Learning Excellence. Her mixed-methods research examines ally behavior, interventions to increase understanding of intersectionality and privilege, prejudice reduction, and creation of inclusive workplace and education settings. She is the author of *Deconstructing Privilege: Teaching and Learning as Allies in the Classroom* (2013) and *Intersectional Pedagogy: Complicating Identity and Social Justice* (2017), both published by Routledge. The Society for the Psychological Study of Social Issues previously honored Dr. Case with the Outstanding Teaching and Mentoring Award and the Innovative Teaching Award. The Society for the Teaching of Psychology named her as the 2018 Robert S. Daniel Excellence in Teaching Awardee for her nationally recognized pedagogical advancements. Her scholarship, blog, and teaching resources are available online (https://www.drkimcase.com).

Wendy R. Williams, PhD, is a professor of psychology and women's studies at Berea College. She received her PhD in social psychology from the University of California, Santa Cruz, in 2005. She was previously an associate professor and director of women's studies at Marshall University. Her teaching and research interests focus on stigma and prejudice, specifically around issues of social class, including documenting the lived experiences of low-income and working-class Americans, as well as examining the personal and political consequences of how low-income people are perceived. She regularly teaches courses both in the core of the psychology major (e.g., Introduction to Psychology, Statistics, Research Methods, Social Psychology) and in her areas of research interest (e.g., Psychology of Women & Gender, Psychology of Poverty & Social Class), and she incorporates service-learning and other experiential learning pedagogies into her teaching. She has published 17 papers, including a book chapter on how experiential learning can raise awareness of social class privilege. In addition, she has won awards for her research, teaching, service, mentoring, and leadership.

Contributors

Scott M. Barrera, MA, is a doctoral candidate in counseling psychology at Ball State University. He has completed numerous teaching assistantships through his program, including teaching courses on human sexuality and interviewing skills. His research interests broadly focus on diversity and resilience with the integration of neuroscience methodologies. His previous research has focused on social ostracism and racial identity development among Latinx individuals. He served as a campus representative for the Society for the Psychological Study of Culture, Ethnicity and Race (APA Division 45).

Darren R. Bernal, PhD, is an assistant professor in the department of psychology at the University of North Carolina at Asheville. He is an early-career psychologist who earned his counseling psychology degree from the University of Miami in 2014. A recipient of four teaching awards, Dr. Bernal teaches courses focusing on sociocultural factors that affect psychological, sexual, and social functioning. He has taught at graduate and undergraduate levels in public and private universities, as well as internationally. As part of The Catalyst study-abroad program, he teaches courses on mindfulness, sexuality, and well-being. His research focuses on the measurement and role of socioeconomic status in mental health disparities, mindfulness and performance, and psychological well-being. He is the chair of the American Psychological Association's Committee on Socioeconomic Status and serves on the Psi Chi board as the Southeastern Region Vice President.

Guy A. Boysen, PhD, is a professor of psychology at McKendree University. He received his bachelor's degree from Saint John's University and his PhD from Iowa State University. His scholarship emphasizes the teaching of psychology, professional development of teachers, and stigma toward mental illness. He is the author of the book *Becoming a Psychology Professor: Your Guide to Landing the Right Academic Job* and coauthor of *An Evidence-Based Guide to College and University Teaching: Developing the Model Teacher.* Dr. Boysen's scholarship has led to consulting editor appointments for the journals *Teaching of Psychology* and *Scholarship of Teaching and Learning in Psychology.*

Salena M. Brody, PhD, is a senior lecturer in psychology at the University of Texas at Dallas. She earned her BA in psychology from Boston College in 1998 with a concentration in faith, peace, and justice studies, and her master's and doctoral degrees in social psychology from the University of California, Santa Cruz. Dr. Brody's research has investigated the mechanisms underlying attitude change in service-learning contexts; her collaborations also include several book chapters on intergroup contact and prejudice reduction. She is an active member of the Society for the Psychological Study of Social Issues (SPSSI; APA Division 9) and currently chairs the Teaching and Mentoring Committee. She is a past winner of the SPSSI Innovative Teaching Award and the Collin College Outstanding Professor of the Year award. She is active in her community as a diversity speaker and was recognized at the 2017 Women Leading in Diversity event at the University of Texas at Dallas for her efforts to advance multicultural education.

Lisa M. Brown, PhD, is a professor of psychology at Austin College. She did her undergraduate work at Harvard and Radcliffe Colleges and her graduate work at the University of Michigan. At Austin College, she currently serves as the dean of social sciences and is cochair of the President's Committee on Inclusion and Diversity. She is a social psychologist whose research focuses on identity, primarily ethnic identity. Her publications related to ethnic diversity and higher education include articles in *Personality and Social Psychology Bulletin* and the *Journal of Social Issues*, and the edited book *Gender Differences in Mathematics*. She teaches or coteaches a variety of courses related to human variation and stratification, including Health Psychology, Human Sexuality, Cultural Psychology, and Stigma and Prejudice. As a means of reaching the broader public, she did a TEDxAustinCollege talk on improving intergroup relations entitled "Who Gets the Benefit of the Doubt? And Who Shouldn't?"

Matthew Calamia, PhD, is an assistant professor of psychology at Louisiana State University and an adjunct assistant professor at the Institute for Dementia Research and Prevention at Pennington Biomedical Research Center. He is a licensed clinical neuropsychologist. His research focuses on improving the measures used in neuropsychological assessment and examining predictors of cognitive aging and associations between cognition and psychopathology. His teaching includes both undergraduate courses (e.g., Introduction to Psychology and Introduction to Research) and graduate-level courses in psychological assessment. He has more than 50 peer-reviewed publications and has coauthored a chapter on neuropsychological assessment for the textbook *Clinical Psychology: A Global Perspective*.

Samuel M. Colbert, MA, is a doctoral candidate in counseling psychology at Ball State University. Sam's teaching experience includes undergraduate courses in Human Sexuality, Multicultural Counseling, and Fundamentals of Counseling Skills. One of Sam's professional passions is presenting and facilitating difficult discussions advocating for marginalized communities. Prior to graduate school, he conducted 261 LGBTQ cultural competency trainings with varied audiences ranging from elementary school students to university faculty and staff. His recent LGBTQ cultural competency work includes presenting skill-building presentations and workshops at the American Psychological Association's national convention and the annual national Rehabilitation Psychology Conference. His clinical interests include couple's counseling and working with individuals from marginalized communities. Sam's research interests include exploring factors leading to the health and well-being of gender and sexual minority people possessing intersecting identities.

Asia Eaton, PhD, is an associate professor of psychology at Florida International University. As a feminist social psychologist, she explores how gender intersects with identities such as race, class, and sexual orientation to affect individuals' access to and experience with power in intimate partner relationships and in the workplace. Her scholarship has shed light on how gender influences power dynamics in heterosexual relationships, how gender and sexuality affect people's access to power in organizations, and factors that contribute to relationship well-being for racial and sexual minorities. Dr. Eaton is the recipient of the 2019 Emerging Leader Award from APA's Committee on Women in Psychology, the 2019 Outstanding Teaching and Mentoring Award from the Society for the Psychological Study of Social Issues

(SPSSI; APA Division 9), and the 2016 Michele Alexander Early Career Award from APA Division 9. She also serves as head of research for the Cyber Civil Rights Initiative, which is working to understand and end nonconsensual porn. Her self-care activities include attending peer support groups, jogging, and learning from and with her students.

J. J. Garrett-Walker, PhD, is an associate professor in the Department of Psychology at the University of San Francisco, where she teaches African American Psychology, Psychology of Sexuality, and Research Design. She earned her BA from the University of San Francisco and her PhD from The Graduate Center of City University of New York. Dr. Garrett-Walker examines multiple identities (racial, religious, and sexual) for Black LGBTQ+ emerging adults. Additionally, Dr. Garrett-Walker implemented a university-wide *Check Your Privilege Campaign* that sought to raise student, faculty, and staff awareness around social inequalities and privilege. She has become increasingly interested in the ways in which shared educational privilege impacts colorblind racial ideologies and privilege awareness. The campaign went viral on the internet and has been implemented at universities from Canada to New Zealand.

Susan B. Goldstein, PhD, is a professor of psychology at the University of Redlands, where she teaches psychology of prejudice and discrimination, cross-cultural psychology, and study abroad predeparture and reentry courses. She received her BA from Oberlin College and her PhD from the University of Hawaii, Manoa while a grantee of the East-West Center Institute of Culture and Communication. She is the author of *Cross-Cultural Explorations: Activities in Culture and Psychology* (3rd ed.; 2019) and has published on intercultural attitudes and training, social justice allies, stigma, and strategies for diversifying the psychology curriculum. Her most recent journal articles have focused on various aspects of study abroad, including predictors of immersion preferences, barriers to equitable participation, and national identity and stereotype threat. She developed the *Making Connections With Social Issues* website, which was supported by the APS Fund for Teaching and Public Understanding of Psychological Science.

Patrick R. Grzanka, PhD, is an associate professor of psychology and chair of the interdisciplinary program in women, gender, and sexuality at the University of Tennessee (UT). His research on complex inequalities at the nexus of race, gender, and sexualities has been funded by the National Science Foundation and published in a wide range of academic journals. He is the 2018 recipient of the Michele Alexander Early Career Award from the Society for the Psychological Study of Social Issues (SPSSI; APA Division 9). His book, *Intersectionality: Foundations and Frontiers* (Routledge, 2019), is now in its second edition, and his new book (under contract with Cambridge University Press) traces the social and legal implications of scientific debates about the etiology of sexuality orientation. He has published several articles and chapters on social justice-focused pedagogy and won multiple awards for his teaching and mentoring. At UT, he regularly teaches a social justice practicum, research design, psychology of gender, and introduction to women, gender, and sexuality studies.

Tana M. Luger, PhD, MPH, is a health psychologist and public health researcher with the Greater Los Angeles Veterans Affairs Healthcare System. Her work aims to improve health care delivery for special veteran populations, such as older adults and women, by leveraging health information technologies to provide more convenient and effective care. She has designed and taught courses about health psychology, health inequity, mental health, and health informatics as a visiting professor at the University of Illinois Urbana–Champaign and Pitzer College. She currently serves on the editorial board for the *Journal of Behavioral Medicine*.

Ryan M. Pickering, PhD, is an assistant professor of psychology at Allegheny College in Pennsylvania. His teaching and research interests include the psychology of prejudice, the psychology of social class, and social psychophysiology. He is currently the vice chair of the American Psychological Association's Committee on Socioeconomic Status and recently finished his term as cochair of the Society for the Psychological Study of Social Issues (SPSSI; APA Division 9) Early Career Scholars Committee. He also recently received an Honorable Mention for SPSSI's Innovative Teaching Award.

Desdamona Rios, PhD, is an associate professor of psychology and director of the Latinx and Latin American Studies program at the University of Houston-Clear Lake (UHCL). She holds a joint doctorate in psychology and women's studies from the University of Michigan and teaches courses on personality; social psychology; and psychology of gender, race, and sexuality. She has published on intersectionality in the academy, including pedagogical practices and faculty experiences. She is the recipient of national teaching awards from the American Psychological Association's Society for the Teaching of Psychology (Division 2), Society for the Psychological Study of Social Issues (SPSSI; Division 9), and the Association for Women in Psychology. She is also the recipient of UHCL's Hayes Diversity Award for her work with underrepresented groups in academia. She currently serves as consulting editor for *Psychology of Women Quarterly*, Secretary for the Texas Association for Chicanos in Higher Education's Gulf Coast Region, and as a council member for SPSSI.

David P. Rivera, PhD, is an associate professor of counselor education at Queens College, City University of New York (CUNY), where he is also the founding director of the CUNY LGBTQI Student Leadership Program. He holds degrees from Teachers College, Columbia University; Johns Hopkins University; and the University of Wyoming. His research focuses on issues impacting the well-being and marginalization of oppressed sociocultural groups, with a focus on microaggressions. His work has been published in top journals and his coedited book, *Microaggression Theory: Influence and Implications*, was released in 2019. Dr. Rivera holds leadership positions with the American Psychological Association, CLAGS: Center for LGBTQ Studies, The Steve Fund, and The Council for Opportunity in Education. He has received national honors from the American Psychological Association, the American College Counseling Association, and the American College Personnel Association.

F. Tyler Sergent, PhD, is a scholar–activist and associate professor of history and general studies at Berea College. He teaches courses in ancient and medieval history, especially the Viking Age and medievalism, as well as research and writing courses on religious extremism, race, class, gender, and Appalachia. His scholarly activism focuses on the current (mis)use of history by white supremacists and other extremist groups in North America and Europe plus rights and protections for DACA students in higher education. He coauthored the book chapter "Strengthening the Sanctuary: Institutional Policies to Support DACA Students" (2018). He won the MUOnline Teaching Award at Marshall University in 2009 and the Mortar Board Honor Society Faculty Appreciation Award at Berea College in 2016. His other research relates to 12th-century Cistercian history and thought, particularly William of Saint-Thierry. He is director-at-large and secretary of the Cistercian Publications board of directors.

Lisa S. Wagner, PhD, is an associate professor and chair of the Department of Psychology at University of San Francisco. She completed her BA in English language and literature at the University of Michigan, and her PhD in social and personality psychology at the University of Washington. Through a grant from the National Institute on Aging, her research has examined age-related stereotypes and older adults' experience of stereotype threat. Her recent research promotes intergenerational interactions between younger and older adults and examines effects of these interactions on attitudes toward both age groups. She teaches courses on social psychology, psychology of prejudice, social psychology of aging, adulthood and aging, and a unique intergenerational course, Generation to Generation, that enrolls traditional college-age students and retired older adults. Her publications include a coauthored book, *Aging and Diversity: An Active Learning Experience* (3rd ed.), examining how diversity affects the aging experience (Mehrotra & Wagner, 2018).

Leah R. Warner, PhD, is an associate professor of psychology at Ramapo College of New Jersey. Dr. Warner received her dual PhD in social psychology and women's studies from The Pennsylvania State University. Her interdisciplinary teaching addresses controversial social issues, working with students to address social inequality through constructive dialogue, social science methods, and activism. She received the 2019 Society for the Psychological Study of Social Issues Teaching Innovation Award for these efforts. Her scholarship concerns intersectionality, having written widely on the challenges and transformative potential of integrating intersectionality into psychological research. She also engages in the scholarship of pedagogy, which includes coreceiving an Association for Psychological Science Teaching Grant to develop a demonstration on gender inequity in the workplace. Finally, she has held numerous positions at her institution to promote diversity and inclusion, including Faculty Fellow for Equity and Diversity Programs. Her self-care activities include exercising, immersive theater, and drag.

Amanda J. Wyrick, PhD, is an associate professor of psychology at Berea College, where she focuses on teaching clinical applications of psychology. She received her PhD in counseling psychology from the University of Louisville. From a humanistic perspective, she believes in promoting academic environments and assignments that encourage student growth in scholarly and personal development. To further her focus on holistic student development, she is a campus Safe Zone trainer. In this role, she facilitates workshops and presentations on LGBTQ identity and gender-inclusive language, to promote welcoming and affirming classrooms and campus spaces for historically marginalized populations. At her previous institution, she also spearheaded the development of a campus common diversity read on sexuality. Her research interests include LGBTQ issues, faculty well-being, and factors that increase student emotional health and resilience. In addition, she was recently honored for her role as an outstanding mentor.

Preface

The sun shone brightly in Santa Cruz, California, when 12 feminists—all women—arrived at 312 Pelton Avenue, one hundred steps from Steamers' Lane, a favorite spot for surfers. The date was October 6, 2017. That night when the traffic noise abated, everyone in the group imagined that she could hear the waves of the Pacific Ocean.

This was the 87th meeting of a group known by the unlikely name of "Nag's Heart." The name had been proposed in 1995 by the scholar Louise Kidder to the enthusiastic applause of 12 other feminists gathered in Amherst, Massachusetts. The Amherst group was united in rebellion against the patriarchal undertones of workshops that occurred in Nags Head, North Carolina. Although the in-joke lost a little of its luster after everyone sobered up, the name stuck. The Amherst group applied the name retrospectively to all the meetings that had previously occurred and declared themselves the 15th Nag's Heart meeting.

At both the 87th and the 15th sessions, and at all the other sessions before and after, participants have been invited to come to a workshop on a given topic with a dilemma in mind. They have been assured that the group would work collectively, following prescribed procedures, to address everyone's dilemmas. And, as you can tell from the chapters in this wonderful compendium, everyone has taken seriously the instruction to address as forthrightly as possible and with as little defensiveness as possible a conundrum that has arisen in the attempt to teach topics related to social justice.

The focus on dilemmas arose originally as a way to flatten status differences. Rare is the academic gathering in which people share their challenges rather than crow about their accomplishments. Indeed, some critics claim that academia is awash with reminders of status and the not-so-subtle implication that the person who teaches at Princeton University is automatically smarter—better, really—than the person who teaches at Podunk U. Academia is all about grades. Awards proliferate.

Over the years, the Nag's Heart meetings have developed additional ways to attenuate status. Each participant, for instance, is granted the spotlight for exactly the same amount of time—usually 30 minutes. And all participants are in charge of how their 30-minute segments are to be used. Participants can speak for 29 minutes and allow 1 minute of group feedback or speak for 1 minute and allow 29 minutes of feedback from the group.

The end of each 30-minute segment is, furthermore, strictly enforced. Whether the most senior person or the most junior person is speaking, discussion ends when the timer rings. The existence of a "bucket time" at the end of two or three segments allows participants to adhere rather painlessly to the rule of abrupt endings. The facilitator can tell whomever is speaking that there will be a time to come back to the idea even if the speaker at that moment is someone much more eminent than the facilitator.

The emphasis on dilemmas is also consistent with two tenets that undergird much of feminism. First, you cannot solve problems until you acknowledge them. The problem that has no name is sure to persist. Once identified, solutions can be sought. Second, you cannot solve problems alone. Think of the #MeToo movement, and you immediately understand the power of these tenets. Read the chapters in this book, and you will remember their absolute necessity whenever we embark on a path toward social justice. In this collection, linked as it is to the peer-mentoring experiences of a Nag's Heart retreat, you will find peers to mentor you and help you through difficult moments that inevitably arise when we teach controversial topics. Here is feminist pedagogy at its best.

Through observing collective efforts at problem-solving around delineated topics, we have noticed an interesting phenomenon. People can be very insightful about solutions to the problems of others and yet quite blind to solutions to their own problems of a similar nature. Sometimes in the process of analyzing the problems of another, a Nag's Heart participant has an epiphany about how the self-same solution might also prove useful to their own very similar problems. As you read about the situations of others that are similar to your own, you too may experience some epiphanies. At a minimum, I hope you will feel less isolated in your struggles, just as the group did in October 2017.

The three editors of *Navigating Difficult Moments*, Mary E. Kite, Kim A. Case, and Wendy R. Williams, served as organizers and conveners of the Nag's Heart workshop that lasted from October 6 to October 8, 2017. Many, but not all, of the contributors to the present book attended the meeting. But all, as you can see, are willing to lay bare their own struggles in the hope of helping others. I had the privilege of welcoming the group of 12 feminists to Santa Cruz in October 2017. And now I have the privilege of offering this preface to the book that was a prime reason for the meeting and a great result of it. The gratitude that I feel for being part of the enterprise will, I believe, be shared by you as you benefit from the analyses and insights of the brave scholars who have contributed to this book.

—*Faye J. Crosby, PhD*
Distinguished Professor of Psychology
Gary D. Licker Memorial Chair of Cowell College

Acknowledgments

The journey to create this work grew from the generosity and feminist spirit of many people. The result is much more than a gathering of chapters—it is the collective voice of many strong, social justice advocates, some of whom contributed to the volume in written form and some of whom provided the emotional and/or financial support that made this edited book possible.

Because the Nag's Heart experience was instrumental in the genesis of our project, first and foremost we thank Faye J. Crosby, who envisioned a space where feminists could join together in their efforts to enhance equality and inclusion. From its inception, Faye enthusiastically endorsed our idea and, in October 2017, welcomed us into her home for our Nag's Heart retreat. The retreat itself was financially underwritten by generous donors, facilitating our authors' participation by covering all costs except their transportation. During our time in Santa Cruz, Veronica Hall assisted Faye in ensuring that all of our needs were met; this allowed us to focus on the exchange of ideas. In addition to the three volume editors, our Nag's Heart participants included Ella Ben Hagai, Salena M. Brody, Lisa M. Brown, Naomi Buyers-Hall, Asia Eaton, Susan B. Goldstein, Desdamona Rios, Lisa S. Wagner, and Leah R. Warner. Each brought her unique vision for our work together, and words cannot express how grateful we are for their willingness to share their successes and failures as advocates for social justice. All of our chapter authors benefitted in tangible and intangible ways from the Nag's Heart experience.

Through the publication process, a number of people have provided important input and encouragement. We are grateful to Chris Kelaher of APA

Books for recognizing the promise of our book and to Katherine Lenz for her able, encouraging, and thorough feedback during the review process. Our volume is much better due to her expertise. We also thank the production staff at APA Books for bringing our chapters into their final form. Three anonymous reviewers provided sage comments on each and every chapter. They also encouraged us to write a concluding chapter that both highlighted the strengths of our work and pointed to the gaps that we hope others step up to fill. We followed their advice, and a number of their insights are included in that chapter. Their kind but constructive feedback has made the combined volume stronger and was a needed boost to our morale.

Several authors received additional financial assistance during the writing process. Wendy R. Williams was supported by a Faculty Fellowship from the Appalachian College Association and by a Visiting Fellow position at St. Catherine's College of Oxford, England. Lisa M. Brown wrote her chapters while on sabbatical from Austin College, supported by that institution's Richardson Professional Development Fund. Funds from the Society for the Psychological Study of Social Issues supported the editors at a writing retreat, and this was instrumental in the writing of several chapters, including Chapter 1. During that retreat, Ann Johnson and Kent Case provided accommodations, meals, transportation, and care.

In addition to the feedback from other authors, the editors, and the reviewers, several chapters were enriched by the wisdom of expert colleagues. Emily A. Leskinen provided helpful feedback to all of the chapters Leah R. Warner authored or coauthored. The suggestions of our BDU faculty provided a road map for navigating many of the difficult, but critically important, chapters in this volume.

We close by thanking the students who have joined us and all of our chapter authors in our diversity and social justice courses. We suspect that few students realize how much we learn from them and how very much their words of encouragement mean to us as we navigate difficult moments in social justice and diversity teaching. Some of those teachable moments formed the basis of our chapters, others remain to be shared, and still others remain in our hearts and minds. All have made us better teachers, and we hope our shared experiences make you, our readers, more effective teachers as well.

—Mary E. Kite, PhD
—Kim A. Case, PhD
—Wendy R. Williams, PhD

Navigating Difficult Moments in **Teaching Diversity** and **Social Justice**

1   PEDAGOGICAL HUMILITY AND PEER MENTORING FOR SOCIAL JUSTICE EDUCATION

KIM A. CASE, MARY E. KITE, AND WENDY R. WILLIAMS

- "During a guest panel of lesbian and transwomen speaking about their lived experiences, a White woman student raised her hand to ask a question, or so I thought. She proceeded to open her Bible and read Leviticus out loud, condemning the panel to hell."
- "As the social psychology class discussed the differences between prejudice and stereotypes, a White man yelled out across the room that 'All Iraqis are terrorists!'"
- "A student climate-change denier flipped out and flipped me off and told me I was preachy and said 'f**k you' maybe 30 times."
- "After watching the film *Selma* in class, a student critiqued the show for being biased because it did not give equal time to the arguments of the White supremacist counter-protesters."
- "My student asserted that people living in poverty should be 'packed up on a bus and sent back across the border where they came from.'"

---

https://doi.org/10.1037/0000216-001
Navigating Difficult Moments in Teaching Diversity and Social Justice, M. E. Kite, K. A. Case, and W. R. Williams (Editors)
Copyright © 2021 by the American Psychological Association. All rights reserved.

- "After watching a video on consent, I shared a recent news story about a college student who was raped. She had been drinking with a guy, let him sleep in her dorm room, and woke up to him performing sex acts. A male student insinuated it was her fault and likened it to being robbed while walking down the street counting your money out loud."

When we asked a broad range of educators for personal examples from their classrooms of "difficult moments" in teaching diversity, they quickly and easily came up with the quotes above (and many more). Yet, answers for how they handled these moments were offered more slowly and with large doses of humility. After many combined years of teaching social justice courses ourselves, we were not surprised by this. Despite the regular occurrence of such events, faculty teaching diversity and social justice topics often struggle with the question of how to handle these moments pedagogically. We search for answers in scattered journal articles, in random chapters buried in feminist teacher anthologies, or from trusted colleagues—if we are lucky enough to have them. More recently, we turn to online forums, social media collectives, and even anonymous posts within closed groups for advice and support. Despite these desperately needed and much appreciated resources, finding sufficient support quickly and efficiently when these difficult moments occur presents a problem. Rarely do we have time to conduct an extensive review of the literature, confer with a long list of online groups, or even consult a trusted colleague before the next class meeting.

This collection aims to provide a prepared and directly relevant source for some of the most common and challenging dilemmas faced by educators teaching social justice. Some address the "in the moment" events that happen in our classrooms, such as those examples at the beginning of this chapter. Others focus on things we can do to better prepare our students prior to the occurrence of difficult moments, to structure classrooms to prevent them from happening in the first place, or to help instructors regain balance after they have occurred. Our authors also address our roles as teachers inside and outside the classroom. Contributors address topics such as handling personal threats, responsibly incorporating current social justice events, navigating our own stigmatized identities, dealing with bias in teaching evaluations, the need for self-care, and more.

The idea for the book was initially sparked from reading a casebook about how to handle ethical dilemmas in the classroom (Keith-Spiegel et al., 2002). Those authors identified a set of ethical issues from their own and others' experiences and collaborated to offer their best, reasoned advice about how faculty should respond if they faced similar situations. It seemed to me (Mary) that instructors who teach about diversity and social justice related courses would likewise benefit from such a resource. I pitched this idea to Kim and

Wendy and, happily, they agreed to join me on this journey. The resulting collaboration has been restorative for all of us and, thanks to our authors, the result has far exceeded our expectations. Their collective wisdom has resulted in this volume before you. We could not be more grateful for this opportunity.

We (the three editors) determined that the way to build the foundation for this book was to first provide a venue for discussion of the challenges faculty face when teaching about social justice. Thus we began by seeking a way to make our community support model a reality. I (Mary) had attended three Nag's Heart retreats (see Preface, this volume for herstory of Nag's Heart; see also Stockdale et al., 2017) but had never led one. We (Kim & Wendy) were familiar with the format but had not yet attended one. I (Mary) approached Faye Crosby and was delighted when she agreed to accept our proposed retreat. In the Nag's Heart tradition, we aimed to create a trusting, safe space that was, at the same time, unabashedly brave. Trust, courage, and humility are essential when a community shares physical, psychological, and emotional space, as we and our participants would over the course of the retreat. With this goal in mind, and with Faye's guidance, we embarked on our next step: identifying teacher–scholars who could join us for a weekend in the Fall of 2017 at Faye's home in Santa Cruz. We came together to discuss the challenges we knew most, if not all, social justice educators faced.

Because these moments occur in different institutional contexts and student populations, we sought faculty from diverse institutions. Our faculty came from public and private colleges and universities with differing missions, including community colleges, small liberal arts colleges, Master's comprehensive universities, and doctoral research-intensive schools. In addition, these schools included historically Black colleges and universities, Hispanic-serving institutions, and low-income serving schools. Knowing that these moments have different impact depending on career stage, we also sought scholars who represented early, middle, and late career. Finally, our selective process also attended to diversity in terms of intersectional social locations of participants, especially given our (Mary, Wendy, and Kim) homogenous and privileged identities as White, heterosexual, cisgender, able-bodied, U.S. citizen women. Ultimately, we selected nine teacher–scholars with interests and expertise in teaching social justice to join us in person to explore these topics together. Although our authors teach in colleges and universities and based their chapters on experiences in those settings, we firmly believe that the issues they address are relevant to teachers in K–12 institutions and that they, too, will find sage advice in this volume.

As this was my (Kim's) first Nag's Heart retreat, I did not know what to expect. I (Wendy) was a graduate student at UC Santa Cruz when Faye hosted other Nag's Heart retreats, so I knew a little about them through second-hand stories. Participating for the first time as a senior faculty member, in a setting (Faye's Santa Cruz home) that was familiar and beloved, filled me with excitement and trepidation. I (Mary) knew from experience that each Nag's Heart has its own personality and that our retreat's trajectory would depend on our leadership and our participants' willingness to share our vision.

Within moments of arriving, each of us felt the feminist spirit soaring through the house and touching us all. It was immediately clear that the 12 women who attended to discuss difficult dilemmas in teaching social justice brought their full selves. Combined with the care, planning, nourishment, and sharing of brave space, the weekend was a magical and transformational delight. In brave spaces, participants commit to openness, honesty, the courage to learn, and the willingness to be uncomfortable for the sake of learning and supporting others. Collectively, we witnessed interventions to implement self-care, understanding, and compassion. Innovative ideas bounced around the room and deep mentoring relationships formed. Being in the house under one roof, our group members had time not only to process deep and challenging subjects but also to relax while elaborating on ideas and connecting with each other. At our Nag's Heart, there was a collaborative spirit that was absent of academic competitiveness. Breaking bread, sharing rooms and bathrooms, and having coffee (or wine) in our pajamas, we found that the close-knit physical space facilitated openness in a way that a meeting at a hotel or conference center never could.

As the retreat came to a close, participants spoke to the power of peer mentoring in their teaching, roles as mentors, and broader career development. After the weekend, we received overwhelmingly positive feedback speaking to the transformative power of peer mentoring:

- "It truly was a gift to be mentored by such a dynamic group consisting not only of advocates for social justice, but also of people truly passionate about teaching. It was a treat to be among people with such pedagogical creativity and wisdom."—Lisa Brown

- "In an era in which academia has become an increasingly competitive and at times combative environment, our peer mentoring retreat was a creative and effective model for collaborative and productive scholarship." —Susan Goldstein

- "While perhaps unintended, the retreat opened my eyes to possibilities for my teaching, mentoring, and scholarship as an advanced academic, a matriarch. I now have multiple examples of elders I want to emulate, and a vision for my own lifetime contribution to social justice and feminist psychology."—Asia Eaton

Our retreat focused on the difficult dilemmas faculty encounter when teaching social justice topics and courses. Rather than rely on the three editors to identify dilemma topics, prior to arrival we crowd-sourced ideas for the most pressing, common, or traumatizing dilemmas from our scholar-teachers. Most of the chapters in this volume represent the social justice teaching dilemmas that the group shared and analyzed during our weekend retreat. Unfortunately, because of other commitments, not all attendees were able to contribute to this volume. Nevertheless, we are grateful for those participants' sage advice and warm support, which facilitated the thinking of the other chapter authors. The chapter ideas from attendees were then enhanced and expanded on by additional authors who, after the retreat, joined one of our original collaborators as chapter coauthors or wrote their own chapter on a critically important issue. Thus, we were able to go beyond the topics covered at the retreat and provide a more robust coverage of the most typical scenarios we face in our classrooms and on campuses. We are grateful to these additional authors who shared our vision and who adopted the values of the Nag's Heart peer mentoring model as they wrote their chapters. Our original book idea led to the mentoring retreat and also to transformative peer-mentoring with these additional co-authors who shared the philosophy and practice of Nag's Heart to shape their chapters. Our overarching goal was to break pedagogical isolation, model pedagogical humility, and provide peer mentoring to readers.

PEDAGOGICAL ISOLATION

Regardless of discipline or courses taught, the strongest message we receive from social justice educators revolves around pedagogical isolation. We (Kim, Mary, and Wendy) all have experienced this isolation first hand while teaching about diversity and social justice and the controversial topics that are addressed in those courses, including privilege awareness, implicit and explicit bias, and the system-level factors that support the status quo. We have witnessed our peers, mentors, and junior colleagues struggling with contentious classroom discussions, student resistance, and others' discounting the importance of teaching these topics. We also know that quality advice on pedagogical best practices for these challenges is difficult to find.

All too often, our colleagues who believe in the importance of diversity education are the sole instructor in their department or college charged with infusing social justice and diversity content into the curriculum. Accompanying this isolation are worries about the consequences these instructional challenges might have on their career success. For example, when problems arise, faculty may believe they will be judged as inadequate or ineffective teachers, particularly by their colleagues who do not face these difficult dilemmas. Our colleagues may also wonder about the impact of teaching about social justice on their student evaluations, particularly if others fail to understand the unique challenges of teaching about controversial issues (see Dunn et al., 2013). Our colleagues may be further uncertain about whom to ask for help and may find little institutional recognition or support for their work; if this support does exist, they may not know how to access it. This isolation can occur at all faculty ranks but can be particularly difficult for junior faculty who feel too vulnerable to share pedagogical difficulties, especially with those who might later serve on their tenure and promotion committees.

This common and persistent pedagogical isolation may lead to or exacerbate anxiety, imposter syndrome, burnout, frustration, and feeling overwhelmed and demoralized (Ahluwalia et al., 2019). Left without peer support, this isolation may even reduce confidence in their teaching abilities and motivation to teach about these challenging or taboo social issues. We know from our own responses to pedagogical isolation that educators may withdraw from teaching diversity and inclusion by altering the curriculum or stepping away from courses altogether to avoid the difficult dilemmas that often arise. Yet, as our chapter authors attest, diversity educators are not alone. We can, and do, support one another. One goal of this book is to provide this support through our authors' frank and open-hearted discussion of their experiences.

PEDAGOGICAL HUMILITY

Identifying possible avenues for responding effectively to difficult moments in the classroom or on campus requires openness to learning from others and *pedagogical humility*. This term, introduced by Kim Case at the 2018 Annual Conference on Teaching, refers to our obligation to prioritize critical self-reflection and analysis of our own shortcomings and to explicitly acknowledge that we often do not automatically know the best next steps for minimizing harm while maximizing student learning. The most shocking and jarring moments with students or with faculty and staff colleagues offer opportunities to step back and consider what we do not know. Without pedagogical humility, faculty may stay stuck in a range of initial emotions such as outrage, defensiveness, frustration, stereotype threat, hurt, or self-righteousness. Pedagogical humility means assuming we have much to learn about student-centered design and allows us to stay open to the possibility that students might also teach us, that there is value in consistently seeking constructive feedback from students and peers, and that increasing our self-awareness and self-reflection is an ongoing process.

Our challenge as educators is to resist systemic patterns of pedagogical isolation through strengthening our pedagogical humility. In particular, teaching about diversity, inclusion, institutional privilege and oppression, and the many other social justice issues of our times increases our vulnerability within the academy. Through pedagogical humility, faculty can release the expectation that they should magically know the perfect educational path. We can let go of unreasonable self-judgment or internal narratives that tell us we would not encounter difficult moments if only we were better teachers. Pedagogical humility opens the door to break down the isolation and usher in validation, brave spaces, unconditional support, innovation, and creativity. The importance of modeling this approach at the retreat was illustrated by the reflections of our Nag's Heart participants.

- "To promote social justice, we have to take risks in the classroom and try new things. And with risks comes the potential for mistakes or failure. It is so hard to admit that I've failed in the classroom, let alone failed on something so important as addressing prejudice and privilege. Learning from others' experiences helps me lessen the chance of failure and connects me with others who are doing this work."—Lisa Wagner

- "The women generously shared their own stories of feeling isolated, unappreciated, and in some cases, afraid."—Desdamona Rios

- "The retreat introduced me to an amazing group of scholars who were willing to share their experience and wisdom. I appreciated the candid feedback on my own dilemma and the opportunity to think about how my own positionality impacted my teaching style and my reaction to a difficult student."—Salena Brody

- "The retreat was highly impactful for me in terms of my pedagogical approach to social justice. I gained tools to implement in my classroom, but perhaps more profoundly, I felt challenged to address many aspects of myself, such as my privileges and my burnout."—Leah Warner

As Lisa, Desdamona, Salena, and Leah demonstrated, pedagogical humility requires us to open up and share, with the utmost honesty, our missteps, teaching failures, and fears. Mentors and those seeking mentoring must commit to pedagogical humility and be willing to bring emotional vulnerability to this process. As Salena and Leah noted, receiving candid feedback and feeling challenged made an impact on their teaching because they were humble and vulnerable enough to accept constructive criticism coming from a place of unconditional support.

PEER MENTORING IN BOOK FORM

The American Psychological Association's (2013) *Guidelines for the Undergraduate Major in Psychology* identified sociocultural awareness as a major learning goal. This goal focuses on achieving balance between addressing negative motives and situations (e.g., conflict, oppression) and responding to and resolving these issues (e.g., understanding multiple perspectives, appreciation of diversity). To achieve this balance, the guidelines point to the importance of acknowledging that effectively incorporating diversity remains an unmet goal while, at the same time, recognizing positive outcomes that come from promoting diversity.

As editors of this volume, we champion the importance of reaching this goal for each undergraduate psychology major and each psychology graduate student. Faculty in other disciplines, such as sociology, anthropology, social work, ethnic studies, and women's and gender studies, also strive to meet this goal as do teachers in K–12 classrooms. This book serves as a resource for instructors who, like us, have undertaken this journey. As instructors of diversity courses or core courses with social justice approaches, we know first-hand just how challenging this work can be. We know from experience that instructors of diversity and social justice face unique challenges. As mentioned at the beginning of this chapter, students' comments and reactions can sometimes be shocking even to the most experienced instructors. Moreover, the topics covered in these courses often challenge students' worldviews and raise emotional issues that instructors find difficult and draining to address. Faculty must balance the perspectives of privileged students, who differ in their levels of multicultural competence, with the lived experiences of members of underrepresented and marginalized groups. Issues can arise in the classroom that leave faculty unsure of how to proceed or how to maximize students' learning opportunities (see Kite & Littleford, 2015).

The gift of peer mentoring provides the golden opportunity to thrive as educators. When teaching about emotionally and politically charged topics such as racism, privilege, welfare, immigration, transgender rights, or toxic masculinity, trusted peer mentors make a world of difference. Establishing a group of peer mentors, whether within one's own institution or spread across national and international networks, may reduce feelings of isolation and help normalize experiences with microaggressions and seemingly impossible situations in the classroom and beyond. In other words, peer mentors can help correct the gaslighting (Roberts & Carter Andrews, 2013), imposter syndrome (Hutchins & Rainbolt, 2016), and self-doubt that often parallel teaching social justice.

Our book provides a peer mentoring resource that addresses the complexities of teaching diversity and social justice. Our contributors are a vibrant group of feminist and intersectionality scholars who have the experience and expertise to address the pedagogical dilemmas that arise in teaching controversial and taboo topics. Our book comes from a feminist, social constructionist perspective, which is consistent with our reading of the literature on effective strategies for teaching social justice. The dilemmas covered align with extensive research on quality teaching in general and teaching about diversity specifically (e.g., Prieto, 2009; Warner et al., 2013).

The dilemmas we identify come from the authors' own experiences. With the goals of dismantling pedagogical isolation, modeling pedagogical humility, and serving others through peer mentoring, we pushed authors to write from the personal. In stark contrast to our/their positivist training as social scientists, we empowered them to write in the first person from a place of pedagogical humility. We found authors were challenged by the idea of writing about personal experiences and using "I" to discuss what they sometimes viewed as professional failures in the classroom. They tended to write in third person, include lengthy literature reviews, and remove themselves from the dilemmas. In contrast, we advocated for writing in a way that pushed back against our own training to be absent, invisible, "objective," and distant scholars. Knowing that they are all eminent scholar-teachers, we encouraged them, and ourselves, to fight the urge to fade into the background as authors. To encourage pedagogical humility and make room for sharing the personal, we also specifically asked authors to limit research citations. As a result, citations within chapters are intended as starting-points for those curious about the literature or wanting further research-based support for content, rather than as full expositions of the science. As authors, we (Kim, Mary, and Wendy) found the tendency to overcite the literature sometimes crept into our writing, perhaps as a result of feeling more vulnerable. The need to be perceived as legitimate scholars seemed heightened the more we pushed ourselves to express the personal within our own chapters.

DIFFICULT DILEMMA RESOURCES: CHAPTER STRUCTURE

To streamline ease of use and quick access to resources when these difficult dilemmas arise, we designed chapters to follow the same main structure throughout the collection. This consistent chapter structure begins with the dilemma to be addressed. Included dilemmas cover not only pedagogical questions and moments in the classroom context, but also broader challenges associated with our campuses, our colleagues, and institutional barriers. This consistent chapter structure allowed us to maximize peer mentoring: Each chapter reflects the results of peer mentoring among the editors and authors, but also serves as an opportunity for peer mentoring from the chapter authors to the reader. The chapter structure is as follows:

- Summary of Dilemma
- Faculty Reflection
- Considerations of Context and Intersectionality
- Best Practices
- Structural Implications (if relevant)
- Resources
- Chapter References

For example, a chapter tackling the issue of student resistance to learning about transgender perspectives would begin with a description of a classroom interaction. The chapter author(s) would then offer reflections on the approach they took in the moment and potentially what they would have done differently in retrospect. Within Considerations of Context and Intersectionality, contributors offered suggestions for addressing dilemmas across courses, disciplines, career stages, institution types, and more. With respect to intersectional praxis and pedagogy (Case, 2017), chapters may also address the potential ways that instructor social location might affect the teaching dilemma. How does the identity of a White woman teaching about Black Lives Matter influence White students' learning? Does a Latina faculty member face particular stereotype threat challenges with White and African American students who question her expertise?

Although we believe there are clear advantages of using this consistent book structure and a position of pedagogical humility, we also acknowledge that it sometimes resulted in more editorial suggestions than authors typically encounter when writing book chapters about their areas of expertise. In addition, our authors trusted us that sharing their missteps would not diminish them, but rather be enlightening for others. We are forever grateful to our authors for their patience with this process and hope they (and you) agree that the result is a strong, user-friendly resource that upholds the sharing of missteps as a strength, not a weakness.

MAXIMIZING THE IMPACT: HOW TO USE THIS BOOK

For educators like ourselves, this book offers the peer mentoring stories, reflections, guidance, and resources to immediately address difficult moments in the classroom and beyond. A student may express anger at their instructor for challenging stereotypes about undocumented immigrants, or a student may push back on our use of inclusive terminology or may claim we are threatening their "right" to free speech. We aim for this collection to serve as a go-to guide in these moments that cause confusion, frustration, and even deep emotional and psychological pain for educators. By going directly to the one or two chapters that reflect the difficult dilemma at hand, educators can use the authors' reflection, best practices advice, and contextual considerations to reflect on their own experiences and possible next steps. If needed, the resources section could be used to pursue additional support. The chapters also offer strategies for creating classroom environments that can reduce the possibility that these painful moments arise.

USE BY ADMINISTRATORS

Department chairs, deans, and faculty development directors may also use the book to become more effective mentors of faculty teaching diversity and social justice courses. Our lived experiences and the stories we gather from colleagues consistently illustrate the lack of support faculty receive from administrators who evaluate them for merit review and promotion and tenure. Administrators sometimes assume that difficult dilemmas arise because of deficits within the educator (e.g., incompetence, attitude). We urge them to instead refer to these chapter dilemmas as a means for supporting faculty who willingly take on these intensely challenging topics. Faculty development leaders may consider providing copies of this collection to incoming faculty who will be teaching courses that address diversity topics or use social justice pedagogical approaches. In addition, administrators must pay significant attention to how these dilemmas impact underrepresented faculty. Although any faculty member teaching diversity and social justice may face these difficult moments, marginalized and underrepresented faculty often experience increased frequency and intensity of incidents (Gutiérrez y Muhs et al., 2012; Plaut et al., 2014; Rockquemore & Laszloffy, 2008). Acknowledgment and validation of this reality for marginalized faculty, along with offering this peer mentoring guidebook, could signal a more developed and institutionalized culture of administrative support.

COMMUNITY BUILDING FOR THE FUTURE OF SOCIAL JUSTICE EDUCATION

The original and persistent goal of the Nag's Heart peer mentoring model is to build feminist communities that grow well beyond the time-limited weekend retreat. In fact, Nag's Heart participants report lasting connections, friendships, and support systems that sustain them throughout their careers. We detailed the genesis of this book in the Nag's Heart model because it is formative to understanding how the book came together and how we hope our readers will use it. Through the creation of this book, we formed a feminist academic community of support that is steadfast and long-term, and we were able to extend this community to authors of this volume who could not attend the retreat. With all of our authors, we continue to share resources, celebrate each other's accomplishments, check in on each other, engage in peer mentoring, call when we need to vent, copresent on this work at conferences, attend each other's talks in support, and host each other in our homes when travelling to conferences.

Likewise, we view this book as a source of peer mentoring that supports community-building across the discipline of psychology. We know from our own personal experiences that teaching diversity and social justice leave faculty feeling drained, uncertain, isolated, invalidated, targeted, frustrated, and much more. We most often struggle with these dilemmas in isolation and avoid turning to colleagues for fear of being blamed for the dilemma or labeled as incompetent. Educators may know of no other institutional colleagues teaching these topics, but yet they need a confidential resource to turn to for guidance. Access to the dilemmas described here, along with careful reflection on possible pedagogical strategies and avenues for support could drastically alter faculty experiences when these situations arise.

In the spirit of pedagogical humility and continuous growth, we present this volume as an invitation to a conversation. We view this as the beginning of a dialogue that we hope to see extended across psychology and additional disciplines with faculty teaching diversity and social justice. To be clear, we did not cover all or even most of the difficult dilemmas, but hope this resource reduces pedagogical isolation, promotes pedagogical humility, and provides a source of peer mentoring. We hope that the readers we have not met will reach out to any of the chapter authors either in person or in cyberspace and that they too will extend their expertise and feminist spirit to likeminded colleagues and friends.

REFERENCES

Ahluwalia, M. K., Ayala, S. I., Locke, A. F., & Nadrich, T. (2019). Mitigating the "powder keg": The experiences of faculty of color teaching multicultural competence. *Teaching of Psychology, 46*(3), 187–196. https://doi.org/10.1177/0098628319848864

American Psychological Association. (2013). *APA guidelines for the undergraduate psychology major: Version 2.0.* Author. https://www.apa.org/ed/precollege/about/psymajor-guidelines.pdf

Case, K. (Ed.). (2017). *Intersectional pedagogy: Complicating identity and social justice.* Routledge.

Dunn, D. S., Gurung, R. A. R., Naufel, K. Z., & Wilson, J. H. (Eds.). (2013). *Controversy in the psychology classroom: Using hot topics to foster critical thinking*. American Psychological Association. https://doi.org/10.1037/14038-000

Gutiérrez y Muhs, G., Niemann, Y., González, C. G., & Harris, A. P. (Eds.). (2012). *Presumed incompetent: The intersections of race and class for women in academia*. University of Colorado Press.

Hutchins, H. M., & Rainbolt, H. (2016). What triggers imposter syndrome among academic faculty? A critical incident study exploring antecedents, coping, and development opportunities. *Human Resource Development International, 20*(3), 191–214.

Keith-Spiegel, P., Whitley, B. E., Jr., Balogh, D. W., Perkins, D. V., & Wittig, A. (2002). *The ethics of teaching: A casebook* (2nd ed.). Lawrence Erlbaum.

Kite, M. E., & Littleford, L. N. (2015). Teaching about diversity across the undergraduate psychology curriculum. In D. S. Dunn (Ed.), *The Oxford Handbook of undergraduate psychology education* (pp. 129–141). Oxford University Press.

Plaut, V. C., Fryberg, S. A., & Martínez, E. J. (2014). Officially advocated, but institutionally undermined: Diversity rhetoric and subjective realities of junior faculty of color. *The International Journal of Diversity in Organisations, Communities and Nations, 11*(2), 101–116.

Prieto, L. R. (2009). Teaching about diversity. In R. A. R. Gurung & L. R. Prieto (Eds.), *Getting culture: Incorporating diversity across the curriculum* (pp. 23–39). Stylus.

Roberts, T., & Carter Andrews, D. J. (2013). A critical race analysis of the gaslighting of African American teachers: Considerations for recruitment and retention. In D. C. Andrews & F. Tuitt (Eds.), *Contesting the myth of a "post racial" era: The continued significance of race in U.S. education* (pp. 69–94). Peter Lang.

Rockquemore, K. A., & Laszloffy, T. (2008). *The Black academic's guide to winning tenure without losing your soul*. Lynne Rienner.

Stockdale, M. S., Chrobot-Mason, D. M., Chance, R. C., & Crosby, F. J. (2017). Peer mentoring retreats for addressing dilemmas of senior women in STEM careers. In A. J. Murrell & S. Blake-Beard (Eds.), *Mentoring diverse leaders: Creating change for people, processes, and paradigms* (pp. 218–234). Routledge. https://doi.org/10.4324/9781315747569-12

Warner, C. B., Phelps, R. E., Pittman, D. M., & Moore, C. S. (2013). Anticipating and working with controversy in diversity and social justice topics. In D. S. Dunn, R. A. R. Gurung, K. Z. Naufel, & J. H. Wilson (Eds.), *Controversy in the psychology classroom: Using hot topics to foster critical thinking* (pp. 143–156). American Psychological Association. https://doi.org/10.1037/14038-009

2
GROUND RULES FOR DISCUSSING DIVERSITY
Complex Considerations

SUSAN B. GOLDSTEIN

Although it is certainly jarring when offensive or insensitive statements derail class discussions (see Kite et al., Chapter 4, this volume), the more frequent dilemma I have encountered in teaching diversity-related courses it is that of students staying silent. Often those who remain silent during class will express their thoughts at other times, such as in their written work or through comments made to me after class. These writings offer clues about their reluctance to engage. For example, students with important and insightful perspectives disclose that they are "tired of having to explain prejudice to those who just don't understand" or of "hearing ignorant comments." Others state that they are afraid to speak out in class since "what is politically correct changes constantly" or they feel as if they are "walking on eggshells" to avoid offending anyone. How can instructors ease students' concerns about participating in discussions of diversity and social justice while at the same time encouraging them to do so in a constructive manner?

https://doi.org/10.1037/0000216-002
Navigating Difficult Moments in Teaching Diversity and Social Justice, M. E. Kite, K. A. Case, and W. R. Williams (Editors)
Copyright © 2021 by the American Psychological Association. All rights reserved.

FACULTY REFLECTION

Like most college faculty, I see classroom discussion as integral to my students' learning and my own pedagogical approach. Over 80% of faculty surveyed by the Higher Education Research Institute report using class discussions in all or most of their courses (Eagan et al., 2014). Students also increasingly value in-class participation as recent cohorts seek a more interactive college experience (Rocca, 2010). In fact, there is strong evidence for the benefits of class participation, including gains in motivation, confidence, critical thinking, communication skills, and memory for course content (Rocca, 2010; Weaver & Qi, 2005). Yet despite this overall positive assessment of class participation by both faculty and students, the number who actually participate is small. Rocca's review of several decades of research on student participation indicates that a small group of students is generally responsible for the vast majority of comments and questions within any given classroom.

Although there may be several reasons for students choosing not to participate in class discussions, there is evidence that apprehension about discussing sensitive issues plays a significant role. Consistent with the statements in the above dilemma, students express concern about eliciting criticism from their peers, with those from non-dominant groups feeling particularly at risk of being disputed or disbelieved (Fournier-Sylvester, 2013; Walls & Hall, 2018). Discussions addressing issues of diversity draw immediate attention to participants' multiple social identities (Young, 2003) and require that most students acknowledge some form of privilege among these identities which may evoke strong emotions (Spencer, 2015). For example, much research indicates that when White students explore the ways they have benefitted from racism, feelings of guilt, shame, discomfort, and hopelessness may result, particularly for those encountering issues of privilege for the first time (Boatright-Horowitz et al., 2012).[1] As a result of this emotional arousal among students, learning, problem-solving, and productive communication may be impaired (Vespia & Filz, 2013; Young, 2003).

Faculty also report apprehension about discussing sensitive issues and may avoid doing so due to concerns about accusations of trying to push a political agenda, ambiguity about the role of their own identity, the unpredictability of student reactions, a lack of experience working with strong emotions, the possibility of revealing their own bias or ignorance to the class, and the

---

[1] The literature on teaching social justice courses is itself limited in terms of diversity in that it has focused primarily on issues of race/ethnicity and the experiences and responses of White students. See, for example, Walls and Hall (2018) on the lack of studies addressing the classroom experiences of African American students in predominantly White colleges and universities.

potential consequences for course evaluations (Boatright-Horowitz et al., 2012; Fournier-Sylvester, 2013; Young, 2003). As is the case with students, faculty from nondominant groups may be particularly vulnerable when discussing sensitive issues, especially when the groups with which they identify are involved (Sue et al., 2011; Walls & Hall, 2018).

Scholars from various disciplines have advocated discussion ground rules as a strategy for supporting both students and faculty in discussing challenging issues (Spencer, 2015). In fact, the use of discussion ground rules has been described as central to the responsibility of college faculty to facilitate an inclusive classroom and campus climate (Boysen, 2012). Discussion ground rules can be instrumental in creating a safe space for students and assisting the instructor in confronting classroom bias and maintaining a collaborative dynamic. These rules, sometimes described as a code of conduct (Landis, 2008), typically address such matters as open-mindedness; tolerance of inadvertent offense; respectful communication in terms of listening, language use, and avoiding personal attacks; and assurances of confidentiality. This latter issue has recently gained importance as conversations increasingly continue outside of class on social media (Kolowich, 2018). A list of sample ground rules that evolved over several semesters of teaching Psychology of Prejudice is provided in Appendix 2.1.

In addition to providing students with the clear expectations and effective communication strategies that increase productive dialogue (Vespia & Filz, 2013), discussion ground rules ideally reduce the likelihood of microaggressions which have significant negative consequences for targets' physical and mental health, social identity, and academic performance and productivity (Sue et al., 2011). In the classroom, these include such behaviors as the use of offensive language, calling on students to represent their identity group, ignoring or diminishing systems of oppression, and reinforcing stereotypes (Walls & Hall, 2018). In addition to reducing these behaviors through explicit directives, discussion ground rules may also create a normative environment which functions to discourage prejudiced responses, particularly when individuals are unable to effectively self-regulate (Buzinski & Kitchens, 2017). Pasque et al. (2013) explained that

> when handled well, classroom conflict can create the dissonance essential for significant learning, permit new and different voices to be heard, clarify important differences, raise issues to a level and place where they can be seen and addressed, and provide students with models for creative engagement and problem-solving. (pp. 13–14)

Implementing discussion ground rules can be key to achieving this dynamic and diminishing the dilemma of silence.

CONSIDERATIONS OF CONTEXT AND INTERSECTIONALITY

Several contextual factors are relevant to decisions about the content and implementation of discussion ground rules. Student characteristics may affect power dynamics in the classroom as well as the relevance of particular rules. Course format is also a consideration in that the optimal approach may differ for required courses as opposed to electives and online courses as opposed to those taught on-site.

Student Characteristics

Discussion ground rules can be helpful regardless of classroom diversity but may be particularly critical in situations in which there are few members of an identity group in the class. For example, African American students attending a predominantly White university overwhelmingly reported decreased participation and unease when discussions turned to issues related to race. These students often found themselves with a "no-win" choice between speaking out and incurring negative consequences or letting ignorant or inaccurate comments stand (Walls & Hall, 2018). Sue et al. (2009) found that for students of color in such situations, the decision to participate is largely dependent on the level of emotional support in the classroom. Ground rules ideally codify this support and encourage members of the class to act as allies in their enforcement. It should be noted, however, that the ground rule of confidentiality may be isolating for students who are the sole member of a nondominant group in the class in that it prohibits seeking support from others with shared experiences who are not members of the class. To address this situation, I maintain the confidentiality rule but encourage students to come to me with any concerns and refer those who do to a trusted Office of Diversity and Inclusion staff member with whom they might speak without mentioning classmates' names.

The academic and disciplinary background of the students is also relevant to establishing ground rules. For example, in my classes that are cross-listed in both the Psychology and Race and Ethnic Studies (REST) departments, the REST students tend to have far more direct experience, knowledge, and sophisticated vocabulary with which to engage in discussions of social justice than do many of the psychology students. They are also more likely to have attended other classes where ground rules were implemented and can easily generate a list with little additional discussion. This creates an interesting dynamic which ironically often disadvantages students from dominant groups. In this situation, I try to reinforce the value of collaboratively generating ground rules so as not to start the semester with one group of students feeling that another has imposed a set of rules upon them.

An additional dimension of student diversity to consider in implementing discussion ground rules is disability. Students with documented disabilities may have permission to record classroom content, primarily to address difficulties with taking or reading notes. This need not conflict with discussion ground rules stipulating confidentiality. According to Section 504 of the U.S. Rehabilitation Act of 1973, recorded material is solely for students' personal educational use and may not be shared with others without the instructor's consent. Yet, in situations where self-disclosure is anticipated and the discussion is not the sole source of tested material, instructors can make a general request that recording devices be turned off and students stop taking notes (The Center for Universal Design in Education, 2019). In my classes, I typically meet privately at the beginning of the semester with students who have this accommodation and indicate that when students are asked not to take notes, recording should also cease.

Finally, instructors should be aware that discussion ground rules may conflict with cultural norms for interpersonal communication. For example, although the use of first person ("I statements") is often promoted as a strategy for reducing generalizations and encouraging ownership of statements and feelings (Kranz & Lund, 2004), such speech may be viewed as unusually egocentric in some cultures, particularly those with a more collectivist orientation (Kashima & Kashima, 1998).

Course Format

In implementing ground rules, instructors might consider whether their course is a requirement or an elective. We can assume that most students who choose to take courses on issues of social justice have lower levels of prejudice and thus are motivated to maintain low-prejudiced attitudes and behaviors (Plant & Devine, 1998). Yet when social justice courses fulfill a requirement, they may enroll students with more polarized beliefs and some resentment about having to engage with the subject matter (Schueths et al., 2013). In this latter situation, I have found that taking specific actions to set the stage for implementing ground rules and creating buy-in (discussed below) is of greater importance.

Courses taught online or with an online component can also benefit from discussion ground rules. Although online communication may be helpful to students who are uncomfortable speaking out in a traditional classroom setting or who prefer to share their thoughts in written form (Fournier-Sylvester, 2013), there is also the potential for what Suler (2004) referred to as toxic disinhibition. Suler suggested that whereas the online format can at times facilitate benevolence, the anonymity and lack of visual feedback for one's behavior can result in rude, critical, or even aggressive exchanges. Vespia and Filz (2013) suggested that faculty teaching online courses have students develop ground rules and directly address and model standards for appropriate virtual communication.

BEST PRACTICES

In reviewing best practices for the use of discussion ground rules below, I explain why faculty may wish to have students take primary responsibility in this process and provide specific models for how this might be accomplished. I also discuss proactive strategies that instructors can take to facilitate the successful implementation of discussion ground rules. Finally, I outline relevant methods of assessment.

Developing Discussion Ground Rules

Although some faculty prefer to begin a new class with a set of ground rules that are included in the syllabus (see, for example, Hammer, 2013), I believe there are several benefits to involving students in the development process. First, the discussion of potential ground rules may itself contribute to raising awareness of social justice issues, a key first step given the nonconscious nature of much bias (Boysen, 2012). Second, this activity gives students the opportunity to get to know each other, and, as a result, they are more likely to participate in class, are better able to communicate with each other, and are less likely to engage in unproductive conflict (Fournier-Sylvester, 2013; Rocca, 2010). Third, involving students in the development of ground rules facilitates the power-sharing that is fundamental to a learner-centered classroom (Spencer, 2015), and finally, taking primary responsibility for developing ground rules creates buy-in and builds trust among students (Landis, 2008).

Several approaches to involving students in the development of discussion ground rules have been detailed. For example, Brookfield and Preskill (2005) suggested initiating this process by having students identify the characteristics of the best and worst group discussions they have experienced. Kite (2013) described an activity aimed at diffusing intergroup anxiety in which students anonymously write one hope, one expectation, one fear, and one concern about discussing diversity on an index card. After the cards are collected, shuffled, and redistributed, students work in groups to write guidelines that address the items on the cards. Landis (2008) described having students work in small groups to list desirable and undesirable classroom behaviors, share their lists with the rest of the class, achieve consensus on a synthesized list which is to be displayed and referred to throughout the semester, and finally determine sanctions for violations of these rules. She noted that faculty should be prepared to negotiate sanctions as those recommended by students may seem unduly harsh.

I typically use the development of discussion ground rules as part of an icebreaker activity on the first day of class. First, I provide an overview of major issues to be addressed over the course of the semester by presenting, one at a time on PowerPoint, 15 to 20 questions for discussion. After each question is presented for a few minutes, students find a different person to introduce themselves to and have a brief discussion. For example, one of the questions used in my Psychology of Prejudice class is "What are your thoughts about the adoption of historically pejorative terms by the communities they target—for example, the use of 'queer' within the LGBTQ+ community?" After students have discussed the questions on each slide, I ask them to talk about why some questions were more difficult to discuss than others, whether they would feel as comfortable discussing these issues with the entire class as they did in pairs, and what would help them to feel more comfortable in future class discussions. They then work in groups to craft a set of ground rules, which I collect, synthesize, sometimes augment, post on our course management site, and revisit throughout the semester.

Successful Implementation of Discussion Ground Rules

There are several actions that instructors can take to facilitate the successful implementation of discussion ground rules. First, it is useful to frame class discussion as a rare opportunity to engage with alternative viewpoints in a safe and respectful environment (Balls Organista et al., 2000; Hammer, 2013). As Ceci and Williams (2018) explained, "colleges owe it to their students to challenge their views by considering opposing viewpoints, even identity-shattering ones, and to force us to grapple with disconfirmatory evidence" (p. 314). I review the similarity–attraction effect and ask my students to consider how few of their friends have attitudes in opposition to their own. We also discuss the issue of filter bubbles (Pariser, 2011), the algorithms on the Internet and social media that result in isolation from ideas that differ from our own. I stress that the students' decisions about what to say and how to say it are unrelated to issues of free speech (see Warner, Chapter 16, this volume); rather, their choices are about creating an environment that best facilitates learning for all involved.

A second strategy for successful implementation of discussion ground rules is to prepare students for the emotional responses that may be elicited by difficult dialogues and the possibility that one's comments may unintentionally have a negative impact on others. Students tend to be more satisfied with their classes if expectations are met (Green et al., 2015), and they may have inaccurate expectations about the role of emotion in the classroom based on their experiences with courses in other disciplines. Kite (2013) found it beneficial to speak with students about her previous success in helping to manage such emotions. It may also be helpful to specifically address the options students have if they become distressed during class (Vespia & Filz, 2013).

The successful implementation of ground rules may also be aided by explicitly teaching supporting skills and knowledge. Relevant discussion skills include articulating and illustrating complex concepts, identifying connections across contributions, grounding observations in evidence, and mindful listening (Brookfield & Preskill, 2005; Vespia & Filz, 2013). Kite (2013) begins preparing students for difficult dialogues by discussing terminology recommended by professional associations, stereotypes associated with accents and dialects, ethnic slurs, and other forms of problematic language such the use of "they" or "those people" when referring to social groups other than one's own. The discussion of language can itself make for a meaningful lesson in social justice. For example, I explain the rationale for "person-first language" (e.g., "a person with a disability") and "identity-first language" (e.g., "a disabled person") as well as why the latter has recently become popular within some segments of the disability community (e.g., Kenny et al., 2016). I also discuss my own feelings as a disabled individual about such terms, including my aversion to "differently abled" and "physically challenged" despite their appearance in several of the assigned readings, with the intent to illustrate within-group variability in preferred labels. I aim to convey that students should feel comfortable voicing preferences about the terminology used to refer to the groups with which they identify (see also Wyrick, Chapter 13, this volume).

To aid students in adhering to discussion ground rules as well as to increase class participation, it is often helpful to provide opportunities for students to formulate their thoughts in advance of discussion and then to "pilot" them in pairs or small groups (Fournier-Sylvester, 2013). Students can be asked to research or respond to a topic before coming to class or complete brief in-class writing assignments. Kite (2013) noted that for difficult topics, she collects students' answers to focused questions ahead of time to gauge and prepare for students' responses.

Finally, instructors can facilitate the successful use of discussion ground rules by modeling appropriate classroom behaviors (Vespia & Filz, 2013). In addition to the forms of respectful communication outlined in the ground rules, this can include faculty being transparent about their own challenges and limitations in addressing issues of diversity (Balls Organista et al., 2000).

Assessment

On the day the ground rules are developed, I explain that they will be revisited during the semester to check for overall class compliance and for any possible additions or modifications. Although this can take place at any point or points during the course, I link it to a midsemester course evaluation so as to avoid the impression that this assessment is targeting any specific discussion session or individual's comments. Faculty might also indirectly assess the effectiveness of discussion ground rules via measures of class climate, including brief in-class writing assignments, journal prompts, or standardized surveys.

STRUCTURAL IMPLICATIONS

Facilitating difficult dialogues and confronting bias in the classroom can be risky for faculty and requires administrative and structural support (Sue et al., 2011). Miller and Howell (2018) suggested that colleges and universities (a) acknowledge the emotional labor involved in teaching diversity courses, (b) incorporate it into faculty handbooks and tenure and promotion documents, and (c) provide training and recognition for that work. Such actions are critical if faculty are to be successful in implementing ground rules, facilitating discussions of diversity and social justice, and creating an inclusive campus climate.

APPENDIX 2.1
SAMPLE GROUND RULES FOR DISCUSSION

1. Assume good intentions and expect that questions or comments expressed in discussion stem from a desire to gain greater understanding.
2. Allow people to make mistakes.
3. Avoid personal attacks. Criticize the comment rather than the person who made the comment.
4. Stay open-minded and allow for multiple perspectives on a single issue.
5. Be respectful and listen carefully without interrupting others.
6. Try to use language that is not offensive and be willing to respectfully let others know if you are offended by terms used in discussion.
7. Avoid shutting down conversation nonverbally (e.g., rolling eyes, crossing arms).
8. Acknowledge how differences in background and life experiences shape our perspectives.
9. Never ask anyone to serve as a spokesperson for their ethnicity or identity group.
10. Maintain confidentiality—what happens in the classroom, stays in the classroom.
11. Help create an environment in which no one is afraid to voice an opinion.

RESOURCES

American Psychological Association. (2019). General guidelines for reducing bias. *Publication manual of the American Psychological Association* (7th ed., pp. 132–149). American Psychological Association.

These guidelines provide recommendations for reducing forms of biased language in discussion of psychological issues. Although geared toward scientific writing, much of the content is also relevant to language used in classroom discussion.

Antidefamation League. (n.d.). *Toward communication free of gender bias.* https://www.adl.org/education/resources/tools-and-strategies/toward-communication-free-of-gender-bias

This document provides examples of, and inclusive alternatives to, the use of gendered, sexist, and heterosexist language. These examples illustrate how language may unintentionally reinforce stereotypes and convey disrespect.

EdChange. (n.d.). *Guide for setting ground rules.* http://www.edchange.org/multicultural/activities/groundrules.html

Paul C. Gorski and colleagues developed this set of recommendations for generating discussion ground rules. Also included on this site are examples of widely used ground rules, implementation strategies, and a thoughtful piece on how ground rules may inadvertently privilege already privileged groups.

Landis, K., Jenkins, P., & Roderick, L. (2015). *Start talking: A handbook for engaging difficult dialogues in higher education*. University of Alaska–Anchorage.

This 294-page handbook is the product of a Ford Foundation-funded faculty development project. In addition to a lengthy discussion of critical issues in setting ground rules, this volume details a variety of practical techniques and assignments for facilitating controversial discussions.

REFERENCES

Balls Organista, P., Chun, K. M., & Marin, G. (2000). Teaching an undergraduate course on ethnic diversity. *Teaching of Psychology, 27*(1), 12–17. https://doi.org/10.1207/S15328023TOP2701_2

Boatright-Horowitz, S. L., Marraccini, M. E., & Harps-Logan, Y. (2012). Teaching anti-racism: College students' emotional and cognitive reactions to learning about White privilege. *Journal of Black Studies, 43*(8), 893–911. https://doi.org/10.1177/0021934712463235

Boysen, G. A. (2012). Teachers' responses to bias in the classroom: How response type and situational factors affect student perceptions. *Journal of Applied Social Psychology, 42*(2), 506–534. https://doi.org/10.1111/j.1559-1816.2011.00784.x

Brookfield, S. D., & Preskill, S. (2005). *Discussion as a way of teaching: Tools and techniques for democratic classrooms* (2nd ed.). Jossey-Bass.

Buzinski, S. G., & Kitchens, M. B. (2017). Self-regulation and social pressure reduce prejudiced responding and increase the motivation to be non-prejudiced. *The Journal of Social Psychology, 157*(5), 629–644. https://doi.org/10.1080/00224545.2016.1263595

Ceci, S. J., & Williams, W. M. (2018). Who decides what is acceptable speech on campus? Why restricting free speech is not the answer. *Perspectives on Psychological Science, 13*(3), 299–323. https://doi.org/10.1177/1745691618767324

Eagan, M. K., Stolzenberg, E. B., Berdan Lozano, J., Aragon, M. C., Suchard, M. R., & Hurtado, S. (2014). *Undergraduate teaching faculty: The 2013–2014 HERI Faculty Survey*. Higher Education Research Institute, UCLA. https://heri.ucla.edu/monographs/HERI-FAC2014-monograph.pdf

Fournier-Sylvester, N. (2013). Daring to debate: Strategies for teaching controversial issues in the classroom. *The College Quarterly, 16*(3), 1–7. http://collegequarterly.ca/2013-vol16-num03-summer/fournier-sylvester.html

Green, H. J., Hood, M., & Neumann, D. L. (2015). Predictors of student satisfaction with university psychology courses: A review. *Psychology Learning & Teaching, 14*(2), 131–146. https://doi.org/10.1177/1475725715590959

Hammer, E. Y. (2013). Gender matters: Engaging students in controversial issues. In D. S. Dunn, R. A. R. Gurung, K. Z. Naufel, & J. H. Wilson (Eds.), *Controversy in the psychology classroom: Using hot topics to foster critical thinking* (pp. 157–168). American Psychological Association. https://doi.org/10.1037/14038-010

Kashima, E., & Kashima, Y. (1998). Culture and language: The case of cultural dimensions and personal pronoun use. *Journal of Cross-Cultural Psychology, 29*(3), 461–486. https://doi.org/10.1177/0022022198293005

Kenny, L., Hattersley, C., Molins, B., Buckley, C., Povey, C., & Pellicano, E. (2016). Which terms should be used to describe autism? Perspectives from the UK autism community. *Autism: The International Journal of Research and Practice, 20*(4), 442–462. https://doi.org/10.1177/1362361315588200

Kite, M. E. (2013). Teaching about race and ethnicity. In D. S. Dunn, R. A. R. Gurung, K. Z. Naufel, & J. H. Wilson (Eds.), *Controversy in the psychology classroom: Using hot topics to foster critical thinking* (pp. 169–184). American Psychological Association. https://doi.org/10.1037/14038-011

Kolowich, S. (2018, September 28). U. of Nebraska wondered whether conservative students were being silenced. Here's what it found out. *The Chronicle of Higher Education, 64*(5). https://www.chronicle.com/article/U-of-Nebraska-Wondered/244517

Kranz, P. L., & Lund, N. L. (2004). Successful teaching techniques in a race relations class. *The Journal of Psychology: Interdisciplinary and Applied, 138*(4), 371–383. https://doi.org/10.3200/JRLP.138.4.371-384.

Landis, K. (Ed.). (2008). *Start talking: A handbook for engaging difficult dialogues in higher education.* The University of Alaska Anchorage and Alaska Pacific University.

Miller, R. A., & Howell, C. D. (2018, November). *"Constantly, excessively, and all the time": The emotional labor of teaching diversity courses.* Paper presented at the 43rd annual meeting of the Association for the Study of Higher Education, Tampa, FL.

Pariser, E. (2011). *The filter bubble: How the new personalized web is changing what we read and how we think.* Penguin.

Pasque, P. A., Chesler, M. A., Charbeneau, J., & Carlson, C. (2013). Pedagogical approaches to student racial conflict in the classroom. *Journal of Diversity in Higher Education, 6*(1), 1–16. https://doi.org/10.1037/a0031695

Plant, E. A., & Devine, P. G. (1998). Internal and external motivation to respond without prejudice. *Journal of Personality and Social Psychology, 75*(3), 811–832. https://doi.org/10.1037/0022-3514.75.3.811

Rehabilitation Act of 1973, 29 U.S.C. § 701 et seq. (1973).

Rocca, K. A. (2010). Student participation in the college classroom: An extended multidisciplinary literature review. *Communication Education, 59*(2), 185–213. https://doi.org/10.1080/03634520903505936

Schueths, A. M., Gladney, T., Crawford, D. M., Bass, K. L., & Moore, H. A. (2013). Passionate pedagogy and emotional labor: Students' responses to learning diversity from diverse instructors. *Journal of Qualitative Studies in Education, 26*(10), 1259–1276. https://doi.org/10.1080/09518398.2012.731532

Spencer, L. G. (2015). Engaging undergraduates in feminist classrooms: An exploration of professors' practices. *Equity & Excellence in Education, 48*(2), 195–211. https://doi.org/10.1080/10665684.2015.1022909

Sue, D. W., Lin, A. I., Torino, G. C., Capodilupo, C. M., & Rivera, D. P. (2009). Racial microaggressions and difficult dialogues on race in the classroom. *Cultural Diversity & Ethnic Minority Psychology, 15*(2), 183–190. https://doi.org/10.1037/a0014191

Sue, D. W., Rivera, D. P., Watkins, N. L., Kim, R. H., Kim, S., & Williams, C. D. (2011). Racial dialogues: Challenges faculty of color face in the classroom. *Cultural Diversity & Ethnic Minority Psychology, 17*(3), 331–340. https://doi.org/10.1037/a0024190

Suler, J. (2004). The online disinhibition effect. *Cyberpsychology & Behavior, 7*(3), 321–326. https://doi.org/10.1089/1094931041291295

The Center for Universal Design in Education. (2019). https://www.washington.edu/doit/can-faculty-member-forbid-student-disability-use-tape-recorder-class

Vespia, K. M., & Filz, T. E. (2013). Preventing and handling classroom disruptions. In D. S. Dunn, R. A. R. Gurung, K. Z. Naufel, & J. H. Wilson (Eds.), *Controversy in the psychology classroom: Using hot topics to foster critical thinking* (pp. 23–34). American Psychological Association. https://doi.org/10.1037/14038-002

Walls, J. K., & Hall, S. S. (2018). A focus group study of African American students' experiences with classroom discussions about race at a predominantly White university. *Teaching in Higher Education, 23*(1), 47–62. https://doi.org/10.1080/13562517.2017.1359158

Weaver, R. R., & Qi, J. (2005). Classroom organization and participation: College students' perceptions. *The Journal of Higher Education, 76*(5), 570–601. https://doi.org/10.1353/jhe.2005.0038

Young, G. (2003). Dealing with difficult classroom dialogue. In P. Bronstein & K. Quina (Eds.), *Teaching gender and multicultural awareness: Resources for the psychology classroom* (pp. 347–360). American Psychological Association. https://doi.org/10.1037/10570-025

3 SOCIAL JUSTICE BURNOUT

Engaging in Self-Care While Doing Diversity Work

ASIA EATON AND LEAH R. WARNER

Some scholar-activists find balancing personal and professional demands to be an attainable challenge; whether due to judicious and mature life management, personality, privilege, spiritual or religious guidance, sociocultural pressures and supports, or some combination thereof, some individuals can manage their workloads without toxic levels of stress. This chapter is not for them. It is for those of us who have bottomed out, more than once, due to personal and professional overcommitment, fear, and mismanagement. It is for those of us who have teetered between the extremes of enmeshment with work and plans to entirely retreat from our careers. This chapter, we hope, will help social justice scholars suffering from burnout better understand the nature and prevalence of our condition and to begin to envision a way forward.

At the Nag's Heart retreat that gave rise to this book, I (Asia) came prepared to discuss the dilemma of feeling unqualified in my diversity work and the complications of doing work with oppressed populations from a position of privilege. In the last year, I had begun to question my legitimacy to discuss and engage with social justice research in the classroom,

---

https://doi.org/10.1037/0000216-003
Navigating Difficult Moments in Teaching Diversity and Social Justice, M. E. Kite, K. A. Case, and W. R. Williams (Editors)
Copyright © 2021 by the American Psychological Association. All rights reserved.

the community, and beyond. I felt like I was failing on multiple levels, and I didn't know what to do next. Many examples come to mind. In one instance, a colleague and I had written, and collected signatures on, a faculty statement asking our university administration to resist federal pressure to "out" undocumented students. This was shortly after Donald J. Trump was elected president of the United States, and he had promised to terminate Deferred Action for Childhood Arrivals (DACA). We hand-delivered the letter to our university president and provost but never heard back. In another instance, a student[1] texted me to say that border patrol agents were on campus and asked for help investigating and problem-solving. I never got back to her, and when I saw her at a social justice march a few months later, I felt disgusted with myself. I was also feeling like an imposter for doing research on Latinx/Hispanic college students as a White woman at a Hispanic-Serving Institution. I wondered if I should try, at the very least, to get a graduate certificate in Latin American and Caribbean Studies. I felt like I was missing opportunities and letting people down left and right, and the collective actions I was involved with kept hitting dead-ends.

I envisioned that sharing these issues with the Nag's Heart group would result in some concrete suggestions, such as improving my efficacy as a scholar-activist or furthering my expertise in the feminist and critical race literature. I steadied myself for constructive criticism and envisioned a raft of new work assignments to get me on the right course. Surprisingly, the scenario functioned as a canary in the coal mine, notifying my colleagues that I was on my way to burnout, a psychological syndrome consisting of exhaustion, depersonalization, and inefficacy due to chronic emotional and interpersonal job-related stress (Freudenberger & Richelson, 1980; Maslach, 1976). Instead of telling me to enroll in additional classes or take on additional service positions, the Nag's Hearters told me I was already working too hard or, at least, seeing my work in a skewed way. I was experiencing an undue and self-defeating level of personal disappointment and frustration.

Early in our experience at the Nag's Heart retreat, I (Leah) shared with Asia that I felt spread very thin in my life and work; for example, at the time of Nag's Heart, I had accepted most of the diversity positions at my college, including Faculty Fellow for Equity and Diversity Programs; Women's, Gender, and Sexuality Studies minor co-convener; director of a general education course on diversity and inequality (which included course

---

[1] We have made every effort to protect the identities and maintain confidentiality of students and anyone else involved in the examples shared within our chapter. We refrained from using descriptions that could individually identify a person.

development, assessment, and managing 35 sections of a course); and active memberships in the Title IX committee, Diversity Action Committee, the Minority Faculty Staff Association, and the Faculty and Staff Pride Association. These positions formed merely a portion of my service, as I also contributed heavily to four nondiversity committees on campus and to national psychological associations and also served as a member of two editorial boards for academic journals.

Starting in 2016 and beyond, both campus and national climates in the U.S. made social justice activism feel more urgent to me than it had in the past. As a result, I started to place a tremendous amount of pressure on myself to engage in my diversity work and to carry heavy regret when I was unable to fulfill my commitments. For example, in one diversity position I held, I started what I had hoped would be a series of conversations among professional staff about the campus climate. But I only held the first session because I stepped down from the position after recognizing my overburdened schedule. Especially because that first conversation was very generative and folks expressed vulnerable moments of discrimination, I still actively experience guilt a year later. As a "solution" to avoid carrying the guilt of not following through with another initiative, I spread myself so thin across my commitments that I developed a chronic stress-induced health condition.

FACULTY REFLECTION

Ultimately, the Nag's Heart group counseled both of us to engage in this collaborative chapter on self-care and burnout. This process of writing and rewriting gave us the opportunity to learn about burnout in an academic sense, but also to engage in introspection about our motives and payoffs for overwork in the context of social justice and to reflect on what self-defined self-care might actually look like.

Given the personal nature of this topic, we begin with a short description of who we are and what led to our involvement in this work. I (Asia) am a White, heterosexual, cisgender, divorced woman with two small children, and I (Leah) am a White, queer/lesbian, cisgender woman, in a queer relationship, and I have two small children. As scholars, we both hold tenure-track/tenured positions in the psychology departments at our universities, as well as core and affiliate appointments with a host of programs, departments, and centers. In ways both small and large, our involvement in social justice work as teachers, researchers, advocates, and mentors totals over 20 years each. Our engagement in social justice work includes efforts with communities we belong to (e.g., women, mothers, LGBTQ+), as well as allyship with communities we are not members of (e.g., Latinx people, women experiencing homelessness, Black women). Social justice work shapes our identities, blurring the fictional border between our "academic" and "activist" selves (Askins, 2009). Both inside and outside the classroom, we assume roles and responsibilities as social justice advocates and educators.

CONSIDERATIONS OF CONTEXT AND INTERSECTIONALITY

Both personal motives and systemic factors contribute to our burnout. Our own personal fulfillment in engaging in social justice work and our desire to be productive influence our workload. At the same time, institutional contexts increase our commitments and strain, particularly contexts that rely on our "expertise" as members of marginalized groups and ask us to perform unnecessary or unreasonable labor.

Motivations for Engaging in Social Justice Work

Researchers document numerous motives for engaging in diversity work (e.g., Russell, 2011), many which echo our own experiences. More obvious motives include the feeling of accomplishment that comes from improving practices and policies, the joy of sharing in students' self-discovery and expansion, avoiding negative outcomes for ourselves and our loved ones, the intrinsic pleasure of learning, and a sense of belonging and purpose. One of my (Asia's) main motivations is the joy of seeing students gain insights and empowerment through research on issues of power and oppression that affect them personally. From an outsider's perspective, my publication history may look a bit confused and disorganized, ranging from work on gay men employees to social class stigma to the sexual scripts of Hispanic college students. But I know what motivated each and every topic: the interests, needs, and expertise of a specific grad or undergrad student collaborator. And one of the most deeply meaningful outcomes of diversity work for me (Leah) is witnessing the moment when students, faculty, and/or staff gain a true and deep awareness of the lived experiences of a systemically marginalized group for the first time. Their palpable shift towards critical awareness and motivation to engage in social action drives my passion to continue this work.

At the same time, latent motives driving our work can lead to overcommitment and burnout (Gorski, 2019): personal resentments, guilt, the desire to be "productive" or worthy, the knowledge that the voluntary selection of social justice involvements is itself a privilege, and the irrational fear that the success of some movement or action rests solely on our shoulders. For example, one challenge I (Asia) experience in stepping back from work is the knowledge that retreating to my spacious and safe suburban home is not an option for many others. Also, I (Leah) experience painful choices over nurturing social justice work versus nurturing my own children. When I engage in institutional activism at the end of the workday, I wrestle with whether or not to devote my limited remaining time to caring for my children. I know that this choice is a privilege, in that I can choose to walk away from the work, but others cannot choose to walk away from systemic inequities. I also know that my children miss me terribly.

Marginalized Identities

Aside from personal motives, systemic factors lead those who do diversity work to experience overcommitment and/or burnout. For example, diversity work in university settings relies heavily on the volunteer efforts of already marginalized and undervalued scholars and students. In addition, faculty hires and other committees disproportionally ask marginalized scholars to serve as stand-ins for a "diversity perspective" and to provide the checks and balances on campus climate (Ahmed, 2012), which result in systemically overburdening marginalized faculty (Hirshfield & Joseph, 2012). Thus, when overly relying on those personally affected by diversity issues to do this labor, universities support and maintain the systemic inequalities these efforts intend to address.

Gratuitous Labor

Few structural incentives (e.g., promotions or bonuses) exist for serving on diversity and inclusion committees, for infusing social justice into one's syllabi, or for mentoring underrepresented students (O'Meara, 2016). For example, I (Asia) was on 27 dissertation committees during my time on the tenure track, in large part to speak to issues of gender, race, power, and oppression present in the dissertation content. As an untenured professor, I was also a founding, 6-year member of my university's Strategies and Tactics for Recruiting to Improve Diversity and Excellence (STRIDE) committee, which worked to increase the hiring, retention, and promotion of underrepresented faculty through institutional change. These efforts, which were an order of magnitude greater than average, did not translate into comparable professional rewards, making them unpaid (albeit internally rewarding) labor.

In addition, activist work related to social issues involves substantial emotional labor, or managing one's and others' emotions as part of one's work-related responsibilities (Hochschild, 1983). Emotional labor leads to energy depletion and emotional exhaustion—core elements of burnout. This burden can lead to a sense of isolation from mainstream society (Kovan & Dirkx, 2003), especially if activists experience backlash when they engage in their efforts (Gorski, 2019; see also Wagner & Garrett-Walker, Chapter 6, this volume). Given my high levels of activism, I (Leah) worry that others will only see me as causing trouble and, at times, I feel isolated from those who are not directly involved in this work. Furthermore, strain from diversity work compounds other daily stressors that I experience. For example, because I cannot be out about some of elements of my identity, I regularly experience strain from actively concealing elements of my lived experience. Activists who belong to marginalized communities often contend with activist burnout as well as "battle fatigue," which results from facing personal prejudice and discrimination on a daily basis (Quaye et al., 2017; see also Rios et al., Chapter 5, this volume).

Finally, members of social justice circles tend to engage in self-martyrdom, where denial of self-care becomes a part of the culture of activism (Gorski & Chen, 2015; Plyler, 2009; Rodgers, 2010). In an examination of burnout among Amnesty International workers, for example, Rodgers (2010) found that workers perceived burnout as an expected sacrifice as part one's devotion to the cause. They also perceived displays of personal strain as self-indulgent and reported an absence of open discussions about burnout. In the past, I (Leah) participated in this culture by not sharing experiences of burnout with colleagues and by not communicating burnout when taking on new diversity responsibilities.

Taken together, due to intrapersonal, systemic, and cultural factors, scholar-activists who do social justice work are vulnerable to burnout. Burnout can result in poor physical and psychological health (Ahola et al., 2017); strained relationships with partners, coworkers, and others; and reduced work performance (Bakker et al., 2004). Activist burnout also threatens the success of social justice movements more generally (Gorski, 2019; Gorski & Chen, 2015).

BEST PRACTICES

To address the burnout we describe in our dilemmas, we reflect on self-care strategies at the individual, social, and institutional levels. For us, the term *self-care* first conjured images of hand-waving system justification, as corporations and governments have successfully coopted the term to increase profit and to offload responsibility for the welfare of citizens, respectively (Ward, 2015). Today's celebrity corporate shills eagerly define self-care as a superficial and commercial endeavor (e.g., "the new Aveeno hydrating facial";

Gilbert, 2017). Yet the concept of self-care has deep and radical roots and it is necessary for scholar-activists to continue their work (Nadal, 2017).

Defining Self-Care

The term *self-care*, contrary to our first reactions, actually derives from 20th-century literatures in philosophy and medicine. Today, scholars generally define self-care as "engagement in behaviors that support health and well-being" (Lee & Miller, 2013, p. 96) that can prevent and reduce burnout, as well as empower individuals to appreciate and promote their own health in various arenas (e.g., physical, psychological, social, spiritual, and professional health). Scholars disagree, however, over whether to conceptualize self-care as a process or as set of activities and skills (Dorociak et al., 2017; Lee & Miller, 2013).

Current research on self-care in the context of job-related burnout focuses on those in high-stress human service occupations, such as doctors, therapists, and social workers. Professional self-care in these contexts consists of a balance between work and other life arenas, and can include participation in professional development, receipt and cultivation of professional support, and cognitive strategies to manage challenges (Dorociak et al., 2017). At the individual level, self-care can take the form of asking for help, taking vacations, spending time with friends, engaging in physical activities, getting adequate sleep, and slowing down (Adler et al., 2017). At the relational and group level, self-care includes sharing stories, normalizing reactions, encouraging others, witnessing, "caring with," and using humor (Adler et al., 2017; Lopez & Gillespie, 2016).

Self-care, as it relates to activist work, includes the additional recognition that one's work occurs in a societally oppressive context. Thus, beyond neoliberal notions of self-care, which hold the individual solely responsible for and capable of caring for herself (Ward, 2015), care for the self serves as an act of resistance against oppressive systems (Lorde, 1988). For example, in their podcast, Morris and Wortham (2017) described activist self-care as a means "to actively push back against systems that break you down and institutional ways of not being cared for." Thus, activist self-care includes all actions taken to restore and support vitality and balance in a system designed to deplete activists and discourage activism (Lorde, 1988). In an issue of *The Clinical Psychologist*, Norcross (2009) described self-care as "sharpening the saw" (p. 1), a corrective action essential for sustained effectiveness over time. Indeed, in our estimation, self-care goes beyond remediation by amplifying one's strength and precision in future social justice work.

For scholar-activists, we group our recommendations for engaging in self-care into three levels: individual, social, and institutional.

Individual Self-Care

Self-care at the individual level includes the ways scholar-activists change their own behaviors to engage in better safekeeping of one's mind, body, and spirit. For example, by engaging in mindfulness, scholar-activists gain active and purposeful awareness of the present environment. Gorski (2015) found that mindfulness practices helped activists reduce burnout by decreasing the pressure to address all social injustice immediately, reducing the stress and anxiety that result from activism, and reducing guilt for engaging in self-care. Although these may be helpful to some, we qualify recommendations of self-care at the individual level with the acknowledgment that some require economic advantage (e.g., high-quality health care, vacations, and fitness memberships; Plyler, 2009), and replicate oppressive practices (Gorski, 2015), and thus will not be available or healthy for all. For example, economically privileged White people in the U.S. have appropriated yoga and meditation in the name of self-care. Activists should engage in acts of self-care that are critically oriented and draw explicit connections between self and community (see Gorski, 2015).

For those who are used to doing for others and not themselves, this may be easier said than done. For example, inspired by this chapter, I (Asia) endeavored to practice individual self-care by starting a biannual self-care day for my research lab. On one occasion, I purchased watercolors and canvases for lab members, who painted and had snacks on the university lawn. Colleagues from Nag's Heart, however, helped me to see that this activity did not meet the definition of individual self-care; I did not get to tend to my own wants and needs on these days. Instead, I spent time organizing the day for others, consistent with a social or collective form of self-care, which we will describe below. Based on a colleague's suggestion, my new individual self-care tactic is to ask myself, "Do I want to do this, or do I feel that I should?" before agreeing to engagements, to facilitate awareness of whether the activity promotes individual self-care.

Social Movement Self-Care

In addition to promoting one's own welfare, scholar-activists can encourage self-care within their social movements. Despite the culture of self-martyrdom, research suggests that activists long for spaces to discuss burnout openly and without judgment (Gorski & Chen, 2015). To change this culture, activists can demonstrate that self-care facilitates social justice goals. For example, activists can explain that self-care challenges dominant cultures of the Protestant work ethic, which emphasize self-sacrificing, workaholism, and individualistic success at the expense of others (Gorski & Chen, 2015). As a challenge to the Protestant work ethic, activists could emphasize the need to slow down and address one's needs, while promoting an environment in which all activists meet their self-care needs. For example, during a months-long social justice effort in my hometown, the other activists and I (Leah) took turns providing space for each other to reclaim neglected elements of our lives that we had put aside (e.g., time with children, exercise, leisure). Part of this effort involved simply validating for each other that we deserve to take time for these elements of our lives. We also slowed down our efforts and took turns with responsibilities, which involved the hard work of recognizing that our goals would take longer to achieve. Activists can pair this frame with explaining that self-martyrdom places an extra burden on marginalized people and corresponds with increased turnover and other negative consequences for groups (e.g., Rodgers, 2010).

Institutional Self-Care

The last level of scholar-activists' self-care occurs at the institutional level, which involves implementing policies and actions within organizations. Institutions, such as colleges, universities, and professional organizations, should take responsibility for understanding burnout as a workplace hazard, and proactively take steps to ensure the well-being of their workers (Maslach, 2017). Indeed, a recent meta-analysis found that individually focused interventions were not sufficient to alleviate severe burnout (Ahola et al., 2017). Institutional solutions include creating self-care events on campus, such as holistic health assessments or paid work breaks, and making space so that workers receive protected time in which to participate in such activities during the workday.

Institutions can also support self-care of workers by preventing burnout in the first place. In particular, institutions can address the practice of overburdening those who engage in diversity work, particularly the volunteer efforts of marginalized scholars and students (Ahmed, 2012; Hirshfield & Joseph, 2012). To do so, institutions should (a) engage in efforts to better distribute diversity and related service responsibilities across campus (e.g., O'Meara, 2016), (b) better value community-engaged scholarship (e.g., O'Meara et al., 2015), and (c) promote an institutional culture where colleagues support each other's activist scholarship efforts (e.g., Lopez & Gillespie, 2016). In addition, institutions must find ways to measure and reward activist and community work. This may include course releases, valuing activist work as service, and rewarding diversity work at different stages of career development, such as during the promotion and tenure process (Quaye et al., 2017). In addition, scholars can advocate for institutional change by writing about the challenges and opportunities inherent to social justice teaching, and sharing that writing (such as this chapter) with stakeholders who have influence over faculty workloads. At the moment, I (Asia) am lead guest editor for an issue of *American Psychologist* on "public psychology," soliciting papers that describe how community-engaged scholarship involves unique challenges and opportunities across all domains of psychological work. We hope to include papers in the issue that examine how a public psychology framework challenges normative models of hiring, promotion, and evaluation, both inside and outside of academia, and suggests new ways forward. Published papers on this topic are one step toward legitimizing our work at the institutional level.

Efforts at structural change could also take the form of advocating for policies to reduce burnout. These efforts could take place at many levels, including at one's university, relevant consortiums and societies, and/or with local and national representatives. For example, most universities have policies for maintaining fair and equitable workloads. These policies outline opportunities for workload amendments for faculty in response to graduating PhD students, mentoring honors theses, receiving grants, publishing books, or other activities. Faculty who are engaged in social justice work may consider proposing amendments to their workload assignment policies that help recognize their contributions to service and engagement through workload shifts.

Although scholar-activists argue that institutions must facilitate self-care and reduce risks for burnout, an implicit dilemma in this argument concerns how to encourage institutions to do so without creating further responsibilities (and therefore more burnout) for scholar-activists to facilitate these institutional changes. One solution requires allied scholars to take the lead and step in for those from marginalized groups. Additionally, those already in administrative positions should develop their awareness of scholarship on systemic factors involved in burnout and self-care and use their positions and power to incentivize structural change. By the same token, administrators should recognize burnout as a campus climate concern and integrate solutions into diversity strategic plans. Scholar-activists' considerations of whether to add this further institutional activism should abide by the same principles as any other form of activism: that scholar-activists permit themselves to set limits on their responsibilities, that self-care is necessary and not self-indulgence, and that, before taking on more responsibilities, scholar-activists should consider whether the activism is personally nourishing or whether it sets one on the path for burnout.

CONCLUSION

As for ourselves, we persist on the path to expanding our identities as scholar-activists to include recurring self-care at personal, social, and institutional levels. As social justice work remains a marathon, not a sprint, engaging in self-care helps to ensure our sustained efforts. Moreover, practicing self-care enables us to model a more sustainable life as scholar-activists for our students and mentees, who must be willing and able to carry this work into the future. Finally, by sharing the workload with our social movements, allies, and administrators, we will expand our impact, reach and recruit additional allies and activists, and share the fulfillment that comes from using scholarship to improve the lives of oppressed people and groups around the globe.

RESOURCES

Gorski, P. C. (2015). Relieving burnout and the "martyr syndrome" among social justice education activists: The implications and effects of mindfulness. *The Urban Review*, 47(4), 696–716. https://doi.org/10.1007/s11256-015-0330-0
    This resource offers research on the benefits of mindfulness on relieving activist burnout, while also contextualizing mindfulness within U.S. colonialist practices of coopting yoga and meditation and addressing neoliberal tendencies to value the self in terms of productivity.

Nag's Heart. (n.d.). https://www.nagsheart.com/
    Nag's Heart is a collective that organizes small-scale conferences to "replenish the feminist spirit" (Nag's Heart, n.d.). These conferences emphasize self-care within social justice contexts, particularly for (but not limited to) individuals in higher education contexts.

Ortiz, N. (2018). *Sustaining spirit: Self-care for social justice*. Reclamation Press.
    Drawing from her Mestiza community's spiritual traditions, Ortiz provides both reflections on self-care and concrete strategies for activists in social justice movements.

Plyler, J. (2009). How to keep on keeping on: Sustaining ourselves in community organizing and social justice struggles. *Upping the Anti*, 3, 123–134.
    In this resource, Plyler interviews several longtime activists on the factors that sustained them through decades of social justice work, providing solutions both at the individual and the community/movement levels.

REFERENCES

Adler, A. B., Adrian, A. L., Hemphill, M., Scaro, N. H., Sipos, M. L., & Thomas, J. L. (2017). Professional stress and burnout in U.S. military medical personnel deployed to Afghanistan. *Military Medicine*, 182(3), e1669–e1676. https://doi.org/10.7205/MILMED-D-16-00154

Ahmed, S. (2012). *On being included: Racism and diversity in institutional life*. Duke University Press. https://doi.org/10.1215/9780822395324

Ahola, K., Toppinen-Tanner, S., & Seppänen, J. (2017). Interventions to alleviate burnout symptoms and to support return to work among employees with burnout: Systematic review and meta-analysis. *Burnout Research, 4*, 1–11. https://doi.org/10.1016/j.burn.2017.02.001

Askins, K. (2009). "That's just what I do": Placing emotion in academic activism. *Emotion, Space and Society, 2*(1), 4–13. https://doi.org/10.1016/j.emospa.2009.03.005

Bakker, A. B., Demerouti, E., & Verbeke, W. (2004). Using the job demands–resources model to predict burnout and performance. *Human Resource Management, 43*(1), 83–104. https://doi.org/10.1002/hrm.20004

Dorociak, K. E., Rupert, P. A., Bryant, F. B., & Zahniser, E. (2017). Development of the Professional Self-Care Scale. *Journal of Counseling Psychology, 64*(3), 325–334. https://doi.org/10.1037/cou0000206

Freudenberger, H. J., & Richelson, G. (1980). *Burn-out: The high cost of achievement*. Anchor Press.

Gilbert, K. (2017). Jennifer Aniston was into self-care before it was a thing. *Shape*. https://www.shape.com/celebrities/interviews/jennifer-aniston-self-care-fitness-beauty-routine

Gorski, P. C. (2015). Relieving burnout and the "martyr syndrome" among social justice education activists: The implications and effects of mindfulness. *The Urban Review, 47*(4), 696–716. https://doi.org/10.1007/s11256-015-0330-0

Gorski, P. C. (2019). Fighting racism, battling burnout: Causes of activist burnout in U.S. racial justice activists. *Ethnic and Racial Studies, 42*(5), 667–687. https://doi.org/10.1080/01419870.2018.1439981

Gorski, P. C., & Chen, C. (2015). "Frayed all over:" The causes and consequences of activist burnout among social justice education activist. *Educational Studies, 51*(5), 385–405. https://doi.org/10.1080/00131946.2015.1075989

Hirshfield, L. E., & Joseph, T. D. (2012). "We need a woman, we need a Black woman": Gender, race, and identity taxation in the academy. *Gender and Education, 24*(2), 213–227. https://doi.org/10.1080/09540253.2011.606208

Hochschild, A. (1983). *The managed heart: Commercialization of human feeling*. University of California Press.

Kovan, J. T., & Dirkx, J. M. (2003). "Being called awake": The role of transformative learning in the lives of environmental activists. *Adult Education Quarterly, 53*(2), 99–118. https://doi.org/10.1177/0741713602238906

Lee, J., & Miller, S. (2013). A self-care framework for social workers: Building a strong foundation for practice. *Families in Society, 94*(2), 96–103. https://doi.org/10.1606/1044-3894.4289

Lopez, P. J., & Gillespie, K. (2016). A love story: For "buddy system" research in the academy. *Gender, Place and Culture, 23*(12), 1689–1700. https://doi.org/10.1080/0966369X.2016.1249354

Lorde, A. (1988). *A burst of light*. Firebrand Books.

Maslach, C. (1976). Burned-out. *Human Behavior, 9*(5), 16–22. 10.4236/abb.2012.31009

Maslach, C. (2017). Finding solutions to the problem of burnout. *Consulting Psychology Journal, 69*(2), 143–152. https://doi.org/10.1037/cpb0000090

Morris, W., & Wortham, J. (Hosts). (2017, August 24). We care for ourselves and others in Trump's America [Audio podcast episode]. In *Still processing. The New York Times*.

https://www.nytimes.com/2017/08/24/podcasts/still-processing-we-care-for-ourselves-and-others-in-trumps-america.html

Nadal, K. L. (2017). "Let's get in formation": On becoming a psychologist–activist in the 21st century. *American Psychologist, 72*(9), 935–946. https://doi.org/10.1037/amp0000212

Norcross, J. C. (2009). President's column: Psychologist self-care in a workaholic nation. *Clinical Psychologist, 62*(3), 1–5. 10.1037/e619462010-002

O'Meara, K. (2016). Whose problem is it? Gender differences in faculty thinking about campus service. *Teachers College Record, 118*(9), 1–38.

O'Meara, K., Eatman, T., & Peterson, S. (2015). Advancing engaged scholarship in promotion and tenure: A roadmap and call for reform. *Liberal Education, 101*(3), 1–9.

Plyler, J. (2009). How to keep on keeping on: Sustaining ourselves in community organizing and social justice struggles. *Upping the Anti, 3,* 123–134.

Quaye, S. J., Shaw, M. D., & Hill, D. C. (2017). Blending scholar and activist identities: Establishing the need for scholar activism. *Journal of Diversity in Higher Education, 10*(4), 381–399. https://doi.org/10.1037/dhe0000060

Rodgers, K. (2010). "Anger is why we're all here": Mobilizing and managing emotions in a professional activist organization. *Social Movement Studies, 9*(3), 273–291. https://doi.org/10.1080/14742837.2010.493660

Russell, G. M. (2011). Motives of heterosexual allies in collective action for equality. *Journal of Social Issues, 67*(2), 376–393. https://doi.org/10.1111/j.1540-4560.2011.01703.x

Ward, L. (2015). Caring for ourselves? Self-care and neoliberalism. In M. Barnes, T. Brannelly, L. Ward, & N. Ward (Eds.), *Ethics of care: Critical advances in international perspective* (pp. 45–56). Policy Press. https://doi.org/10.1332/policypress/9781447316510.003.0004

4 MISTAKES WERE MADE BY ME

Recovering When an Instructor's Error Affects Classroom Dynamics

MARY E. KITE, SAMUEL M. COLBERT, AND SCOTT M. BARRERA

It could have been better. It should have been better.
—Scott M. Barrera

In that moment, I lost the opportunity to effect change.
—Samuel M. Colbert

I knew right then and there that I had lost my students' trust.
—Mary E. Kite

Facilitating effective class discussion is never easy; sometimes students are reluctant to talk and sometimes students say things that we, as instructors, find frustrating, puzzling, and hurtful. Sometimes we have a visceral reaction to a student's comments; sometimes the entire class shares that reaction. Even the most experienced instructors of diversity-related courses often struggle with how to handle challenging responses—especially those that catch

https://doi.org/10.1037/0000216-004
Navigating Difficult Moments in Teaching Diversity and Social Justice, M. E. Kite, K. A. Case, and W. R. Williams (Editors)
Copyright © 2021 by the American Psychological Association. All rights reserved.

them off guard and unprepared (Vespia & Filz, 2013). Our dilemma addresses how we can recover when our reaction hinders rather than helps and alienates rather than enlightens. This chapter's three authors include both new and experienced instructors. I (Mary) have been teaching for over 30 years; we (Sam and Scott) act simultaneously as students and instructors and can see from both sides how an instructor's response can drastically alter the learning environment.

We could all readily think of times when our responses were inadequate at best and counterproductive at worst. For example, I (Scott), identify as a sexual minority. When I was leading a class discussion on the myths associated with sexual minorities, I was taken aback when one of my students stated that individuals choose to be gay. I was able to manage my own and other students' emotional reactions but was still left feeling defeated and wondering if I could have been better prepared. Prior to entering graduate school, I (Sam) was a guest speaker teaching a cultural competency curriculum. I also identify as a sexual minority and was confident that things would go well because I had conducted over 100 presentations to high school and college students and to community organizations. Yet, a scowling student in the back threw me with his two-word response to a question about same-gender physical behavior: "Ew, gross." My response—"I am going to pretend I didn't hear that"—was unproductive. Afterwards, class resumed but my inadequate reply still echoes in my memory. During a discussion on how social factors led German citizens to be active bystanders during the Holocaust, one of my (Mary's) students said, "the Jews should have known not to get on the trains." I responded by calling out the student for not understanding the readings and succeeded only in hurting the student's feelings. Moreover, and predictable in retrospect, the other students closed ranks in support of the student who had been scolded. This created an instructor-versus-student dynamic that persisted for the rest of the semester; from that point on, discussion was superficial and unrewarding.

FACULTY REFLECTION

The experiences we describe have common elements: The students' comments were unexpected, and our responses were inconsistent with our course goals and the day's planned outcome. All of us found ourselves in a situation that required monitoring, on the fly, our own emotional reactions while still creating an environment that allows every student's opinion to be heard. At first glance, it is easy to conclude that the students' remarks were inappropriate and that our negative reactions were justified. But taking this perspective does little to help individual students develop and can make doing so nearly impossible. Instead, we must take care to avoid singling any student out for expressing an opinion, even an unpopular one. But we also cannot let inappropriate comments stand. For one thing, not responding does nothing to prepare students for navigating an increasingly diverse world (Adams, 2007). Perhaps more important, in the moment these negative remarks occur, others in the class undoubtedly are affected. For example, instructors and students may themselves identify as sexual minorities, as is true for Sam and Scott, or they may have friends and family members who do so. For these individuals, comments that demonstrate sexual prejudice have an especially strong impact.

An important step in managing hurtful comments, especially when they are unexpected, is stopping to consider the source of the students' beliefs. For example, sexual minorities exist in a culture where, not so long ago, homosexuality was considered a pathology and same-gender sexual behavior was deemed illegal and immoral; from this vantage point, perhaps the student's reaction to the topic was unsurprising (see Kite et al., 2019). For us (Sam and Scott), the antecedents of our students' responses were sown long ago and likely seemed reasonable to them. My (Mary's) student grew up in a culture that idealizes individual choice and freedom, making it difficult for them to visualize an environment, such as World War II Europe, where options were severely limited.

When teaching about diversity, we are often asking students to consider and explore material outside the bounds of their emotional safety. For example, our (Sam's and Scott's) students were both young men who may have been responding based on heterosexist, hegemonic masculine ideologies that encourage men to rebel against the specter of anything queer in an effort to protect their own self-image (Pascoe, 2005). Yet even while we recognize these societal pressures, it is difficult to step back and understand how steeped we all are in our cultural history. This includes acknowledging how far we ourselves have come and how easily we can forget how much exposure we have had to diversity issues, compared with our students. It is unrealistic to believe that students can fully grasp these complex issues based on one set of readings or even an entire semester of material. Moreover, as Holmes (2013) noted, if we expect students to examine their biases, we also must be willing to examine our own. Thus, "both students and instructors need to be willing to examine their assumptions about things that seem as obvious as the fact that the sky is blue" (p. 249). For all of us, this is especially difficult for emotional topics.

Our responses are also affected by the image of ourselves as good instructors who provide our students with information that would preclude ignorant remarks. For example, I (Mary) honestly believed the readings were clear and that the students should have readily seen the wisdom and insight they provided. It seemed to me that the students should have understood why the consent and participation of everyday German citizens made it nearly impossible for those identified as "vermin" to avoid being deported to the concentration camps (Goldhagen, 1996). Similarly, I (Scott) had discussed the research demonstrating that sexual orientation has biological, psychological, and social origins (Lehmiller, 2018); thus, the student's comment at once contradicted that research and invalidated the struggles of many sexual minority individuals. My (Sam's) question about same-gender affection was aimed at moving the discussion forward; I had used that approach many times and so was not expecting a negative emotional reaction. When we believe we have done a good job covering the issues or leading a discussion, perhaps it is natural to feel that our teaching ability is being challenged and to respond defensively when students fail to understand or say things we find jarring. In such situations, instructors can engage in the self-serving attribution bias and blame the students rather than themselves (Greenberg et al., 1982). Unfortunately, doing so can close doors and result in lost opportunities.

Where might our defensiveness come from? One answer can be found in the writings of Palmer (2007) who addressed the ways instructors' fear of conflict is heightened when opposing views meet. As Palmer noted, the fear of losing our identity as an effective instructor is tied to our own strongly held beliefs and values. When students' comments catch us off guard, it can call into question our efficacy as an instructor or our role as an authority in the room. In these cases, the resulting fear is a strong motivator that can alter how we would normally respond or can sometimes prevent us from taking action altogether. Thus, in these situations, we might distance ourselves from the interaction, quickly correct the student, or dismiss the student's point, but doing so "distances us from our colleagues, our students, our subjects, ourselves" (Palmer, 2007, p. 36). Distancing allows us to protect our own worldviews, but the result is that we fail to learn about the students' worldviews and knowledge base and what their expertise or perspective can bring to the discussion. Fear in the classroom can lead even the most polished and experienced professor to feel discouraged, ashamed, or defeated. But acknowledging our fears can bring a sense of normalcy and can lead us to a place where we feel encouraged and empowered. When we are open to considering how fear affects our responses, it challenges us as educators and opens us to the possibility of connecting with students and having a positive impact on their development.

Of course, it is natural for us to be affected by the emotional meaning of a student's remark. This meaning is conveyed through verbal content, but also nonverbally. As instructors, we receive information from the student's facial tone, cadence, tone of voice, and body posture (Griffin & Ouellett, 2007). As in any interpersonal interaction, this information affects our own emotional state and can contribute to feelings of being undermined. In these situations, we are likely to perceive a student's reaction as challenging and this may bring up feelings of fear and inadequacy. When these fears are in play, our reaction can be harsh, swift, and counterproductive. In contrast, when we recognize that the students' history and experience influenced their responses, we become open to the ways in which we can educate them without alienating them.

Attachment theory (Bowlby, 1969) offers another lens through which to understand and adjust our responses. Bowlby (1969) proposed that a secure base is a safe haven that people can go to when they become distressed; from this secure place, people can more easily explore the unfamiliar because they know they can return to that which is safe. Ainsworth's (1985) strange-situation paradigm is applicable here. In these experiments, attachment styles to the infants' primary caregiver were tested through exploring the babies' reactions to their mother on reuniting after a separation. Ainsworth found that babies with insecure attachment styles either avoided or were ambivalent toward their mothers on reuniting, whereas those with secure attachment styles happily reunited with their mothers. Those with secure attachment styles fared better with separation and were able to explore their environment when they knew their caregiver was present. In essence, babies who perceived their caregiver as a secure base were better able to deal with distress. At first glance, it seems the classroom should be a familiar, safe place. After all, our students have spent decades in this environment. Yet most of our students have little experience discussing emotional issues and find the prospect of doing so unsettling and even frightening (Vespia & Filz, 2013). Classrooms where difficult dialogues take place may be a strange situation—one in which we ask students to leave the comfort of the familiar and risk exposing themselves to new information and to new ways of seeing the world (Fleming, 2008).

As Fleming (2008) noted, to ensure that students are comfortable with difficult discussions, it is important that the instructor acts as a secure base from which the class can explore new ideas and leave the confines of their previously known environment. Only then can students cross the terrain of what they have previously known to be "true" and move toward that which might have new meaning for them. A classroom where a student's unwelcome remarks are attributed to a lack of understanding and an opportunity to educate is a very different space than one in which those comments are seen as ignorant and deserving of rebuke. When I (Sam) uttered the words "I am going to pretend I didn't hear that," I failed to create a secure base for my student. My response—or lack thereof—resulted in a loss of connection, and I communicated to the entire class that this was not a place of safety. Similarly, for my (Mary's) students, the message was clear: Statements that I did not like would be met with rejection or ignored. The cost was that my students lost a safe classroom environment. Instead, both of us could have reframed the student's remark, focusing on their or others' emotional distress rather than our own. We reflect on possible ways to do this in our Best Practices section.

We are advocating the creation of an environment that allows every student's opinions to be heard, even those who share an unpopular opinion. But we must also be mindful of how hurtful remarks affect the other students in the course. We (Scott and Sam) needed to consider the feelings of the students who identify as sexual minorities or who are allies to LQBTQ+ individuals. The person in power (the instructor) must somehow strike a balance that acknowledges the safety and well-being of all students while directly addressing remarks that invalidate another group's experience. Hitting this mark is far from easy, but the strategies we identify in the Best Practices section can help manage the tension that comes from creating a space where students feel comfortable sharing their views, but naive, hurtful remarks also are fully addressed.

CONSIDERATIONS OF CONTEXT AND INTERSECTIONALITY

The members of Mary's and Scott's class were White students from the Midwest with limited experience with diversity. Sam's students were also mostly White students from the Northeast. If their classrooms had been more diverse, there might have been opportunities for students from different backgrounds to share their experiences and relate them to the readings; however, it is important to ensure that those students are not put in the position of being spokespeople for their group. Other options would be to bring in panelists who could discuss the topic and share their experiences or to find videos or readings that focused on the issues. So, for example, personal accounts from Holocaust survivors might better illustrate the points that were made in the theoretical papers Mary's students read. Scott and Sam could have borrowed one of the experiential activities from the Safe Zone training they have conducted in their university's counseling center; this training is designed to encourage empathy with marginalized communities.

As in many situations, what works for some might not work for others and this can depend on the instructors' social group memberships. For example, male instructors are often given more leeway when directly confronting students, whereas female instructors are generally expected to be warm and caring (Basow & Martin, 2012). Ethnic minority instructors are viewed as more knowledgeable about diversity topics, but as more biased, compared with European American instructors (Littleford et al., 2010) and can be penalized for self-disclosure (Sue et al., 2011). Both majority and minority group instructors will likely find themselves teaching about social groups to which they do not belong; Goldstein (Chapter 15, this volume) provides an excellent overview of the challenges this poses. Furthermore, both students and instructors have multiple intersecting social identities, some of which carry more privilege and power than others. Thus, instructors must be mindful about how their own and their students' privilege might affect classroom dynamics: What might work in one classroom at one moment in time, may not be effective in a different classroom or a different moment (Case, 2017; see Warner et al., Chapter 11, this volume).

BEST PRACTICES: WHAT COULD HAVE BEEN DIFFERENT?

An important goal in education is that the student be able to demonstrate knowledge of and competence in the course content. Thinking back to our scenarios, the students had already been provided with information that should have prevented such comments. If we then conclude that the students' remarks are unwarranted, it is difficult to quickly find an appropriate response. Instead of internalizing these comments or making our own negative remark, however, each of us could have recognized that the students' response reflected their developmental stage or their personal and cultural history and not our teaching ability or their inattention to the course material. From this vantage point, we could aim to facilitate students' learning. We could also model how to appropriately confront prejudice. Effectively doing so has the added advantage of increasing our self-esteem and our feelings of empowerment (Barreto & Ellemers, 2015). Moreover, an appropriate response can result in students seeing us as more effective instructors (Boysen, 2013). We offer several potential strategies for dealing with the unexpected, but also acknowledge that what will be effective will vary by the instructor's approach and the unique situation.

Create Ground Rules

Goldstein (Chapter 2, this volume) highlights the importance of creating ground rules that set the stage for difficult conversations. Instructors are less likely to lose a class by their reaction if they and the students have practiced following these rules. In classrooms where emotional topics are considered, it is important to start small: Use these rules to facilitate discussion of less controversial issues before attempting to lead a discussion on difficult issues. The importance of the instructor–class relationship cannot be undervalued. Using low-risk icebreaker activities at the beginning of the term can be particularly useful. This gives students a chance to share information about themselves while learning about others, often in a fun and amusing manner. Students also find out how the instructor reacts to their comments and hopefully will recognize that this classroom is a safe space.

Acknowledge Your Error

When facing scenarios such as the ones we have described, the first, and perhaps most important step, is to acknowledge our mistake and to apologize. For example, in situations where I (Mary) believe my response is inadequate, I own it. But, I also allow that over the course of a 45-hour semester, it is difficult to never misspeak or inadvertently offend one of the students. So that students can understand this, I talk with them about how complex an instructor's role can be and about how difficult it is to balance covering the material, finding sufficient time for discussion, and making space to address students' needs and concerns. I also make clear that I want students' feedback at the time problems arise; I point out that if students wait until the course evaluations to state their concerns, I will be unable to adequately address the error or make appropriate adjustments. Of course, when students do bring issues up, it is important to hear them out and not respond defensively.

Let Time Pass

Sometimes, the best approach is to not respond in the moment. This gives the instructor time to better consider how to respond. It can be helpful, for example, to wait and circle back to the issue later that day or even the next class day. This also decouples the individual student from the comment so that, when the issue is addressed, that person is no longer singled out as "the problem." For example, in a subsequent class, Scott could have again reviewed the evidence that sexual orientation is not a choice. He could also have described the research showing that people who believe otherwise tend to be more prejudiced (Whitley, 1990). As part of that review, he could have emphasized how hurtful comments can be to sexual minorities and their allies. That said, it is important to recognize that we are not always able— and there is not always time—to address every microaggression or every misstatement. On reflection, the instructor may realize that the comment is best left alone. For example, some students make comments solely with the intent of creating conflict. Reinforcing that behavior may have more costs than benefits. Consultation with other instructors can be a helpful tool here.

Let the Students Respond

Particularly in classes with well-established ground rules, one good option is allowing the other students to respond to the hurtful remark. We have all had the experience of another student giving exactly the right response in a more eloquent way than we could have. When this happens, it makes the classroom experience fulfilling for both the instructor and the other students. Sometimes other students get things wrong; at such times, it is also helpful to look for the kernel of truth in the student's answer, perhaps responding with "I am very glad you brought that point up as many people have similar thoughts." This can create a starting point for discussion while simultaneously signaling that it is okay to answer and get things wrong. Opening the discussion to other students has the added benefit of giving the instructor time to decide how to best respond, particularly if the discussion gets heated.

Model Effective Responding

In the counseling literature, Teyber and McClure (2011) described the idea of a corrective emotional experience where a counselor provides a client with a response to an old relationship pattern that is new and more satisfying than what the client has previously experienced. Applied to the classroom, the instructor provides this experience by responding to a mistake in a way that makes the student feel heard. Thus, Sam could have modeled unconditional positive regard, acknowledging the student's disgust while still exploring the pain it caused others. When the student inaccurately stated that homosexuality is a choice, Scott could have been vulnerable enough to express how those words affected him personally. These responses might be emotionally corrective because the students may not have previously experienced beneficent confrontation. Yet there are risks to personalizing an issue, particularly for faculty from underrepresented groups who teach multicultural classes (Sue et al., 2011). Before self-disclosing, it is important to first assess classroom dynamics and evaluate how the instructor's self-disclosure will affect those interpersonal dynamics. Effective modeling can also be accomplished by using an active learning exercise; for example, Blumer et al. (2013) provided a number of excellent classroom activities that address heterosexual and gender-conforming privilege. During these activities, students can explore what was said and its effect on others, making it more likely that the student who made the comment understands its impact.

STRUCTURAL IMPLICATIONS

Many teaching missteps are easily corrected. If we provide inaccurate or outdated explanations of theories or research results, for example, we can simply acknowledge our error and update students about current thinking. Doing so demonstrates that learning is a lifelong process and that being open to new ideas is a positive thing. The miscalculations that are the focus of our chapter, however, are often not so easily repaired and can sometimes have long-term consequences that extend beyond the classroom. Such risks are higher for graduate student instructors or untenured faculty members, but they can be harmful to seasoned instructors as well. We consider structural barriers that are relevant to our dilemmas, but also point to structural supports that can facilitate recovery from our mistakes.

Structural Barriers

There are many risks, real and perceived, if "things go badly." Teaching evaluations might be lower than desired, and students' comments might be hurtful and difficult to read. If the interaction is described on a website such as RateMyProfessors.com, it may be seen by students and colleagues both inside and outside of one's institution. Word might spread informally to other faculty or students—sometimes without our awareness. Discussions about the event might take place on social media and these can remain visible for indefinite periods of time. When an instructor's actions become part of the gossip mill, it can cause damage to that person's reputation far into the future. Students also might informally report the misstep to an administrator; in some cases, a formal complaint against the instructor could be filed. In either case, the instructor will likely be asked to respond to the student's concern, which can be anxiety provoking and emotionally draining, even if the matter is readily resolved.

Structural Supports

When teaching subjects that might be deemed as controversial, the importance of a supportive colleague cannot be understated. We have found it particularly helpful to consult a faculty mentor who can guide us through the terrain of our particular department and institution. This person can nonjudgmentally guide us through difficult scenarios, empathize with the stress of teaching a diversity class, and help us anticipate the kinds of scenarios described in this chapter.

One useful resource is the faculty and staff of one's university's Center for Teaching and Learning; if a campus does not have a center, excellent advice can be found online. For example, the website of the Society for the Teaching of Psychology (http://www.teachpsych.org) offers a number of resources for teaching diversity. Instructors should also seek out continuing education opportunities, such as instructional lectures offered on their campus. Attending conferences that address teaching excellence can provide information, insights, and networking opportunities (see http://www.teachpsych.org for a current list). In this way, regardless of whether there is structural support, all instructors can take the risks necessary to effectively teach a diversity class.

RESOURCES

Blumer, M. L. C., Green, M. S., Thomte, N. L., & Green, P. M. (2013). Are we queer yet? Addressing heterosexual and gender-conforming privilege. In K. A. Case (Ed.), *Deconstructing privilege: Teaching and learning as allies in the classroom* (pp. 151–168). Routledge.

The authors offer excellent advice about how to address heterosexual and gender-conforming privilege in the classroom. Their activities can be readily modified to address other forms of privilege.

Dunn, D. S., Gurung, R. A. R., Naufel, K. Z., & Wilson, J. H. (Eds.). (2013). *Controversy in the psychology classroom: Using hot topics to foster critical thinking*. American Psychological Association. https://doi.org/10.1037/14038-000

This book includes several chapters that address the difficulties instructors face when teaching about an emotional topic. The editors and contributors offer concrete advice about ways to prevent classroom disruptions and how to handle any conflict that emerges despite a faculty member's best efforts.

Kite, M. E. (n.d.). *Breaking the prejudice habit*. http://www.breakingprejudice.org

This site provides resources for instructors of diversity, including group activities, assignments, videos, and podcasts, and links to other websites that provide advice and hands-on activities.

Palmer, P. J. (2007). *The courage to teach: Exploring the inner landscape of a teacher's life*. Wiley.

Palmer's book provides a thought-provoking account of the fear that is felt both by students and instructors in the classroom. Palmer gives insight into this fear and describes how instructors can use their emotions to connect with students and react to classroom challenges in a nondefensive way.

REFERENCES

Adams, M. (2007). Pedagogical frameworks for social justice education. In M. Adams, L. A. Bell, & P. Griffin (Eds.), *Teaching for diversity and social justice* (pp. 15–33). Routledge. https://doi.org/10.4324/9780203940822

Ainsworth, M. D. (1985). Patterns of infant–mother attachments: Antecedents and effects on development. *Bulletin of the New York Academy of Medicine, 61*, 771–791.

Barreto, M., & Ellemers, N. (2015). Detecting and experiencing prejudice: New answers to old questions. *Advances in Experimental Social Psychology, 52*, 139–219. https://doi.org/10.1016/bs.aesp.2015.02.001

Basow, S. A., & Martin, J. L. (2012). Bias in student evaluations. In M. E. Kite (Ed.), *Effective evaluation of teaching: A guide for faculty and administrators*. http://teachpsych.org/ebooks/evals2012/index.php

Blumer, M. L. C., Green, M. S., Thomte, N. L., & Green, P. M. (2013). Are we queer yet? Addressing heterosexual and gender-conforming privilege. In K. A. Case (Ed.), *Deconstructing privilege: Teaching and learning as allies in the classroom* (pp. 151–168). Routledge.

Bowlby, J. (1969). *Attachment and loss*. Basic Books.

Boysen, G. A. (2013). Confronting math stereotypes in the classroom: Its effect on female college students' sexism and perceptions of confronters. *Sex Roles, 69*, 297–307. https://doi.org/10.1007/s11199-013-0287-y

Case, K. A. (Ed.). (2017). *Intersectional pedagogy: Complicating identity and social justice*. Routledge.

Fleming, T. (2008). A secure base for adult learning: Attachment theory and adult education. *Adult Learner: The Irish Journal of Adult and Community Education, 2008*, 33–53.

Goldhagen, D. J. (1996). *Hitler's willing executioners: Ordinary Germans and the Holocaust*. Knopf.

Greenberg, J., Pyszczynski, T., & Solomon, S. (1982). The self-serving attributional bias: Beyond self-presentation. *Journal of Experimental Social Psychology, 18*(1), 56–67. https://doi.org/10.1016/0022-1031(82)90081-6

Griffin, P., & Ouellett, M. L. (2007). Facilitating social justice education courses. In M. Adams, L. A. Bell, & P. Griffin (Eds.), *Teaching for diversity and social justice* (2nd ed., pp. 89–113). Routledge.

Holmes, J. D. (2013). Using controversies to teach scientific thinking in psychology: Topics and issues. In D. S. Dunn, R. A. R. Gurung, K. Z. Naufel, & J. H. Wilson (Eds.), *Controversy in the psychology classroom: Using hot topics to foster critical thinking* (pp. 245–256). American Psychological Association. https://doi.org/10.1037/14038-015

Kite, M. E., Togans, L. J., III, & Schultz, T. J. (2019). Stability or change? A cross cultural look at attitudes toward sexual and gender identity minorities. In K. D. Keith (Ed.), *Cross-cultural psychology: Contemporary themes and perspectives* (2nd ed., pp. 427–450). Wiley-Blackwell.

Lehmiller, J. J. (2018). *The psychology of human sexuality* (2nd ed.). Wiley.

Littleford, L. N., Ong, K. S., Tseng, A., Milliken, J. C., & Humy, S. (2010). Perceptions of European American and African American instructors teaching race-focused courses. *Journal of Diversity in Higher Education, 3*, 230–244. https://doi.org/10.1037/a0020950

Palmer, P. J. (2007). *The courage to teach: Exploring the inner landscape of a teacher's life*. Wiley.

Pascoe, C. J. (2005). "Dude, you're a fag": Adolescent masculinity and the fag discourse. *Sexualities, 8*, 329–346. https://doi.org/10.1177/1363460705053337

Sue, D. W., Rivera, D. P., Watkins, N. L., Kim, R. H., Kim, S., & Williams, C. D. (2011). Racial dialogues: Challenges faculty of color face in the classroom. *Cultural Diversity and Ethnic Minority Psychology, 17*(3), 331–340. https://doi.org/10.1037/a0024190

Teyber, E., & McClure, F. (2011). *Interpersonal process in therapy: An integrative model* (6th ed.). Cengage Learning.

Vespia, K. M., & Filz, T. E. (2013). Preventing and handling classroom disruptions. In D. S. Dunn, R. A. R. Gurung, K. Z. Naufel, & J. H. Wilson (Eds.), *Controversy in the psychology classroom: Using hot topics to foster critical thinking* (pp. 23–32). American Psychological Association. https://doi.org/10.1037/14038-002

Whitley, B. E., Jr. (1990). The relationship of heterosexuals' attributions for the causes of homosexuality to attitudes toward lesbians and gay men. *Personality and Social Psychology Bulletin, 16*, 369–377. https://doi.org/10.1177/0146167290162016

5

WHEN THE PROFESSOR EXPERIENCES STEREOTYPE THREAT IN THE CLASSROOM

DESDAMONA RIOS, KIM A. CASE, SALENA M. BRODY, AND DAVID P. RIVERA

When marginalized students face stereotype threat in academic settings, it may be affected by classmates, the faculty member, and/or context. *Stereotype threat* occurs when a person encounters a particular situation or context that results in feeling that they may confirm a stereotype about their ingroup (Steele & Aronson, 1995). For example, a female professor of aeronautical engineering may feel stereotype threat when presenting a conference talk. Although student academic performance has been a central focus of stereotype threat research, students are not the only ones who are nervous or apprehensive at the start of the semester. Faculty wonder about how the personalities, backgrounds, identities, and attitudes of the students in our classrooms might shape classroom dynamics. Early days in the semester involve faculty and students sizing each other up and making assumptions about each other. Some expectations facilitate a successful semester, such as students expecting clearly articulated syllabi or faculty expecting students to arrive on time. Other expectations arise from stereotypes about particular facets of a faculty member's identity, which in turn may negatively impact

https://doi.org/10.1037/0000216-005
Navigating Difficult Moments in Teaching Diversity and Social Justice, M. E. Kite, K. A. Case, and W. R. Williams (Editors)
Copyright © 2021 by the American Psychological Association. All rights reserved.

students' perceptions of the faculty member. In some cases, student behavior signals a lack of confidence in the instructor which can heighten anxiety and negatively affect classroom climate and faculty well-being. As these experiences repeat consistently over time, the threat of confirming stereotypes may carry forward and begin to alter our classroom behaviors as educators. In this chapter, we explore scenarios where faculty members experienced stereotype threat in the classroom and the impact those threats had on faculty well-being and teaching.

EXAMPLES OF STEREOTYPE THREAT IN THE CLASSROOM

We outline dilemmas we have faced related to stereotypes about social justice educators, people of color, and feminists, and our observed compromised performance as a reaction to the threat. These stereotype threats occur whether they originate with students, faculty colleagues, or administrators, and they can emerge across academic contexts (e.g., the classroom, committee meetings, conferences, interviews).

Desdamona's Story

In the context of stereotype threat, my threatened identities include Chicana, woman, and politically liberal. As a junior faculty member, I was the only underrepresented woman of color in my department, and I am now the only tenured person of color in the department. I frequently encounter confusing and hurtful comments (in class and in course evaluations) and nonverbal behaviors from students. Diversity discussions in committees would result in colleagues rolling their eyes after I found the courage to offer my input. These stereotype threatening moments often resulted in me getting physically and psychologically flustered, nervous, worried, and disoriented, which then led to stuttering, stammering, and being unable to clearly articulate my thoughts into words.

Student qualitative comments within official course evaluations revealed negative feedback, including the following:

- "A really nice lady, but . . ."
- "Mastery is demonstrated by quality, not quantity. Shorten the articles."
- "I enjoy your class and teaching methods; however, I wish you didn't push your political agenda down our throats."
- "I would change the teaching style and exams. The instructor did not disseminate information in a way I was able to apply when taking the exam."

Some students make comments indicating I am condescending in tone or angry, which contradicts other student comments about being a "really nice lady" but not a knowledgeable one. These descriptions feel extreme given that I strive to support, encourage, and lift students up as a mentor and academic guide. After several years struggling to shift to meet students' needs, I noticed that certain negative comments never go away. In fact, I began to recognize three stereotype spheres of student feedback present in course evaluations, during class, and within face-to-face meetings:

- Woman: bossy, nice but not smart
- Chicana/Latina: lacks intelligence, hates White people
- Feminist: angry, rigid, man-hater, cold, unavailable

Once quite confident in my extensive pedagogical training and teaching abilities, over time I became less secure and unsure of how to improve my courses.

Kim's Story

When I think about my own encounters with stereotype threat, my threatened intersectional identities include my background as a first-generation, working-class academic and my role as a female professor. My personal and professional focus on social justice education and community activism with regard to antiracism, sexual minority and transgender rights, and feminism also impact my experiences of stereotype threat in the classroom and broader academy. My early career days in the classroom included weekly encounters with rude, dismissive, disruptive student behavior from a wide range of races, ages, and genders. White students, some from conservative backgrounds, pushed back when learning about the social psychology of prejudice, calling me biased or accusing me of grading them low due to their belief systems. A White male student once spent every single class session interrupting, mocking, and heckling me from the back of the room. A White woman in one of my women's studies courses refused to return to class after I provided a research-based response during class discussion to her statement that poor people do not want to work. After I denied her request for an extra week to study for an exam, a Latina student accused me of not caring about women's issues (although her request was due to forgetting the exam date and unrelated to gender issues).

These persistent microaggressions and microassaults on my credibility and ethics as a professor took a psychological and an emotional toll on me during the vulnerable tenure-track phase of my career. At first, I was fearful of firmly addressing problematic behavior in these students and allowed them to create toxic learning environments for other students, who seemed eager to learn. I had no expectation that administration would support me if disgruntled students complained because of my identities and social justice pedagogies. At the same time, I suspected my whiteness would carry a lot of privilege and protection if such an occasion were to arise.

Salena's Story

In the context of stereotype threat, my threatened identities include social justice professor and feminist. I consistently worry about being sufficiently open to opposing viewpoints in the classroom. In courses that are nonrequired diversity electives, many students may self-select into the course because of their interest in social justice issues. This often results in a lopsided classroom dynamic with few students voicing dissenting opinions. When this happens, my thoughts circle around to whether my behaviors signal inclusion in classroom discussions (see Brody & Bernal, Chapter 7, this volume). At the heart of my worry is the thought that dissenting students stereotype professors, particularly those teaching diversity content, as having liberal bias and being unreceptive or intolerant to other perspectives.

Some arguments imply being a liberal professor teaching a social justice-oriented course means an adequate range of views are not presented in my class, and this ruffles my feathers. I know that my course exposes students to a wide range of material representing diverse viewpoints and requires them to be active, critical readers of the news. Yet, the threat of being perceived as biased still manages to get under my skin despite my acknowledgment that this stereotype does not reflect the reality of my classroom. In this case, I have not internalized the stereotype, as in Desdamona's example, but it nonetheless affects the way I encounter students with dissenting viewpoints. For example, after students post their first response to the online discussion board, I carefully comb through the responses to make sure that the excerpts I highlight in class include a dissenting voice in the classroom. As the semester progresses, I make extra efforts to give students ample airtime to counter the stereotype that I am unwelcoming of different viewpoints. This stereotype changes the way I would naturally and organically welcome and include divergent voices by making me hyperaware of my level of inclusiveness as a faculty member. This change in my teaching has resulted in a disproportionate advantage to the most privileged students in my classroom rather than a climate that serves the best interests of all students.

David's Story

In the context of stereotype threat, my threatened identities include social justice scholar and man of color. Many faculty from marginalized backgrounds report that they contend with stereotypes directed toward them from the recruitment phase through retention and promotion phases (e.g., Niemann, 2012). For example, when presenting a faculty position job talk on racial microaggression research, a senior White faculty member repeatedly interrupted my talk, suggesting microaggressions do not exist. In reflecting on my experience, these kinds of challenges are less about the actual sociopsychological construct of microaggressions and more about stereotyping faculty of color as intellectually inferior and overly sensitive. Systemically, and not so coincidentally, this example is a common microaggression theme (ascription of intelligence) experienced by many marginalized people across contexts (e.g., Rivera et al., 2010). These experiences carry through to the classroom, leading us to second-guess our approaches to teaching psychology, whether we have sufficient knowledge about the topic, and our ability to understand or gauge the relevance of social issues in our students' lives.

FACULTY REFLECTION

As demonstrated in the stereotype literature, rather than using cognitive resources toward teaching and scholarship, threatened faculty use their energy questioning their competency, intelligence, and expertise. Facing threats of negative stereotypes and evidence that students were perceiving me (Desdamona) in stereotypical ways, I began to internalize these messages. As a scholar of feminist theory, critical race theory, and intersectional theory, the frequent threat of being stereotyped wore me down to the point of doubting myself. The direct challenge to my (David's) intellect during my interview caused me to momentarily question the veracity of my work, which was a threat to my presentation performance in that setting and in the classroom. These types of questions and challenges based on perceived identity, rather than actual content and competency, create an additional layer of burden that saps cognitive energy, which further complicates the faculty member's ability to perform most optimally.

Heightened Anxiety

One symptom of stereotype threat is heightened anxiety (Baysu & Phalet, 2019). In the case of teaching social justice, for faculty who experience stereotype threat or for allies who witness it, performances may be compromised by experiencing heightened anxiety before, during, or after teaching a lesson. In my (Salena's) experience, the stereotype that faculty have a liberal bias and are therefore unreceptive or intolerant of dissenting voices has been amplified by popular media sources and conservative outlets (e.g., Sunstein, 2018). Students who espouse similar ideas may enter a class with social justice themes expecting a professor to be a radical liberal, have an agenda, be unwelcoming to diverse viewpoints, and be intolerant of opposing views. For example, an official student course evaluation of mine (Kim's) declared that I had an "LGBT agenda" as a professor teaching Psychology of Race and Gender.

Chasing Perceived Neutrality

To avoid offending students, all of us have unconsciously responded in various ways, including being overly nice, apologetic, and/or accommodating, which then redirects cognitive energy away from critical discussions about social issues to our efforts to appear unbiased, neutral, and grounded in psychological science. Examples of apologies include prefacing lectures on racism, heterosexism, transphobia, and other oppressive systems with "not all men . . ." or "not all White people . . . ," which privileges the most powerful groups and waters down the oppression experienced by marginalized groups (Onwuachi-Willig, 2012). Being overly critical of our performance as social justice educators has often left us feeling we should be stronger/smarter/neutral/more competent. Contrary to current higher education trends, neutrality in the classroom does not necessarily define excellent teaching. As I (Kim) noted in my model for intersectional pedagogy, we must resist the neutrality myth that claims all voices deserve the same level of legitimacy and validation within the classroom (Case, 2017).

Stereotype Threat Impact on Performance

Stereotype threat theory proposes that knowledge of the negative stereotype, without the requirement of internalizing the stereotype, is enough to impair performance on a task when one's target identity is salient. Stereotype threat research illuminates the consequences of negative stereotypes on performance. For example, women reminded of their gender before taking a math quiz performed worse than women who did not encounter gender identity cues that trigger negative stereotypes of women as bad at math (Spencer et al., 1999). As an example of racial stereotype threat, research findings illustrated that African Americans intellectual test performance suffered compared to Whites when race was emphasized (Steele & Aronson, 1995).

The stereotype threat scholarship advanced our understanding of how the threat of confirming a negative stereotype can have severe consequences for test-taking, college admissions exams, performance on graduate school and job interviews, and more (Harrison et al., 2006; Steele, 2011). Yet, specific challenges arising for faculty who experience stereotype threat in the classroom remain unaddressed. Women and men of color, as well as White women and men who speak up as antiracist allies, may be unaware of stereotype threat having an impact on their own responses to student behavior and negative feedback. Even those of us well versed in the stereotype threat literature are not immune to awareness of negative stereotypes about our in-groups. Even simple awareness, without internalizing or believing a stereotype, can result in stereotype threat negatively impacting performance.

CONSIDERATIONS OF CONTEXT AND INTERSECTIONALITY

As implied by the title of Claude Steele's (1997) groundbreaking article "A Threat in the Air," the potential for activating stereotype threat exists because of the insidious nature of stereotypes, and no one is immune to internalizing stereotypes about others and the self (David, 2013). Just as every person holds multiple identities that interact to create a particular worldview, people also hold awareness of various stereotypes within their culture attached to their coconstructed identities. Of course, cross-cultural and transnational variations in stereotypes may prevent exposure and awareness of a stereotype's existence, and therefore, prevent the threat. Our awareness of the potential for stereotyped beliefs to exist in all contexts creates a climate for stereotype threat to manifest by the threatened individual confirming and enacting the stereotype. Over time, engaging in behaviors that students perceive as stereotypical may contribute to internalization of the stereotype, such as believing we are incompetent or unintelligent.

There are multiple avenues for stereotype threat to influence faculty performance across academic contexts, creating heightened anxiety. For faculty from groups who have historically been viewed in the United States as less intelligent, including Native and Indigenous, Black, Latinx, and working-class faculty, knowledge of those stereotypes may especially compromise performance. These threats come from many sources. Students may perceive us as not having mastered the disciplinary material. Faculty colleagues and administrators may perceive us as unqualified, incapable, bad departmental citizens, or inarticulate. Evaluators of our research, such as journal reviewers or the audience of a presentation, may see us as biased.

In the case of teaching social justice across the psychology curriculum, there are several ways our performance may be compromised due to Steele's (1997) proposed threat in the air. Students often stereotype us as radical, having a hidden agenda, or aiming to convert students into raging liberal activists. For faculty who identify as feminists and, in particular, as intersectional feminists, attention to various social identities may trigger different students for different reasons. For example, a White intersectional feminist who addresses racism may be perceived as anti-White by some students and a man-hater by others (Case et al., 2012). As a White woman, my (Kim's) student evaluations have included comments labeling me as racist against White people. For all of our dilemmas, whether grounded in our identities as marginalized faculty and/or social justice educators, stereotype threat cause us to question whether we should pull back, refocus that job talk, stay silent in committee meetings, water down the curriculum, reduce our academic rigor, and be overly apologetic for our inclusive pedagogies.

BEST PRACTICES

A strength of intersectional theory is the emphasis on understanding a person in context, meaning systems of oppression such as racism, classism, sexism, and heterosexism may be experienced differently yet simultaneously depending on their positionality within social hierarchies (Cole, 2009; Collins, 1990; Crenshaw, 1991). This perspective can provide a framework for best practices for addressing stereotype threat.

Fix the System, Not the Professor

Recommendations for faculty members with a stereotyped identity should not solely focus on "fixing themselves," with suggestions for improving the clarity of their lectures, being more available to students, or spending infinite hours monitoring their responses to student feedback. These efforts to improve our pedagogical practices will not prevent us from continuing to experience backlash from students or colleagues who perceive us as incompetent, inaccessible, or politically biased against them. Instead, addressing stereotype threat at the personal and systemic levels is necessary for exposing implicit bias and accepted practices that harm stereotyped faculty. Importantly, we can implement person-level strategies without victim blaming or assigning deficits to the instructor. As we discuss below, personal and professional responsibility to address implicit bias also rests on allies who seek to support marginalized and minoritized faculty.

Focus on Students' Development

It is important to reflect on the fact that embedded in our social justice pedagogy is the challenge of privilege. Students are often uncomfortable in the process of learning about their own privilege (Case, 2013; Case & Cole, 2013; Rios et al., 2017). By recognizing this discomfort, educators can facilitate student empowerment toward using their privilege to improve their communities (Case, 2013, 2017; Rios et al., 2017). Doing so can reduce negative performance outcomes and allow social justice-oriented teachers to facilitate the development of critical thinking in our students and their application of psychological science to address social inequities. For example, students who complete our courses learn to use their privilege to make things better and also become more aware of what is happening in their communities.

Look for the Positive

As a self-care practice, it can be helpful to look at aggregated evaluation scores in "core" psychology courses where diversity is not the focus, compared to diversity courses where our students may expect to engage with social justice issues. Additionally, remembering positive student feedback, as opposed to one or two negative comments, reminds faculty of why social justice pedagogy matters (Rios et al., 2017). For example, students often notice our passion and commitment and remind us that they appreciate our dedication to addressing the injustices of all people. We find that returning to positive comments from our own students is an important self-care practice reminding us of the powerful transformations that result from social justice pedagogy. Reviewing positive feedback affirms not only our teaching effectiveness, but also that we care for our students enough to facilitate their growth as critical thinkers and community leaders. In spite of challenges faced, we are often encouraged by students' written comments such as "Thank you for your passion and commitment. It is hard to find people who are so dedicated to [addressing] the injustices of all peoples" and "Dr. [X] is a great professor and pushes students to become better people, not just students."

Institutional Interventions and Policy

Administrators who do not consider the deleterious effects of stereotype threat in their contexts are, in essence, allowing the institution to enter into a symbiotic and collaborative relationship with stereotype threat. Doing so maintains systems of privilege and oppression that in turn create the various disparities experienced by marginalized members of the academic community, including faculty (Stewart & Valian, 2018). Institutions can attend to stereotype threat in academic contexts by simply educating the community about the existence of this harmful phenomenon.

Research suggests that the knowledge of stereotype threat and how it subconsciously motivates a person to confirm a stereotype is, in and of itself, an intervention that effectively reduces the negative impact on performance (Johns et al., 2005). This knowledge may work in both directions, as folks who may be potential instigators of stereotype threat can develop a conscious awareness of their role in this process and decrease their negative impact. As diversity, equity, and inclusion efforts are ramping up on many campuses across the country, stereotype threat can be used as a lens to analyze policies and procedures as well as the evaluative feedback that is given to marginalized and minoritized faculty across the recruitment, retention, and promotion process. A stereotype threat lens can help peer evaluators and administrators understand when policies, procedures, or evaluative feedback are unfairly influenced by stereotype threat. This awareness can prevent others from making the common misattribution that the faculty member is to blame from what appears to be problematic performance.

Find Administrator Allies

An administrator ally believes faculty when they describe their experiences in the classroom and does not assume that the faculty's race, gender, or politics are the most salient feature of their identity all the time. An administrator ally can serve as a mentor who helps faculty navigate backlash in the classroom, provides constructive and fair feedback on how to improve teaching practices, reminds faculty of their strengths as a professor and scholar, and publicly promotes the value of teaching social justice in the psychology classroom. Administrators unfamiliar with stereotype threat and the larger challenge of retaining faculty of color and faculty who seek to diversify their psychology curriculum could start by reviewing relevant literature and resources, like those listed at the end of this chapter. Administrators must support underrepresented faculty and faculty who do social justice work in their classrooms by believing and affirming their experiences.

For concrete illustration of how administrators play a role in stereotype threat, we provided an example of when an administrator failed to act as an ally. When a White female student met with me (Desdamona) after being disappointed in her grade, she refused to answer my questions about her plagiarism and secretly recorded me in an attempt to turn the Dean of students against me. Incidents like this one left me with persistent anxiety about how my work is perceived by those who write my annual merit evaluations and my promotion letters. In other words, the teaching context of stereotype threat without institutional support for women of color faculty like myself resulted in questioning my own perceptions of reality. The university systems designed to "protect" students from faculty who are presumed incompetent (Gutiérrez y Muhs et al., 2012) leave us walking a tightrope without a net and questioning our very sanity.

When considering context, administrators responsible for evaluating faculty should create policies that address how stereotype threat may impact performance by faculty of color in the classroom. Administrators should also introduce and support policies that consider types of courses taught by marginalized faculty including core/required courses versus elective/diversity courses. The American Psychological Association (APA) prioritized the need "to respond to the issues and importance of diversity" (Sliwa, 2016, p. 11) across its membership, training initiatives, and institutional relationships, yet the mainstream psychology curriculum does not reflect the diversity of the U.S. population nor international perspectives. Therefore, students may not expect to wrestle with issues related to diversity and social justice issues in core/required courses. Faculty who integrate social justice into the core psychology curriculum are likely to find students who are resistant and less prepared to engage with social justice issues. In this case, administrators who are solely focused on student evaluations may overlook challenges faced by faculty who diversify the curriculum (see Boysen, Chapter 17, this volume). Outcomes such as lower evaluations may result from student perceptions of a professor being too political or biased about race, gender, or other issues related to social identities (Littleford & Jones, 2017). Therefore, penalizing faculty for lower evaluation scores or negative comments from students about the personality of the professor (e.g., "too political") would be in line with practices that harm faculty of color and faculty who promote social justice in their classrooms. Additionally, the provision of educational materials about stereotype threat and implicit bias to tenure/promotion committees could potentially minimize another level of biased evaluation of marginalized and minoritized faculty.

Strategies for Peer Allies

Colleagues who are knowledgeable about the value of diversifying and teaching social justice across the curriculum can take on the burden of educating their scholarly community by offering their knowledge and sharing relevant materials. Supportive colleagues can also sing the praises of faculty who do the heavy lifting of updating curriculum, whether through direct teaching practices or scholarship on teaching and learning, to meet current APA standards of diversifying across the psychology curriculum. Colleagues who consider themselves allies can also support marginalized faculty by reminding them of the importance of serving as an exemplar and role model for others, peers and students alike. Supportive colleagues will remind faculty that teaching in a way that sheds light on typically invisible diversity issues matters because it has the potential to minimize inequality and maximize inclusive practices in the classroom and wherever our students take their knowledge.

Strategies for Student Allies

Students can, in fact, be powerful sources of support, even if they are not always aware of this role. Encouraging students to document in their course evaluations what they learned versus describing a faculty member's personality will highlight the pedagogical talents of faculty who creatively apply science to social issues. Encouraging students to write notes of praise (rather than the more common complaints) to administrators, or directly to the faculty member, helps document how critical thinking skills are encouraged in the social justice classroom. Another strategy is collective action by students. For example, in one particularly challenging semester, former students learned that I (Salena) was not doing well after a particularly difficult semester (see Brody & Bernal, Chapter 7, this volume). They organized to write letters of support, and two students delivered the 10 letters to me with a gift. The heartfelt letters reflected how impactful the class had been for them and how they continued to benefit from the knowledge. I was really lifted up by these letters during a difficult time and later shared them with administrators when discussing promotion.

Calling for Faculty Stereotype Threat Awareness

As faculty who have experienced stereotype threat in the classroom and as intersectional allies to our marginalized faculty colleagues, we urge academic leaders, peer mentors, and educators training the next generation of faculty to purposefully raise awareness of this form of stereotype threat. Despite the vast literature on negative student outcomes associated with stereotype threat, faculty facing these same threats in the classroom and across the broader academic landscape typically do not recognize this phenomenon and its serious impact on performance, stress, anxiety, and overall mental and physical health. As allies to our ingroup and outgroup members, we can all serve to inform our students, colleagues, and administrators about the consequences of stereotype threat faced by faculty.

RESOURCES

Case, K. (2017). Insider without: Journey across the working-class academic arc. *Journal of Working-Class Studies, 2*(2), 16–35.

    This piece weaves together the personal and academic, addressing the positionality of working-class academics within a middle-class normative structure through an intersectional lens. Case artfully recounts stories of a class consciousness in the academy while addressing privilege along other social identities.

Dews, C., & Law, C. (1995). *This fine place so far from home: Voices of academics from the working class.* Temple University Press.

    This anthology includes autobiographical accounts of self-described "working class academics." Chapter 7 shares a first-person account by a Latina scholar and addresses a lack of formal support and mentorship in academic spaces for women/mothers and people of color. The contributor shares her experiences countering the hostile myth that people of color are only hired to fulfill affirmative action quotas and the lack of confidence to take up space as a woman of color in the academy. She shares strategies that nontraditional students can emulate to buffer against hostility and build solidarity in higher education.

Gutiérrez y Muhs, G., Flores Niemann, Y., González, C. G., & Harris, A. P. (Eds.). (2012). *Presumed incompetent: The intersections of race and class for women in academia.* University of Colorado Press.

    Excellent resource for women of color in academia. The second part of the edited volume focuses exclusively on faculty/student relationships and includes a chapter on how student evaluations particularly impact women and people of color.

Rockquemore, K., & Laszloffy, T. (2008). *The Black academic's guide to winning tenure without losing your soul.* Lynne Rienner Publishers.

    Chapter 7 addresses defensive teaching and the hostility professors of color experience in the classroom.

REFERENCES

Baysu, G., & Phalet, K. (2019). The up- and downside of dual identity: Stereotype threat and minority performance. *Journal of Social Issues, 75*(2), 568–591. https://doi.org/10.1111/josi.12330

Case, K. (Ed.). (2013). *Deconstructing privilege: Teaching and learning as allies in the classroom.* Routledge. https://doi.org/10.4324/9780203081877

Case, K. (Ed.). (2017). *Intersectional pedagogy: Complicating identity and social justice.* Routledge.

Case, K., & Cole, E. (2013). When students resist deconstructing privilege: The journey back into the community of engaged learners. In K. Case (Ed.), *Deconstructing privilege: Teaching and learning as allies in the classroom* (pp. 34–48). Routledge. https://doi.org/10.4324/9780203081877

Case, K., Miller, A., & Jackson, S. B. (2012). "We talk about race too much in this class!" Complicating the essentialized woman through intersectional pedagogy. In S. Pliner & C. Banks (Eds.), *Teaching, learning, and intersecting identities in higher education* (pp. 32–48). Peter Lang.

Cole, E. R. (2009). Intersectionality and research in psychology. *American Psychologist, 64*(3), 170–180. https://doi.org/10.1037/a0014564

Collins, P. H. (1990). *Black feminist thought: Knowledge, consciousness, and the politics of power*. Routledge.

Crenshaw, K. (1991). Mapping the margins: Intersectionality, identity politics, and violence against women of color. *Stanford Law Review, 43*(6), 1241–1299. https://doi.org/10.2307/1229039

David, E. J. R. (Ed.). (2013). *Internalized oppression: The psychology of marginalized groups*. Springer. https://doi.org/10.1891/9780826199263

Gutiérrez y Muhs, G., Niemann, Y. F., González, C. G., & Harris, A. P. (2012). *Presumed incompetent: The intersections of race and class for women in academia*. University of Colorado Press.

Harrison, L. A., Stevens, C. M., Monty, A. N., & Coakley, C. A. (2006). The consequences of stereotype threat on the academic performance of White and non-White lower income college students. *Social Psychology of Education, 9*(3), 341–357. https://doi.org/10.1007/s11218-005-5456-6

Johns, M., Schmader, T., & Martens, A. (2005). Knowing is half the battle: Teaching stereotype threat as a means of improving women's math performance. *Psychological Science, 16*(3), 175–179. https://doi.org/10.1111/j.0956-7976.2005.00799.x

Littleford, L. N., & Jones, J. A. (2017). Framing and source effects on White college students' reactions to racial inequity information. *Cultural Diversity & Ethnic Minority Psychology, 23*(1), 143–153. https://doi.org/10.1037/cdp0000102

Niemann, Y. F. (2012). The making of a token: A case study of stereotype threat, stigma, racism, and tokenism in academe. In G. Gutiérrez y Muhs, Y. F. Niemann, C. G. González, & A. P. Harris (Eds.), *Presumed incompetent: The intersections of race and class for women in academia* (pp. 336–355). University of Colorado Press. https://doi.org/10.2307/j.ctt4cgr3k.33

Onwuachi-Willig, A. (2012). Silence of the lambs. In G. Gutiérrez y Muhs, Y. F. Niemann, C. G. González, & A. P. Harris (Eds.), *Presumed incompetent: The intersections of race and class for women in academia* (pp. 142–151). University of Colorado Press. https://doi.org/10.2307/j.ctt4cgr3k.17

Rios, D., Bowling, M. J., & Harris, J. (2017). Decentering student "uniqueness" in lessons about intersectionality. In K. A. Case (Ed.), *Intersectional pedagogy: Complicating identity and social justice* (pp. 194–213). Routledge.

Rivera, D. P., Forquer, E. E., & Rangel, R. (2010). Microaggressions and the life experience of Latina/o Americans. In D. W. Sue (Ed.), *Microaggressions and marginality: Manifestation, dynamics, and impact* (pp. 59–83). Wiley & Sons.

Sliwa, J. (2016, January). APA brief affirms benefits of racial and ethnic diversity on campus: Psychological research demonstrates value of diversity in higher education. *Monitor on Psychology, 47*(1), 11.

Spencer, S. J., Steele, C. M., & Quinn, D. M. (1999). Stereotype threat and women's math performance. *Journal of Experimental Social Psychology, 35*(1), 4–28. https://doi.org/10.1006/jesp.1998.1373

Steele, C. M. (1997). A threat in the air. How stereotypes shape intellectual identity and performance. *American Psychologist, 52*(6), 613–629. https://doi.org/10.1037/0003-066X.52.6.613

Steele, C. M. (2011). *Whistling Vivaldi: How stereotypes affect us and what we can do.* W. W. Norton & Company.

Steele, C. M., & Aronson, J. (1995). Stereotype threat and the intellectual test performance of African Americans. *Journal of Personality and Social Psychology, 69*(5), 797–811. https://doi.org/10.1037/0022-3514.69.5.797

Stewart, A. J., & Valian, V. (2018). *An inclusive academy: Achieving diversity and excellence.* MIT Press. https://doi.org/10.7551/mitpress/9766.001.0001

Sunstein, C. (2018, September 17). *The problem with all those liberal professors.* Bloomberg News. https://www.bloomberg.com/opinion/articles/2018-09-17/colleges-have-way-too-many-liberal-professors

6

BECOMING A TARGET

Anonymous Threats While Teaching Diversity Courses or Working on Social Justice Issues

LISA S. WAGNER AND J. J. GARRETT-WALKER

Teaching can be a challenging enterprise given that instructors are placed in a uniquely vulnerable position.[1] They are charged with helping students learn while simultaneously evaluating those students on their progress. Negative student reactions directed at faculty are not ubiquitous but are also not rare (Lampman, 2012; Lampman et al., 2016). The term *contrapower harassment* (CPH) has been used to describe situations where someone with less institutional power (such as a student) harasses someone with ostensibly more institutional power (e.g., a professor; Benson, 1984). Women, people of color, and younger faculty report greater levels of student incivility and/or bullying (Lampman, 2012). Faculty who teach courses on diversity or social justice–related issues face an additional challenge. Their course content challenges the status quo and may make students uncomfortable as they learn facts that go against their current worldview (Case & Cole, 2013; DiAngelo, 2011). Students from groups that are privileged in society (e.g., White,

---

[1] For the purpose of clearly demonstrating the issues discussed in this chapter, derogatory and in some cases violent language is included verbatim from threats received.

https://doi.org/10.1037/0000216-006
Navigating Difficult Moments in Teaching Diversity and Social Justice, M. E. Kite, K. A. Case, and W. R. Williams (Editors)
Copyright © 2021 by the American Psychological Association. All rights reserved.

male, heterosexual, able-bodied) may react defensively when learning that their social position is, in part, the result of unearned, systemic privilege that contributes to the oppression of other groups (Bonilla-Silva, 2014; Case & Cole, 2013; DiAngelo, 2011). Some of these students, in turn, may be more likely to react against the faculty members who raise these issues, particularly if they are women and/or people of color, by means of negative course evaluations or even verbal threats (Huston, 2006). Thus, we think faculty who teach courses on social justice issues may face a unique combination of defensive negative reactions to social justice course material and contrapower harassment. Given the current political climate in the United States, work on social justice issues is often covered in the media, which further opens up faculty members to be targeted from people outside of the university community (e.g., Cuevas, 2018; Howey, 2018; White, 2015).

Although research has shown that aggressive student behavior exists and that women and faculty of color are more likely to be targeted by this behavior (Huston, 2006; Lampman et al., 2016), little research specifically examines the threats received by faculty teaching courses on diversity or social justice–related issues. Similarly, although student threats to faculty are named through CPH, threats that appear to come from people outside the academic institution are not named and have not been systematically studied. As colleagues at our institution, where we both teach courses related to diversity and social justice issues, we became aware of our shared experience of anonymous threats through ad hoc conversations. After talking with colleagues outside of our university about their similar experiences, we decided that increased faculty and administrator awareness of these threats is important. We present three examples of threats received by faculty while teaching or working on diversity-related issues in a university setting. These examples are described here with permission from the faculty members who experienced them. We present the threats exactly as they were written, including leaving the actual slurs intact. We made this choice because removing parts of the threats lessens their impact and, given the context and audience for this book, we wanted to convey at least some of the experience of what it is like to receive one of these threats.

We want to raise awareness of the difficulties that people teaching and working on these issues face. Our goals in discussing these kinds of threats are threefold:

1. To let faculty teaching diversity-related courses or working on social justice issues know that they are not alone. They have fellow instructors around the country who have been targeted in similar ways. Breaking the sense of isolation that can come from being targeted may help instructors step

back from the threatening message itself and see options for support from others and for their own response.

2. To increase awareness of this type of threat for faculty who sit on salary/merit or tenure and promotion committees and evaluate faculty, especially those who do not teach social justice courses, and for administrators who work with and/or evaluate faculty. Recognizing that certain groups of faculty may be more likely to be targeted both from students and from people outside the university puts into context student evaluations and the lived experiences of these faculty members. Raising awareness is especially important at institutions where such threats have not occurred (or perhaps have not yet been reported) or where threats are not taken seriously.

3. To communicate both the range of reactions to these threats and the range of options available to people who experience these threats.

Our hope is that knowledge of these situations will lead to creation of systematic institutional procedures and policies that will support faculty.

EXAMPLE 1 – ANONYMOUS EMAIL

In November 2012, an instructor for the course Psychology of Prejudice received a threatening anonymous email. The instructor was a White, cisgender, heterosexual woman and a tenured professor in her late 40s; the email used slurs to attack her gender, made inaccurate assumptions about her sexual orientation, and wished her dead. She received the email after giving critical feedback to the students in her classes. To not know whether this email was sent by a student or by a random outsider made her anxious about returning to the classroom. She also was not sure if she was targeted specifically due to her gender or whether the sender was simply attacking randomly. These uncertainties gave renewed weight to the experience of attributional ambiguity that members of oppressed groups face when they are not sure whether negative behavior is directed toward them because they are members of a particular group (Crocker et al., 1991).

Email Text

You don't know anything about Psychology. You're a stupid BITCH. Hope you die! Lesbian looking cunt. You treat students like elementary kids.
Everyone at [university abbreviation] hates you.

Faculty Response

The faculty member's initial response was shame, hurt, and concern about what she had done to incite this. Similar to reports from research on CPH and student incivility and/or bullying (Lampman, 2012; Lampman et al., 2016), the faculty member was worried that others might evaluate her negatively and question her teaching ability if she reported it. She was anxious about teaching the next class period and felt vulnerable. The energy consumed by anxiety and the numerous questions about the threat was immense. Ultimately, concern that this kind of attack might become more common if not reported and might spread to more vulnerable people such as untenured faculty, combined with concern from a close colleague about the implied death threat ("Hope you die!") led her to contact her university's human resources office; their staff referred her to the university's Office of Public Safety. Public Safety assessed the threat, had Information Technology Services try to trace the email (which, unfortunately, originated off campus and was not traceable via their means), and made recommendations for safe behavior. She was satisfied with the expertise of the public safety threat assessors and their recommendations and hoped they were right that this was likely a one-time event. She also felt somewhat comforted—but also distressed—to learn that threats like this were not uncommon and that other faculty members on her campus had also received threats. Finally, it was reassuring to know that Public Safety had experience in dealing with situations like these.

EXAMPLE 2 – ANONYMOUS EMAIL WHILE ORGANIZING A BLACK STUDENT ORIENTATION

In August 2017, while developing a Black student orientation (BSO) to improve Black students' adjustment to a university setting, a faculty member received a threatening and racist anonymous email. The faculty member was a Black queer woman, early-30s, nontenured faculty member who had organized a privilege campaign that went viral a couple of years earlier. During that campaign, she had received many similar emails and voicemails and had the occasional anonymous negative student evaluation attack described in the CPH research (Lampman, 2012).

Email Text

> Subject line: You leftist fuckin nigger! Dont waste
> Message body: time having a special "black orientation" jigaboos are too stupid to be in any school!
> White and "right" in Arizona

Faculty Response

The faculty member was not shocked but instead felt a deep reminder of the permanency of racism in the United States. She explained that when someone is a person of color and racist things happen, that has an emotional response on them that isn't quite anger, or fear, or frustration, but its own unique feeling. It is perhaps like despair, or just reality. Although this individual email threat did not stay with her, the culmination of all the hate mail she has gotten over the years follows her wherever she goes. The knowledge that people honestly do not believe in or understand structural inequalities stays with her. The faculty member does not normally report any of these kinds of threats (because they happen so frequently), but, because she was worried about the safety of the students, she contacted the Offices of Student Life and Public Safety. She requested that Student Life refrain from publicizing the location of BSO (so that outsiders would not know where it was located). Public safety was asked to increase plainclothes security at the BSO, which they did. She had previously had her office number removed from any online directories at the university so that outside individuals could not easily locate her.

EXAMPLE 3 – ANONYMOUS ONLINE COMMENT MADE WHEN FACULTY ORGANIZED TO HAVE A SANCTUARY CAMPUS

In December 2016, a news organization picked up the story of two faculty who were organizing to have their campus become a sanctuary campus. The subsequent online comments on these media reports, as well as direct emails and postal mail to their campus address, included calls to have the faculty fired and implied death threats (the text of the comment follows). The two faculty members were always identified in the media together. One was a White, heterosexual cisgender woman, mid-30s, tenure-track faculty member, and the other was a White, queer man, mid-30s, Marxist, tenure-track faculty member.

Online Comment Text

"Sounds like it's time to take a trip to [state where university was located] FULLY ARMED to remove all those who aid or abet ILLEGALS!!!! And I really mean remove . . . FROM LIFE!"

Faculty Response

The two faculty members had somewhat different responses. The threats did not surprise the woman faculty member because they came after the 2016

U.S. presidential election at a time when she was starting to accept the fact that the country is filled with people who are "willfully ignorant cowards," and she imagined that the people writing these comments had no guts, integrity, or credibility. She found that these threats supported her concern that many in the United States did not care if immigrants, women, and/or people of color live or die. She did not share these messages with anyone. She thought there were more important things to worry about, such as her students being deported. The threats to others around her seemed more real than the virtual threats to herself. The other faculty member responded differently. He was concerned about his personal safety, and so he forwarded some of the threats to the university police, who sent an email response thanking him for notifying them and asking him to forward any related messages.

FACULTY REFLECTION

The examples described above are clearly horrific, but because a systematic study of these types of threats has not occurred, we do not know how representative they are. We chose these examples because they cover a span of time (including an example much earlier than the 2016 U.S. presidential election) and a range of attackers (the first likely a student and the other two likely from outside the institution). We also do not know whether threats like these occur outside of the United States in countries where hate speech is more (or less) highly regulated and restricted. Similarly, just as the examples are not necessarily a representative sample, the faculty responses are also not necessarily representative. For example, unlike the faculty member of color in the second example, some faculty of color may be shocked if they receive a threat and might react in ways that are more similar to the instructor from the first example. Some people may understandably see the threats as all-consuming, and others may set the threat aside, perhaps for self-preservation. A range of emotional reactions are reasonable and normal.

When we presented these examples at a national teaching conference in 2018, responses to the poster, although not from an unbiased sample, were still telling. In general, attendees who were White men expressed shock that any instructor might receive such horrible comments, attendees who were White women were saddened to receive additional evidence that the world can be an awful place, and people of color attendees tended to simply acknowledge that these experiences are a common reality. Our goal in sharing these anecdotal examples highlights that some groups of faculty seem unaware that other groups of faculty are targeted (if not regularly, at least not infrequently), whereas for other groups of faculty, the threats are always a real possibility.

Although we are especially concerned about the effects of these threats on the most vulnerable (e.g., adjunct faculty, untenured junior faculty who are members of oppressed groups), greater awareness of these threats would be beneficial for all. Faculty, both junior and senior, may develop courses on diversity and may end up receiving threats. Knowing about the possibility of threats in advance may help them be better prepared if they receive one. Similarly, faculty who are from oppressed groups may receive threats like these in nondiversity courses as well. Faculty of color who are not aware of, or have not received, threats may even respond by blaming a colleague when they hear the person received a threat, perhaps to psychologically distance themselves from the threat. Given that these threats are not uncommon, having broad awareness that threats do occur will ultimately help everyone.

CONSIDERATIONS OF CONTEXT AND INTERSECTIONALITY

Faculty members from certain groups may be more likely to be targeted for CPH or other kinds of threats. For example, research on CPH found that women, people of color, and younger faculty report greater levels of student incivility and bullying (Lampman, 2012). More systematic research studies are needed of both those who hold majority identities and those who do not; thus examining both the characteristics of faculty who teach diversity-related courses and the incidence of receiving threats while teaching such courses is important. There are examples in the media of faculty members who are White men receiving threats due to the content of their course (e.g., White, 2015), but it is not clear whether these men are also members of other oppressed groups (e.g., LGBTQ+, non-Christian religious group). One interesting question worthy of future research is whether White, heterosexual, cisgender men are less likely to teach diversity-related courses or work on social justice issues. If so, is this by choice, social design, or both? If it is true that faculty members who are White men and not members of an oppressed group are less likely to teach these courses (Ahluwalia et al., 2019), then they may not understand the experiences of faculty who do and have been threatened. Given that faculty have historically been predominately White, heterosexual, and cisgender men, this creates a situation where the senior faculty evaluating the junior faculty for tenure and promotion may have not taught any diversity or social justice–related courses and may be completely unaware of the challenges faced in teaching such courses or doing such work. Similarly, White, heterosexual faculty might be great allies for people experiencing these threats, even if they never teach a diversity class themselves, and thus they need to be aware of the challenges faced by people who do.

We also wonder, as with CPH, whether members of oppressed groups are more likely to be threatened, whether certain intersections of characteristics may increase that likelihood even further, and whether faculty characteristics might affect how seriously administrators take the threat. For example, what roles do gender and race play in the likelihood of being threatened? Are women more likely to be threatened than men? Does holding a double minority status (e.g., being a woman of color) increase this likelihood? Do threats vary across certain identity groups (e.g., sexual orientation, gender identity, gender presentation, and religious-group membership)? If our suppositions about the increased likelihood of threat for some intersections of characteristics are accurate, it highlights the importance of discussing this issue widely as members of privileged groups are less likely to have experienced these types of threats and thus might not understand the experiences of their fellow faculty members. Greater awareness helps everyone because anyone can get targeted regardless of what they teach.

BEST PRACTICES

Teaching diversity-related courses and working on social justice issues is an essential task that, unfortunately, comes with additional challenges. Although we do not think that anonymous threats to faculty who take on this important role are ubiquitous, we do think that they are not uncommon. To sustain oneself through what can be a wrenching experience, we suggest that faculty prepare in advance for such threats. Finding supportive colleagues, having a good knowledge of an institution's support structures, and considering how events like these may be communicated in the classroom will have positive effects even if one never receives an anonymous threat. Ideally this preparation would be done early in one's adjustment to an institution, given that younger, less experienced faculty are more likely to experience CPH and perhaps more likely to be teaching diversity and social justice–related courses. But senior faculty who are new to teaching diversity, or even veteran social justice workers can, unexpectedly, receive threats, so these best practices apply to everyone.

Find Supportive Colleagues

New faculty orientation is certainly an important place to discuss student incivility and bullying behaviors, ways to respond to these behaviors, and resources on campus to report them. Faculty orientation and welcoming events are also good places to begin to look for supportive colleagues (and for more seasoned faculty to seek out junior faculty who might be assigned these courses). Finding colleagues who teach similar courses in one's department, college, or university is often a good avenue for making these connections. Many institutions have organizations within the institution that promote diversity and inclusion. Staff and faculty affiliated with those groups can help connect new faculty with local colleagues. If understanding colleagues cannot be found in one's department or at least on campus, associates outside of one's institution can be found through the internet. Examples include online discussion forums on the *The Chronicle of Higher Education* website or private Facebook groups for identity groups in higher education (e.g., women, people of color, LGBTQ+ people). Divisions within national organizations such as the American Psychological Association (APA) can be a good source for finding people in similar situations who might serve as allies and advisers (see Resources, below). Joining a division listserv can be a relatively easy way to start connecting with colleagues from other institutions. For example, within APA, faculty can join divisions that relate to their teaching or research area (e.g., Society for the Psychological Study of Social Issues; Society for Personality and Social Psychology, Society for the Psychological Study of Culture, Ethnicity and Race, Society for the Psychology of Sexual Orientation and Gender Diversity, or the Society for the Teaching of Psychology), join the division listserv (if available), or, in some divisions, request a mentor.

Safety Is Key

Faculty and staff should become familiar with their university threat assessment team, ideally before a problem arises. Everyone should know who to contact if a disturbing or threatening message is received or seen. Some individuals (both the recipient of the threat or the person notified of the threat) may be tempted to minimize any potential danger that may follow the threat. A calm, yet firm reminder that everyone has a duty to protect the instructor, students, and staff usually nudges those individuals into a more appropriately cautious stance. The correct official to notify may vary by institution, but the most common offices include human resources, public safety, crisis response team, university ombudsperson, and diversity and inclusion. This is where an on-campus supportive colleague can be very helpful. This person can help to determine the appropriate official by placing strategic calls to determine what steps to follow if an instructor was threatened. This avoids the targeted instructor from having to retell the threat details through repeated layers of bureaucracy that may involve student workers and unrelated staff. Sometimes the threat recipients themselves need encouragement to report the situation. Again, a reminder that protecting students and staff (in addition to the instructor) is very important and may help nudge the person into action. That said, reporting may not be the best option for everyone. Individuals who have received threats may have a real and justified need not to engage in a reporting process that might further victimize them. Having trusted, supportive colleagues to help assess different reporting choices is important.

Documenting the Threat and the Response

If one receives a threat or finds a threatening message, everything should be carefully documented. This includes documenting not only the actual threat (e.g., saving the email or voicemail) but also the response received by the relevant campus official(s). If these officials appear to discount the threat, checking in with one's supportive colleagues (both inside and outside of the institution) can help determine whether moving beyond that campus official (e.g., from an academic dean to human resources) would be appropriate.

Returning to the Classroom

Depending on the type of threat, sharing the event with the class can be empowering for the instructor and educational for students, but careful thought should go into the decision to do so. Some faculty members report having mixed feelings about using personal self-disclosure when teaching about diversity (Ahluwalia et al., 2019). There are also safety concerns to consider. In our first threat example, the Department of Public Safety recommended not mentioning it to the students due to the likelihood that the threat had come from someone in the class. Their thought was that bringing attention to the message might embolden the student further. If threat assessment staff recommend that the instructor not discuss the threat with the class, then their advice should be considered. Yet, faculty members have the power to tell, or not tell, their stories in the ways that feel most comfortable to them. If the threat comes from an outside source, as in the second and third threat examples, sharing these experiences with students in diversity courses could be very educational. Students from privileged social groups may have never had someone close to them be exposed to such hatred. Discussing a tangible act of hatred in the context of the course may facilitate a greater understanding of the pervasive nature of prejudice. Students from marginalized social groups may see that even people in respected positions are targets of hatred, and this realization may give them some comfort that they are not alone as they recognize the systematic nature of prejudice that does not reflect on them personally. Hirabayashi (2000) movingly described his experience with a voicemail death threat received while teaching an Introduction to Asian American Studies course, and how his psychological processing was facilitated by sharing the threatening voicemail with his classes and having them answer probing questions. His example also illustrated that some faculty have been receiving these kinds of threats long before our current national political situation. Of course, handling this situation appropriately in the classroom is important so that recognition does not become overwhelming and instead can be turned into empowerment (see Brown, Chapter 8, this volume).

Self-Care

Teaching and doing diversity-related work can be challenging, but it is essential to examining, understanding, and addressing prejudice. Given how taxing justice work can be, it is important that faculty teaching these courses or developing university-wide efforts to promote diversity make time and space for self-care around these challenging issues (see Eaton & Warner, Chapter 3, this volume). It is also imperative that they get the support and resources that they need to help them navigate the challenging aspects, which will sustain them in the work long term. For example, taking a break from teaching these courses may help restore one's energy to be able to continue this important work later.

Administration's Support

Ideally, administration will be proactive in discussing with the academic community in advance about the kinds of communication allowed at the university and also be swift in response to violations of these communication standards. Although administration may not be able to prevent these kinds of attacks from happening, how they respond to such attacks affects not only the faculty member's experience of the threat but also sets the tone about what will and will not be tolerated in the academic setting. Institutions should have procedures for what will occur when a faculty member is targeted either from within the institution or, as is becoming increasingly likely, anonymously from outside the academic setting (Cuevas, 2018; Howey, 2018; Scott, 2018). The University of Iowa (2018) has a faculty/staff support policy in place and prominently links this guide on its faculty resource page. This guide clearly delineates the roles, actions, and resources for each individual within the university (e.g., faculty, department chair, collegiate administration, central administration) with links to relevant resources.

How should institutions respond on behalf of faculty members? Although systematic studies examining outcomes of different strategies have not been done, media reports of institutional responses include complete silence from the institution, temporary removal of the faculty from the classroom, and proactive statements supporting the faculty and condemning the attack (Cuevas, 2018; Scott, 2018). Institutional silence has not stopped escalation of the threats, nor has removal of the faculty from the classroom, whereas institutional denunciation of the attack and support for academic freedom and the targeted faculty member appear to be the best route (Scott, 2018). When the university denounces an attack, it sends a public message that these threats are unacceptable. Cuevas (2018) further suggested that administrators who speak out against these attacks may even play a role in decreasing future attacks by stating that those who share disinformation can be sued for slander.

STRUCTURAL IMPLICATIONS

Anonymous threats to faculty teaching diversity-related courses or working on social justice issues occur within an existing power structure of the university setting where continued employment is determined by students' and colleagues' evaluation of their teaching (see Boysen, Chapter 16, this volume). Given that women, people of color, and younger faculty are more likely to experience student incivility (Lampman, 2012), and that faculty who teach diversity-related courses tend to be from marginalized groups (e.g., women, people of color, LGBTQ+, non-Christian religious groups), faculty evaluations by senior colleagues who may be the least likely to have experienced these threats is problematic. Faculty with the least experience and job security are the most vulnerable to negative effects from these threats.

Increasing awareness of the prevalence of threats made and the personal cost to the people who teach courses and work on diversity and social justice related issues is important. Although research demonstrates that CPH, when someone with less institutional power (such as a student) harasses someone with ostensibly more institutional power, takes a significant emotional and time-consuming toll on faculty (June, 2010; Lampman et al., 2016), little research has focused on incivility and bullying experienced by faculty who work in diversity-related fields. Administration and senior faculty, especially those likely to be making tenure-related decisions, should be made aware of and be sensitive to the fact that certain groups of faculty members (e.g., women, people of color, people who are LGBTQ+, people from non-Christian religious groups) may be more likely to be targeted with threats like these. Recognizing the threats that faculty members teaching diversity-related courses face and then determining how best to support these colleagues are important aspects in efforts to challenge prejudice and social injustice.

Justice-related conversations that happen at colleges and universities are essential to students' learning. These conversations help students become more well-rounded and critical thinkers and are considered primary learning goals for an undergraduate psychology education (APA, 2013). Without the efforts of faculty who engage in diversity and social justice–related work, the conversations around these topics would be halted within the academy. Although faculty who teach these courses often carry a very specific burden, we speculate that they continue to teach these classes for the good of humanity. Even with the known challenges, we implore all faculty to consider how they can infuse conversations about diversity and social justice into their classes so that the burden of this work does not fall on a select few faculty members.

RESOURCES

Case, K. A., & Cole, E. R. (2013). Deconstructing privilege when students resist: The journey back into the community of engaged learners. In K. A. Case (Ed.), *Deconstructing privilege: Teaching and learning as allies in the classroom* (pp. 34–48). Routledge.

Wise, T., & Case, K. A. (2013). Pedagogy for the privileged: Addressing inequality and injustice without shame or blame. In K. A. Case (Ed.), *Deconstructing privilege: Teaching and learning as allies in the classroom* (pp. 17–33). Routledge.

    The edited book *Deconstructing Privilege: Teaching and Learning as Allies in the Classroom* (Case, 2013) contains helpful information to consider when teaching courses on diversity and social justice issues, and the two chapters listed here may also be helpful when faced with anonymous threats from within the class.

Engaging difficult dialogues in higher education. Difficult Dialogues. https://www.uaa.alaska.edu/academics/institutional-effectiveness/departments/center-for-advancing-faculty-excellence/difficult-dialogues/

    The website Difficult Dialogues provides strategies, resources, and information about engaging campus communities in challenging conversations around issues such as race, religion, and academic freedom.

One Faculty, One Resistance. (n.d.). *Targeted harassment of faculty*. American Association of University Professors. https://onefacultyoneresistance.org/faculty-attack-fighting-targeted-harassment/

    One Faculty, One Resistance is a campaign by the American Association of University Professors to fight harassment, protect academic freedom and the right to conduct research freely, and unite faculty. They track faculty reports of targeted harassment and offer resources for faculty concerned about these issues.

University of Iowa. (2018). *Faculty support and safety guidance*. https://provost.uiowa.edu/sites/provost.uiowa.edu/files/Faculty_Support_Safety_Guidance.pdf

    This guide provides a model for how institutions might support faculty and staff who have been targeted by individuals or groups outside of the institution. It offers detailed information on the roles, actions, and resources for individuals ranging from faculty members to central administration. For each individual, detailed recommendations about actions they should take and links to additional information are given. This guide is prominently linked on the university's faculty resource page.

The following organizations have divisions, committees, or forums that can serve as resources for finding support when teaching courses related to diversity and social justice and supportive colleagues outside of one's current workplace:

- Chronicle Forums: Diversity in the workplace or in the tenure track or nontenure track forums. *The Chronicle of Higher Education*. https://www.chronicle.com/forums/?cid=UCHESIDENAV1

- Society for Personality and Social Psychology. http://www.spsp.org/

- Society for the Psychological Study of Culture, Ethnicity and Race (Division 45 of APA). http://division45.org/

- Society for the Psychological Study of Social Issues Diversity Committee. https://www.spssi.org/index.cfm?fuseaction=Page.ViewPage&pageId=541

- Society for the Psychology of Sexual Orientation and Gender Diversity (Division 44 of APA). https://www.apadivisions.org/division-44

- Society for the Teaching of Psychology (STP) Diversity Committee and Diversity Resources. http://teachpsych.org/page-1537443

REFERENCES

Ahluwalia, M. K., Ayala, S. I., Locke, A. F., & Nadrich, T. (2019). Mitigating the "powder keg": The experiences of faculty of color teaching multicultural competence. *Teaching of Psychology*, *46*(3), 187–196. https://doi.org/10.1177/0098628319848864

American Psychological Association. (2013). *APA guidelines for the undergraduate psychology major: Version 2.0*. https://www.apa.org/ed/precollege/undergrad/index.aspx

Benson, K. A. (1984). Comment on Crocker's "An analysis of university definitions of sexual harassment." *Signs: Journal of Women in Culture and Society*, *9*(3), 516–519. https://doi.org/10.1086/494083

Bonilla-Silva, E. (2014). *Racism without racists: Color-blind racism and the persistence of racial inequality in America* (4th ed.). Rowman & Littlefield.

Case, K. A., & Cole, E. R. (2013). Deconstructing privilege when students resist: The journey back into the community of engaged learners. In K. A. Case (Ed.), *Deconstructing privilege: Teaching and learning as allies in the classroom* (pp. 34–48). Routledge. https://doi.org/10.4324/9780203081877

Crocker, J., Voelkl, K., Testa, M., & Major, B. (1991). Social stigma: The affective consequences of attributional ambiguity. *Journal of Personality and Social Psychology, 60*(2), 218–228. https://doi.org/10.1037/0022-3514.60.2.218

Cuevas, J. A. (2018, January–February). A new reality? The far-right's use of cyberharassment against academics. *Academe.* https://www.aaup.org/article/new-reality-far-rights-use-cyberharassment-against-academics#.XjUGGxeIbjA

DiAngelo, R. (2011). White fragility. *The International Journal of Critical Pedagogy, 3*(3), 54–70.

Hirabayashi, L. R. (2000, May 12). How a death threat became an opportunity to connect with my students. *The Chronicle of Higher Education, 46*(36), B10.

Howey, B. (2018, October 30). Right-wing groups are recruiting students to target teachers. *Reveal.* https://www.revealnews.org/article/right-wing-groups-are-recruiting-students-to-target-teachers/?fbclid=IwAR08_ZjdQHJLpJrssshJ4dPfqv_bry3-JaqRUt0p3LbidOhnb5aKCsX0K3w

Huston, T. A. (2006). Race and gender bias in higher education: Could faculty course evaluations impede further progress toward parity? *Seattle Journal for Social Justice, 4*(2), 591–611.

June, A. W. (2010, August 1). When students become class bullies, professors are among the victims. *The Chronicle of Higher Education.* https://www.chronicle.com/article/When-Students-Become-Class/123733

Lampman, C. (2012). Women faculty at risk: U.S. professors report on their experiences with student incivility, bullying, aggression, and sexual attention. *NASPA Journal About Women in Higher Education, 5*(2), 184–208. https://doi.org/10.1515/njawhe-2012-1108

Lampman, C., Crew, E. C., Lowery, S., Tompkins, K. A., & Mulder, M. (2016). Women faculty distressed: Descriptions and consequences of academic contrapower harassment. *NASPA Journal About Women in Higher Education, 9*(2), 169–189. https://doi.org/10.1080/19407882.2016.1199385

Scott, J. W. (2018). *Targeted harassment of faculty: What higher education administrators can do.* Association of American Colleges and Universities. https://www.aacu.org/liberaleducation/2018/spring/scott

University of Iowa. (2018). *Faculty support and safety guidance.* https://provost.uiowa.edu/sites/provost.uiowa.edu/files/Faculty_Support_Safety_Guidance.pdf

White, K. (2015, March 30). ASU prof receives hate mail over "Problem of Whiteness." *The Republic.* https://www.azcentral.com/story/news/local/tempe/2015/03/30/asu-prof-receives-hate-mail-problem-whiteness/70679650/

7
INCLUSION–EXCLUSION

Balancing Viewpoint Diversity and Harmful Speech in the Multicultural Classroom

SALENA M. BRODY AND DARREN R. BERNAL

The classic country hit "The Gambler" tells the tale of a seasoned card shark delivering wisdom to his playing companion on a long train ride (Rogers, 1978). "You've got to know when to hold 'em/know when to fold 'em," he advises, hinting at a meaning beyond card games. This philosophy certainly resonates with faculty who teach social justice classes. Faculty members can feel a bit like gamblers while navigating difficult, often uncomfortable discussions with diverse groups. When identities, politics, and positionalities collide in classroom discussions, every pedagogical decision feels high risk. Faculty must decide in the heat of the moment when to push students through discomfort or to pull back and cut losses. We gamble, hoping that the risks taken yield high rewards and knowing that the decisions we make can have lasting, significant consequences. The Gambler's advice holds for faculty as well as gamblers: Understanding who is at the table means the difference between a win, lose, or draw.

When members of underrepresented and or marginalized groups speak candidly in a social justice–oriented class, it often stirs up feelings of guilt, shame, anger, or defensiveness for majority group members. The practice of

---

https://doi.org/10.1037/0000216-007
Navigating Difficult Moments in Teaching Diversity and Social Justice, M. E. Kite, K. A. Case, and W. R. Williams (Editors)
Copyright © 2021 by the American Psychological Association. All rights reserved.

social justice educators to feature the histories and experiences of marginalized groups contributes to a new positionality of White students within the classroom. Specifically, White students who learn a more complete history may perceive racism differently and reframe how they view their own ingroup status (Nelson et al., 2013). The experiences of White students on the receiving end of this education can vary from extremely positive (an identity of "woke" allyship) to extremely negative (active resistance and defensiveness regarding new information). We will focus on the latter possibility. Specifically, we address two dilemmas experienced in our classrooms. In both, students responded to faculty's attempts to balance viewpoint diversity and harm with resistance and defensiveness, altering classroom dynamics. We will explore how the identities and positionalities of the students and instructors contributed to each outcome.

DILEMMA 1

Our first dilemma centered on inflammatory remarks Donald J. Trump made about Mexican people. In a midsemester unit about immigration and xenophobia, I (Salena) projected the text of candidate Trump's remarks of June 16, 2015, in his presidential announcement speech: "When Mexico sends its people, they're not sending their best. They're sending people that have lots of problems. They're bringing drugs. They're bringing crime. They're rapists, and some, I assume, are good people" (cited in Lee, 2015). At this point in the course, students were accustomed to discussing current events facilitated by me, an Indian American woman.

A White student, Shannon,[1] self-identified early on in the course as a conservative Christian—an identity that is the majority in the community outside the classroom—and expressed excitement when the slide text was presented. "He's absolutely right!" she said as she narrated his words to the class. Her enthusiastic behavior about the slide prompted a Mexican American student, Maricela, sitting in front of her to reply with a tone of disgust, "I'm sorry we are all rapists." The two began to argue while I repeatedly attempted to interrupt the escalating exchange without success. This culminated with an enraged and emotional Shannon launching into a curse-laden monologue about being persecuted in the class for her viewpoint. The outburst continued as she dramatically gathered her things and stormed out the door. I ran after

---

[1] All student names have been changed throughout this chapter to maintain the student's anonymity.

her, frantic and frazzled, hoping to repair the situation. Shannon continued her march from the classroom, refusing all requests to stop or communicate with me. I returned to a classroom to find Maricela distraught and a classmate (also a woman of color) attempting to support and comfort her.

DILEMMA 2

The second dilemma (Darren) occurred after the 2016 election in the fifth week of a required graduate course, Multicultural Counseling. During the weekly check-in before a unit on gender in counseling, a student, Ted, expressed anger that he was being blamed by the class as the "source of all evil" as a White American male. My (Darren) initial reaction was uncertainty if Ted was using humor to address his discomfort. In the spirit of inclusion of experience and thought, I asked Ted to say more. Ted elaborated that he felt judged based on his skin color and that his opinion was being suppressed by the ethnocultural minorities in the class. I embraced the tension in the room that signaled the type of teaching "hold 'em" moment that produces big gains in student awareness and an opportunity to demonstrate to the class of future therapists how to build insight.

The course is built around exploration of self and multicultural science, so we discussed and unpacked Ted's feelings of persecution for approximately 30 minutes. The response from the other students was mixed, with students expressing concern, shame, disagreement, and exasperation. Ted did not appear to be either soothed or to have gained insight by the end of the conversation. As an immigrant male person of color, I also used my own negative experiences of being judged in an attempt to facilitate perspective taking and to decenter Ted's point of view. Finally, members of the room drew parallels between Ted's feelings and the daily experiences of bias, stereotype threat, misogyny, and xenophobia. Appearing unconvinced, Ted (re)expressed resignation as the class was redirected to scheduled course content.

FACULTY REFLECTION

With time and space from these incidents, we appreciate how our White students' "outsider" status within the social justice classroom community and "insider" status outside of the classroom contributed to the reactions of the main players. Although the issues we discuss here featured cross-racial interactions about racial threat, we have also experienced challenging classroom interactions across various identities and issues that suggest that similar dynamics and solutions may apply. Although we will primarily focus on the race-related aspects of these dilemmas, we also acknowledge that our gender identities (in particular, but along with other differences) likely contributed to how our students perceived our authority and responses.

It sometimes happens that students present negative, incorrect information about ethnocultural groups to which the instructor belongs. For example, when I (Darren) was told that immigrants of color overuse health services and are bringing down the USA, I had to model a professional response to a well-intentioned, but xenophobic, remark rather than treat it as a legitimate difference of opinion. In this scenario, marginalized students may be particularly attuned to what the instructor will do next, hoping the instructor can right the wrong of the xenophobic remark. This puts additional pressure on the instructor to hit the mark, while simultaneously having to suppress an emotional response about the comment itself. Add these dynamics to a publicly held exchange with a power differential between the student and instructor, and approaches to teaching must be particularly sensitive.

Positionality of Faculty in the Classroom

Reflecting on *positionality*, or one's relative status, power, and privilege in a context, can be a useful frame for analyzing classroom dynamics (Maher & Tetreault, 2001). Positionality not only refers to the social location of an individual in a particular context but also the negotiation of identities that follows (Cooks, 2003). As Cooks (2003) discussed, faculty—like students—are influenced by their own positionality in the classroom, and the various identities and composition of a particular classroom contribute to complex interactions and consequences for all involved. It is not reasonable to expect any members of the classroom community to be divorced of their own identities and emotions, especially in challenging, unexpected, socially charged incidents like these.

Positionality of Students in the Classroom

Ethnocultural minority students often have different expectations entering social justice-oriented classrooms than do White students. They perceive these spaces as a welcome respite from having to defend and justify their existence. This feeling of "safe space" may be strengthened by having an ethnocultural minority as an instructor. Yet because of this sense of safety, students with marginalized identities outside the classroom may raise issues that place the instructor in a difficult position and hold professors of color to a high (or impossible) standard when it comes to social justice activism. This can lead to a "call-out culture" in the classroom where the professor who is perceived as not perfectly "walking the walk" loses credibility with students who hold marginalized identities. White students may respond in different ways as they witness students of color holding a professor of color to a sometimes unreasonable standard. Some may shut down and choose silence, nervous that any future missteps will be harshly criticized or called out. Other White students may opt to signal their allyship and/or wokeness by piling on to the critique.

Teaching Strategies Used by Faculty of Color

As White students are often learning about historical and modern-day racism in-depth for the first time in a social justice–oriented course, faculty, and particularly faculty of color, often develop pedagogical strategies to mitigate resistance to new and challenging information (Bohonos, 2019; Perry et al., 2009). Faculty of color prepare for challenges to their credibility and authority and often scaffold and supplement curriculum in diversity-focused courses. Perry and colleagues (2009) termed this strategy *anticipatory teaching* and discussed how physically and emotionally taxing this strategy can be for faculty.

In reflecting on the teaching strategies we personally use, it can mean we do extra preparation for classes, as we expect to be questioned more, or hyperfocusing on our presentation style and word choice, knowing that our actions may be under a microscope. We also employ another common strategy, "disarming," which involves purposefully cultivating a nonjudgmental, inclusive classroom environment where diverse political viewpoints are welcome (Perry et al., 2009). Syllabi, first day of class overviews, and explicit discussion expectations serve to make this point clear to students.

Specifically, we find that syllabi for social justice–oriented courses can sometimes read like waivers for a skydiving adventure. A laundry list of what the class is and is not, the expectations for behavior, the topics covered, and the emotions you might experience, our introductions to the course early on suggest to students that they are embarking on something that is exciting, a little unpredictable, and maybe a wee bit dangerous. We ask them to consider their abilities to do the workload, consider new perspectives, and handle emotionally sensitive material. Sometimes students hear these "warnings" and withdraw from the course, while others gear up for an adventure. We prepare students that the examination of self and identity in the context of our courses might produce discomfort and encourage them to examine that discomfort in the service of learning. The syllabi and first-day descriptions prime students to expect a range of emotional responses and provide expectations that members of the classroom community might "misstep" while learning. We design this permission to err specifically to encourage students to take risks and speak candidly.

For years, the anticipatory teaching and disarming strategies worked well in our classes to produce a classroom culture where White students who were less experienced talking about race often felt comfortable speaking up and sharing their perspectives. Describing the classroom environment as a place to stumble, misstep, ask questions, and rethink seemed to encourage White students, who were often the numerical minority in the classroom, to fully participate in class discussions. Many years of this approach led to fruitful discussions and some significant self-reflection as White students listened, shared their perspectives, and asked questions of their peers. These students often reported the greatest growth at the end of the semester. The waiver was working!

In addition, this teaching approach seemed to be well-received by students of color who wanted opportunities to practice emotionally charged dialogue with White students in a controlled environment. Because there were sometimes only a handful of White students in the classroom, the perspectives of these individuals were often amplified as they were sometimes given a disproportionate amount of airtime in the service of these dialogues. The trade-off to give White students more speaking time in these dialogues in order to give students of color an opportunity to practice difficult cross-group dialogue often seemed appropriate to classroom goals.

As our scenarios suggest, however, the strategies do not always result in positive outcomes. Positionality can inform why the timing, social locations, and identities of the players might lead to fruitful conversations in one semester and chaos and harm in another. When professors start the semester by overly attending to the needs of one student's opposing viewpoint for the sake of viewpoint diversity, they may establish patterns that amplify a perspective that is already well-established outside the classroom. While a divergent viewpoint can serve the instructor and the discussion dynamics, equal time may not mean equal representation. Giving one student who is advancing a majority viewpoint out of the class equal airtime as the rest of the class will result in a disproportionate amount of commentary in each class session. The pedagogical approach of "disarming" and giving resistant White students more than their share of classroom time takes a different shape when the views are both extreme and amplified or normalized outside the classroom by inflammatory political rhetoric. Add to this the perceived expectation from marginalized students to create a safe space in the social justice classroom during turbulent political times, and the instructor's range of options seem narrow. Additionally, explicit mention of viewpoint inclusivity early in the course can be interpreted as equal airtime and embolden students like Shannon to demand more and more time to vocalize an already amplified perspective.

Course content on its own can produce resistance and defensiveness that students lob against the instructor and class, as was the case with Ted. At first, the resistance might be thought of as an opportunity for the instructor or classmates to work through by sharing stories, perspectives, and experiences with the resistant student. When there is a lack of progress with countering resistance, it may become a source of resignation for some students as they become aware that making someone face their positionality can be a laborious and unsuccessful process. Both Ted and Shannon vocalized not feeling that their viewpoints were valued despite the amount of time devoted to their viewpoints and early support from their peers.

CONSIDERATIONS OF CONTEXT

(Over-)Accommodating Multiple Viewpoints in a Politically Divisive Climate

Making extra accommodations for students in the service of disarming them likely set the stage for the later disruptive behavior discussed in our dilemma. Given the especially divisive sociopolitical climate and increasing public pressure to achieve "viewpoint diversity" in the classroom (Kristof, 2016), accommodating an oppositional role in discussions seemed necessary at the time. In retrospect, the pressure to appear "fair and balanced" inadvertently emboldened Shannon and Ted to be demanding and disruptive. In the emotionally charged political climate, catering to White people and White norms became confounded with the idea of valuing viewpoints and intellectual diversity. In this way, a commitment to inclusion and viewpoint diversity really translated to a commitment to prioritizing White voices and perspectives.

Holistic Impact and "Invisible" Consequences

Students like Shannon and Ted present a particular challenge to those who are aiming for viewpoint diversity in the classroom and who seek constructive dialogue. Upon reflection, the greatest lesson from our experiences is that the students of color, who were visibly harmed after each incident, were invisibly harmed in all the weeks prior and for weeks after. We refer to *invisible* in this context as indirect, intangible, and subtle repercussions.

Allowing an emotionally disruptive student disproportionate airtime in the name of inclusion does little to improve the lives of people of color, nor does it result in meaningful learning or growth on the part of the White student. A lone student who is unwilling to consider new perspectives should not be afforded a disproportionate amount of class time in the service of inclusion.

The impact of Shannon and Ted's behavior also had an invisible impact on the class as a whole. Students who identify with and as minorities may suffer in these situations, but they may serve as bellwethers for a larger problem involving all members of the course (see Warner, Chapter 16, this volume). Negative repercussions such as outbursts of bigotry can affect the classroom culture, and the morale of all present in the room (other students, the resistant student, and the instructor). For instructors, the morale element can make it very difficult to approach the class with the same vulnerability as before. In Salena's case, the exhaustion of supporting the harmed students and continued effort to reach out to Shannon took a physical and emotional toll. Each week became a practice in putting on a brave face and showing students what it looked like to stay engaged with the conversation. Doing so came at the cost of well-being. Students and the instructor personally reached out to Shannon to check on her well-being and welcome her back to class. These efforts did not elicit a positive response from Shannon, but she did return to class, no longer verbally participating but completing and submitting assignments. From the top down, the class community suffered in this uncomfortable environment; no one felt safe to speak freely.

Ted, on the other hand, appeared to make an earnest attempt to understand how the intersection of his race and gender influenced his interactions with society. Yet for Ted, the salience of his status as a person of low income appeared to supersede other dimensions of his identity for him and interfered with his ability to be introspective or to perspective take. He was unable to see his privilege but rather only his disadvantage.

INTERSECTIONALITY

An intersectional approach considers how identities (race, gender, social class, faculty classification and rank) may pressure faculty to make difficult choices in the classroom. In addition to the aspects of intersectionality we have already described, some additional factors are important to attend to in these situations. Specifically, contingent faculty and those without tenure may be particularly wary of rocking the boat in the classroom (Taber, 2014). Accusations of bias or promoting an agenda are powerful grenades in an academic setting. Complaints that faculty have an "agenda" may appear more legitimate when lodged against faculty of color than toward White faculty. White students who feel challenged or threatened by course content might also feel like they can reclaim lost power by filing complaints within the university or by submitting a professor's name to the Professor Watchlist, a site dedicated to compiling names of "biased professors." Faculty of color trying to maintain a positive atmosphere in the classroom may feel particularly pressured to appease defensive or reactive White students to avoid these professionally harmful outcomes. This pressure is in conflict with department and university pressures that many faculty of color experience to be diversity experts and to carry the load of "diversity work" in service of institutional core values (Perry et al., 2009).

BEST PRACTICES

In an ideal world, the 15-week courses on social justice themes we have carefully crafted would lead to a transformational experience for each of our students. As experience has taught us, there are a number of factors that change the dynamics in the classroom and a number of strategies to prepare for situations that may arise. Our suggestions for faculty seeking to be prepared for the unexpected focus on strategies to minimize harm, using positionality as a pedagogical tool, practicing self-compassion, increasing institutional support, and recognizing the long-term nature of social change and the work we do. The best practices described in this section acknowledge that many of the decisions social justice educators make while facilitating difficult discussions require a complex balancing act of reading the dynamics in the room, practicing emotional regulation, and showing care for the educational process of each student. This work is not easy, and sometimes the decisions are "best we can do" practices.

Minimize Harm

While students of color bear the brunt of the negative consequences from a pedagogical approach that prioritizes White comfort and normalizes White outbursts, the entire class community suffers when harmful dialogue is unsuccessfully resolved. White students don't learn inclusion, minority students face being retraumatized, and the instructor may be drained and attenuate their message. Students of color benefit from practicing cross-group dialogue in a structured setting, but when the circumstances intensify the impact of the rhetoric inside the classroom, steps must be taken to minimize the harm to students. An approach to "walking the walk" about viewpoint inclusion might take into account how prevalent the extreme view is outside of the classroom. The instructor then uses this information to calibrate how much more of this viewpoint is necessary to include in class, thereby balancing the competing needs of inclusion and harm reduction. In the case of Trump's inflammatory rhetoric about Mexican immigrants, one might take a value-added approach to examining whether and how much further input is needed. Instructors should examine whether a disproportionate amount of classroom time is devoted to extreme, hardened views and recenter the conversation accordingly.

The dysfunctional pattern of behavior evidenced in the first scenario developed as early as the first day of class. Noting inflammatory behavior and responding appropriately (ignoring it, questioning it, or shutting it down) in the early stages would be more productive than allowing it to continue in the name of inclusion. In both scenarios, it is important to note that there were other reasonable White students in the class who did not behave as Shannon or Ted did. These students also missed out on important opportunities for learning and self-reflection. By handling a student like Shannon or Ted in the semester, the entire class (including Shannon and Ted) might have benefitted from watching meaningful cross-group dialogue between the students of color and White students.

We have found perspective taking, modeling, and clarifying to be helpful, but equally important is instilling structure. Unconstrained exploration of negative views can make the class as an organism unhealthy. Instructors need to ask themselves if (a) the viewpoint is well-understood and represented to students outside the classroom already and (b) the particular student espousing the hurtful or damaging rhetoric has been granted more classroom time than other students. Stating "Thank you for that perspective, I think we understand your point of view now" and pivoting to ask for other perspectives can be a practical strategy for moving forward in the moment. When a particularly polarizing or bigoted statement occurs, a response might sound something like "Let's hit pause for a moment and talk about what you just said. If I'm understanding correctly, you are saying [paraphrase of student's comment]. . . . Is that correct? . . . Have you thought about how the words you've chosen might impact others in the room?" If the student doesn't have a response, the instructor or another student might jump in to create a learning opportunity about language and inclusion. This kind of conversation is delicate, but modeling compassion for the student while also creating structure and protection for marginalized students can be powerful for everyone involved.

Use Positionality as a Pedagogical Tool

Difficult moments are multilevel problems that need multilevel solutions. Relles (2016) suggested using positionality as a method for teaching for inclusion. The technique of incorporating positionality acknowledges that dynamics of "power, privilege and difference . . . exist between teacher and her or his students" (p. 313). An examination of positionality as a pedagogical tool in the social justice classroom can be used to enhance learning for all students. Takacs (2002) suggested that by bringing identities to the foreground, instructors can create an asset model of multicultural education where no one student's opinion is privileged. The context of the conversation dictates who is in the best position to enhance student learning. Instructors and students should actively identify instances where discussions of prejudice have been coopted by privileged students. Takacs noted that when White students feel entitled to dominate a discussion based on a dominant position outside the classroom,

> to deny that white student a voice may shut him [sic] down and help to build a barrier to genuine constructive listening; to allow that student to dominate a discussion may alienate students of color in the classroom. Here enters the joy—and a contribution to social justice—that focusing on the positionality-epistemology connection brings. (p. 176)

He then suggested that essential learning comes from examining the power dynamics occurring in the classroom and whose voices are privileged as a result. It is constructive to address positionality early on in the course to give students a vocabulary for what they might experience. Asking students to think about how expressing their positions outside the classroom feels in contrast to expressing them inside the classroom might also be an avenue to reach a student who is in unfamiliar territory.

In classroom discussions, positionality as a pedagogical tool can be applied in three ways: *positionality-on-action*, *positionality-in-action*, and *positionality-for-action* (Takacs, 2002). Instructors use positionality-on-action when they draw attention to bias after it has happened. Positionality-in-action involves a spontaneous acknowledgment of bias that happens in the midst of discussion. Positionality-for-action is forward-looking, asking students to use their understanding of bias to improve classroom equity as the course moves forward.

For example, positionality-on-action incorporates the difficult past situation as a part of the curriculum moving forward, allowing future students to think more critically about classroom dynamics and their own positionality. I (Salena) now use the Shannon incident itself as part of my course content, and I find it a useful vehicle to discuss classroom power and dynamics. Assignment suggestions that use the positionality-on-action approach are included in the Resources section at the end of the chapter.

Giving Compassion to Yourself

The same compassion and patience afforded to the students in the course must be applied to the instructor. Navigating difficult moments can be emotionally taxing, and missteps will likely be part of the process (see Kite et al., Chapter 4, this volume). These conversations may continue to feel like walking a tightrope, but a proper safety net of supportive colleagues, friends, and mentors can make it much easier to move forward after a misstep (see also Eaton & Warner, Chapter 3, this volume for suggestions on social justice burnout). Moments such as those with Shannon and Ted are a microcosm of issues that are widespread in society, and expecting instructors in social justice courses to consistently have neat answers to these classroom dilemmas creates unnecessary stress and models unrealistic behavior for students. Instead, students can learn from an instructor who models authenticity and honest dialogue during and after challenging classroom incidents. This may mean revisiting a misstep in the next class and acknowledging their own emotional fallout in a situation. It may be appropriate at times to offer an apology to the class. When faculty misstep but show vulnerability in offering an authentic apology, it can be transformative and informative for the class community. It shows that we expect missteps to happen and that there is a path forward to restore communication.

Acknowledgment at the Institutional Level

The professional impact of teaching these courses should be considered at a departmental and institutional level. Students' strong reactions can skew instructor ratings directly through negative student evaluations or by negatively influencing peers (see Boysen, Chapter 17, this volume). Diversity-related courses can often be unpopular to teach and not valued by colleagues; further, faculty of color can feel pressured to assume responsibility for these courses. The tax of teaching a course that is personally and professionally challenging can be intensified by the context of departments that question the value of diversity-related courses. Thus, institutions also need to value the extra work involved in balancing a diversity of viewpoints, while minimizing harmful attacks and student defensiveness.

Taking a Long View to Social Change

Healthy expectations include recognizing that students and faculty will stumble in class and that growth often occurs outside the classroom, sometimes long after the course is over. The compassionate permission to stumble, misstep, ask questions, and rethink should apply as much to faculty as to students as they navigate difficult moments in the classroom together. Teachers should appreciate the value in planting seeds and providing the tools for future growth. Students have a lifetime of acculturation into the implicit attitudes and beliefs we examine in our classes; the expectation to alter within the span of a semester is sometimes unrealistic. The age of the typical college student coincides with developmental grappling with multiple identities. Consciousness raising on top of that can feel overwhelming and emotionally wrought in a way that might feel different in later adulthood. Teaching these courses may require faculty to gamble on the long game, counting successes long after our classes are over.

RESOURCES

Accapadi, M. (2007). When White women cry: How White women's tears oppress Women of Color. *College Student Affairs Journal, 26*, 208–215.
    This short news piece describes the impact of "white tears" in a social justice classroom. Students read the article and discuss the relationship between emotion and power and strategize how students and instructors should handle situations where students center the discussion around their own discomfort. In this way, students are dictating their own discussion expectations in a way that doesn't put a particular student on the spot.

"The Anatomy of an Apology." https://youthrex.com/wp-content/uploads/2019/02/Anatomy-of-An-Apology-Rania-El-Mugammar.pdf
    Social justice activist Rania El Mugammar offers a helpful framework for properly apologizing. Her piece walks the reader through the required elements for moving forward after a misstep. The piece can also be assigned during the course for students to analyze the effectiveness of public apologies.

Mun Wah, L. (2014). *If these halls could talk* [DVD]. StirFry Seminars & Consulting.
    Another assignment that uses the positionality-on-action approach asks students to screen Lee Mun Wah's film *If These Halls Could Talk*. This documentary film features a group of college students discussing and grappling with difficult issues related to race, religion, and privilege. The film involves several emotionally charged scenes where discussants specifically call out more privileged members of the group and create discomfort among the group. The film creates an opportunity for viewers to talk about dynamics of power and privilege and position as it relates to the cast of the film, rather than themselves. A film guide is available at https://www.ifthesehallscouldtalk.org/.

REFERENCES

Bohonos, J. W. (2019). Including critical whiteness studies in the critical human resource development family: A proposed theoretical framework. *Adult Education Quarterly, 69*(4), 315–337. https://doi.org/10.1177/0741713619858131

Cooks, L. (2003). Pedagogy, performance, and positionality: Teaching about whiteness in interracial communication. *Communication Education, 52*(3–4), 245–257. https://doi.org/10.1080/0363452032000156226

Kristof, N. (2016, May 7). A confession of liberal intolerance. *The New York Times*, p. SR1.

Lee, M. Y. H. (2015, July 8). Donald Trump's false comments connecting Mexican immigrants and crime. *The Washington Post.* https://www.washingtonpost.com/news/fact-checker/wp/2015/07/08/donald-trumps-false-comments-connecting-mexican-immigrants-and-crime/

Maher, F., & Tetreault, M. (2001). *The feminist classroom: Dynamics of gender, race, and privilege* (Expanded ed.). Rowman & Littlefield.

Nelson, J. C., Adams, G., & Salter, P. S. (2013). The Marley hypothesis: Denial of racism reflects ignorance of history. *Psychological Science, 24*(2), 213–218. https://doi.org/10.1177/0956797612451466

Perry, G., Moore, H., Edwards, C., Acosta, K., & Frey, C. (2009). Maintaining credibility and authority as an instructor of color in diversity-education classrooms: A qualitative inquiry. *The Journal of Higher Education, 80*(1), 80–105. https://doi.org/10.1080/00221546.2009.11772131

Relles, S. (2016). A call for qualitative methods in action: Enlisting positionality as an equity Tool. *Intervention in School and Clinic, 51*(5), 312–317. https://doi.org/10.1177/1053451215606690

Rogers, K. (1978). "The gambler" [Song]. On *The Gambler*. United Artists.

Taber, N. (2014). Critiquing war in the classroom: Professor positionality, vulnerability, and possibility. *New Horizons in Adult Education and Human Resource Development, 26*(4), 1–17. https://doi.org/10.1002/nha3.20081

Takacs, D. (2002). Positionality, epistemology, and social justice in the classroom. *Social Justice, 29*(4), 168–181.

8

THE EFFICACY PARADOX

Teaching About Structural Inequality While Keeping Students' Hope Alive

LISA M. BROWN

There are times when I am concerned that students feel overwhelmed by the pervasiveness and persistence of structural inequality given the repeated exposure to research about, and examples of, privilege, prejudice, and discrimination presented by me and themselves throughout my Stigma and Prejudice class. Rarely are any of them surprised that privilege and prejudice exist. Nevertheless, the many forms of privilege and prejudice, how widespread they remain, and the severity of their consequences sometimes surprise some, if not all, of my students. I see them shaking their heads in disapproval, saying, "That's messed up." Their emotional responses vary including despondence, anger, guilt, outrage, bitterness, cynicism, and disgust. All of these emotions may be associated with feeling that their efforts cannot change the intractable nature of inequality. Given that research has found that feelings of efficacy promote social justice action intentions and behavior (van Zomeren et al., 2008), instructors can channel students' myriad of negative emotions into efficacy that leads to positive social change through action.

https://doi.org/10.1037/0000216-008
Navigating Difficult Moments in Teaching Diversity and Social Justice, M. E. Kite, K. A. Case, and W. R. Williams (Editors)
Copyright © 2021 by the American Psychological Association. All rights reserved.

FACULTY REFLECTION

Concern about my students' emotional responses and the ways they affect their sense of efficacy often stands in juxtaposition to my own emotional responses to teaching about social injustice. I feel incredibly fulfilled teaching about injustice because I believe that such knowledge will help my students be part of incrementally making the world a more just, equitable, and inclusive place. I have taught a Stigma and Prejudice course since 1993. The crux of the class is to critique older theories suggesting that members of negatively stereotyped groups internalize negative views of their respective groups and end up with poor well-being and low self-esteem (i.e., self-hatred). Contemporary research has largely found that members of negatively stereotyped groups do not necessarily have low self-esteem compared with majority group members (Crocker & Major, 1989; but see Schmitt et al., 2014). I spend the bulk of the class highlighting ways members of negatively stereotyped groups actively participate in the construction of their impressions to various others as a means of managing their marginalized identities. This focus is in contrast to many classes on the topic that focus on the majority group's perceptions and experiences. I provide this background to convey that I go into the class centering the perspective, agency, and resilience of individuals in negatively stereotyped groups as active agents in social interactions. This framing is part of why I do not feel discouraged, but rather emboldened, by the subject matter. A tacit theme of the course is resilience and resistance in the face of adversity.

Someone once asked me why teaching about pervasive and persistent privilege and prejudice did not depress me. I was dumbstruck. I honestly had not previously entertained the thought. And the person asking seemed equally perplexed given the perception that I was a dispositionally optimistic individual teaching a demoralizing subject. I did not have an immediate answer. Upon reflection, I came to this conclusion. My maternal grandmother was born a Black woman in 1915 in the integrated North and went to integrated high school in Boston. When she was a young woman and went to apply for a cashier's job at a downtown department store, she was told that perhaps she could get a job as an elevator operator—and that was only because she was light-skinned—but there was no way she could get a job as a cashier. My paternal grandmother did not even have these opportunities as she was born Black in the segregated, rural South in 1917 where the local Black school went only to 10th grade. I find it encouraging and remarkable that these women have a Black grandchild who has a PhD from an institution that once did not enroll Black people and also teaches White students in an ethnically diverse student body at a college that once was only for Presbyterian, White men. Do things still need to change? Absolutely (Kraus et al., 2019). But have things changed for the better? Absolutely. My grandmothers' pride and amazement at that transition in just two generations are not lost on me. Also, I readily admit that perhaps I can withstand teaching about injustice day in and day out because I am just a "glass half full" kind of person. That optimism and sense of efficacy frame the way I view the world—including injustices. I always believe things can and will get better because people—including myself—can and will do better.

But my students are not all raving optimists.

The Efficacy Paradox

Teaching about social justice involves a paradox. In order to raise the students' consciousness about social justice, typically instructors help them discover the pervasive, enduring, and intractable nature of social injustice. Instructors teach them about the ways ostensibly fair (and thus accepted and highly regarded) social systems and structures perpetuate inequality (Banks et al., 2006). Instructors teach them about ways unconscious biases may be a factor in wide-ranging forms of discrimination. Examples range from the benefits physically attractive individuals receive relative to less attractive individuals (Langlois et al., 2000) to the harsher punishment Black students receive for the same infraction as White students (Okonofua & Eberhardt, 2015) to redlining as a form of U.S.-government-imposed racial and economic segregation (Woods, 2012). At the end of the semester, students understand the ways in which structural systems and individual biases have maintained inequalities and continue to do so. Yet witnessing their emotional responses raises a concern that some of them leave classrooms feeling convinced that these systems resist change and little they can do will have any effect. Given that research on efficacy suggests that perceiving a situation as intractable undermines efficacy to change it (Bandura, 2006), what are ways instructors can help their students both to recognize structural forces and also to maintain a sense of efficacy to combat these forces?

Psychological Underpinnings of the Paradox

This focus on structural factors is additionally paradoxical because it sits at odds with typical ways that people are socialized in Western cultures to explain events (Lopez et al., 1998). Attribution theory addresses ways people explain why an event happened or someone acted a certain way;

was it something about the situation, or was it something about the person? Many college students in the United States were socialized to underestimate situational causes (e.g., long-term effects of residential segregation) and overestimate dispositional causes (e.g., personal choice, willpower) of inequality (Miller, 1984). Thus, when instructors teach students about structural inequality, initially some students may question the validity of the evidence because it so contradicts their default attributional tendencies.

Students' Emotional Responses

Well-being among most people socialized in individualistic cultures correlates with viewing oneself as efficacious (Myers & Diener, 1995), and perceiving oneself as inefficacious evokes negative emotions that people often want to avoid. In fact, depression involves negative attributions about the self that are internal ("this bad thing is something about me"), global ("it is everything about me"), and stable ("it will not change"; Seligman et al., 1979). After accepting that structural inequalities exist, students may believe that people, including themselves, can do little to effect change over these inequalities, incorporating two components of depressive attributional style: the global component ("this is pervasive") and the stable component ("this has always existed, still exists, and will continue to exist"). In fact, research finds that among people in marginalized groups, perceptions of pervasive discrimination are associated with lower well-being (Schmitt et al., 2014).

Although some students may feel despondent, others may feel outrage. Students may realize that the world is not just and that certain people are wronged for no fault of their own. These students may respond with this sense of outrage, as anger typically results when individual harm is perceived to be unfair (Rozin et al., 1999). But how are they to mete out justice? The structure that perpetrated the injustice may seem beyond their reach, as are the victims of it. Thus, these students may leave the class feeling angry, frustrated, disgusted, or overwhelmed. Regardless of the specific emotion, faculty may aim to translate students' emotions into efficacy that ideally leads to social change.

Faculty Responsibility

Let me be clear: I am not advocating that instructors should shield students from feeling negative emotions in class. These emotions are reasonable responses to learning about injustice and its pervasiveness. Yet instructors who have some responsibility over the welfare of these students should not trivialize possible consequences of the emotional work students may do in these classes (Young, 2003). In addition, psychology instructors in particular should be cognizant about the effect these classes may have on students' well-being. As Tatum (1992) argued,

> Heightening students' awareness of racism [and other forms of injustice] without also developing an awareness of the possibility of change is a prescription for despair. I consider it unethical to do one without the other. Exploring strategies to empower students as change agents is thus a necessary part of the process of talking about race [and other identities] and learning about racism [and other systems of oppression]. (pp. 20–21)

In addition, arguably the goal of education is not to make the students comfortable but to prepare them to participate in civic society. Education may be seen as a means to prepare people for engagement in democracies in which individuals are exposed to different viewpoints and have the freedom to engage in political participation. Globalization and increasing demographic diversity have only made this preparation more essential. For many people teaching about social justice, a goal is not only to raise the consciousness of students by evoking strong emotions but also to increase their civic participation. Fortunately, much previous research finds that experiences with diversity (including learning about social injustice) in college foster a variety of positive outcomes, including intentions for civic participation (e.g., Gurin et al., 2004). In addition, beliefs in collective efficacy in response to white privilege foster positive social action to promote social change (Stewart et al., 2010). Moreover, feeling outrage at injustice paired with feelings of efficacy (van Zomeren et al., 2008) and hope (Greenaway et al., 2016) allow collective action to follow.

CONSIDERATIONS OF CONTEXT AND INTERSECTIONALITY

Specific factors may affect the dynamics of a given class. One approach, expectation, or practice does not fit all classroom situations generally, let alone when teaching about diversity. This subject matter in particular requires being sensitive to classroom dynamics and adjusting accordingly. Relevant factors include the context of the class and the intersectionality of identities of both students and instructors.

Contextual Factors

My Stigma and Prejudice class is an upper-level course that majors can opt to take. Most of the students want to be there and have previously had me as a professor. It is exceptionally rare that students in my class do not already believe that privilege and prejudice are still problems, and I realize that I am fortunate to have that experience. Many faculty who teach about issues of social justice often face blatant and subtle hostility and questions of their credibility (Rios et al., Chapter 5, this volume). This latter classroom experience may be far more common when diversity classes are required and students cannot self-select away from the topic.

Intersectionality

Even someone as fortunate as I have been in the classroom has battle scars. After a lecture in my Stigma and Prejudice class during my first year as a faculty member, a White, male, undergraduate student asked me about a claim I made in lecture. I assumed he had not understood the material, so I repeated the claim. He questioned me again. It was then I realized the issue was he did not *believe* the claim. I went through each of the steps of my argument with a citation and empirical finding for each step. At that point he said, "Well, I guess you are smart after all." Of course, I will never know for sure, but I just do not think an undergraduate student would have so dismissed the credibility of a White male professor, let alone admitting it to that professor's face. Students may challenge faculty who have a marginalized identity until those faculty become "known quantities" or are perceived to be "old and wise."

Perhaps that student's comment cemented the following tendency of mine: Throughout all of my courses, I attempt to model good information literacy and scientific thinking by presenting empirically based claims in class. I am explicitly clear when some statement is my opinion or a hypothesis versus an empirical fact. Thus, I set the expectation that claims require evidence and reasoned arguments. Although some of this tendency is just my personality (I was skeptical even as a child), some of it is likely also a strategy to compensate for the chance people may question my credibility because I am a Black woman. I will often supplement citations from the empirical literature with personal anecdotes to illustrate a point or claim as students may find them more relatable, accessible, and memorable (Adams & Marchesani, 1997). For example, as mentioned above, I can harken to family history and readily cite examples of intergeneration change and progress as well as changes in my own lifetime to engender hope.

In addition to my own interconnected identities, intersectionality relates to my students' emotional responses. Students with different identities tend to have different responses. For example, although some of my White students feel some level of guilt in response to the material on racism, my students of color virtually never do. Disgust and contempt are more typical emotional responses from students of color. In most classes, crying is not normative. Yet guilt can at times bring tears, particularly from my White female students. This, in turn, may evoke gestures of sympathy from other students. For example, in response to a neutral discussion question directed at White students, a White, female student teared up while responding. Gauging the situation, and having had this student in class before, I felt that I did not need to intervene. In the next class period, however, the two Latina students who asked the question wanted to create rules that no one could "get called out" in discussion. I talked with the Latina students after class, and they felt gravely responsible for upsetting a fellow student and wanted to prevent it from happening in the class again. I told them that their question was legitimate and that there was nothing accusatory in the way they asked it, so I was pretty sure the White, female student did not feel attacked by the question. I assured them that I would follow up with her just to make sure. The White female student confirmed that she cries when talking about herself in such ways and that she did not feel that anyone had done anything hurtful against her.

I try to make sure that all emotional responses carry equal weight and try not to cater to the tyranny of visible tears. The type of crying mentioned in the example should be recognized but not privileged above any other responses to the material. All students should have the same opportunity to receive empathy and support—not because they cry but because they personally or their group(s) experienced an injury. Often instructors feel the responsibility to fix our students' discomfort at all costs or to avoid upsetting them out of concern for the potential effect on our class evaluations (Boysen, Chapter 17, this volume; Kite et al., Chapter 4, this volume). The reality is that sometimes what students learn is upsetting. Although no students should end up wounded in classes, instructors need to learn to be at peace with students' being appropriately upset and to facilitate the decentering of privilege when studying inequality (see Brody & Bernal, Chapter 7, this volume).

Students' past experiences also inform their reactions in class. Often students who belong to a marginalized group are less surprised by the pervasiveness of privilege and discrimination and thus less emotionally upset in the immediate classroom situation. At the same time, it is also the case that students in dominant groups who have had much contact with and exposure to members of marginalized groups often are not surprised either. For example, White students who attended majority Black and Latina/o/e high schools and nondisabled students who have a family member with a disability often are familiar with ways in which privilege, prejudice, and inequality operate in everyday life. In contrast, at times I have found that students of color whose parents are highly educated immigrants are surprised by the systemic inequalities, presumably because their families had economic and educational privilege in their homelands and voluntarily came to the United States perceiving it as a land of opportunity and fairness.

BEST PRACTICES

Thoughtful planning before class begins may reduce the chance that students will become demoralized throughout the semester. The following recommendations include responsibilities of the instructor and construction of assignments for the students.

Implement Intentional Class Design

Being intentional about class design can help to stave off negative emotions and low sense of efficacy that may fester rather than lead to positive social action. Having interventions throughout the course rather than none or just at the end of the course can help to counteract the cumulative toll of negative emotions on efficacy. Providing students with options for action in the classroom can help to alleviate some of the heaviness of the subject matter (see the Resources section). Moreover, even if the entire class does not work on a social change project, all students can report to the entire class on their experiences and findings and benefit from hearing about those who did. Instructors may provide a road map for the emotional journey of the class by forewarning students about the possible emotional reactions that the course may stir up, offering guidelines for ways to respond to each other, and setting expectations for ways the instructor will respond.

Lay a Foundation of Hope

From the outset of classes, instructors can lay the groundwork for students to maintain or establish a sense of efficacy in terms of combatting injustice and inequality. Instructors may provide students with examples throughout the course that engender hope by including historical accounts, media accounts, and repetition and reflection.

- *Historical Accounts.* Whenever the students in my Stigma and Prejudice class seem to need a morale boost, I often recount the revelation that

I came to about my grandmothers—always highlighting that there is still much work to do but things are changing for the better. Connecting this progress to students' own experiences should help to reinforce their hope (Adams & Marchesani, 1997). For example, I mention that same-sex marriage is now legal in the United States and many parts of the world, when that would have been inconceivable when I went to college in the 1980s. Today's students have witnessed a major societal transformation that would not have been imaginable a few decades earlier.

- *Media Accounts.* A similar strategy is to use media to convey that small changes may cumulatively have impact and that everyone has a role no matter how small the change they effect. The late environmental activist and Nobel Peace Prize winner Wangari Maathai tells a fable of a hummingbird fighting a forest fire in a clip "I will be a hummingbird" (*Dirt! The Movie*, 2010). It is a call for everyone to do the best they can no matter how insignificant the effects of their individual actions may seem. Instructors may enhance a sense of collective efficacy by pointing out that coordinated efforts may have much more impact than individual efforts.

- *Repetition and Reflection.* An instructor may communicate such conveyors of hope early in the course and reinforce them throughout it. Students may write papers on their experiences in class and from campus events to reflect upon their emotional responses and what next steps they imagine. These infusions of hope may help to buffer them from being overwhelmed by negative emotions that foster hopelessness and inaction.

Teach the Students About Specific Methods of Successful Collective Action

Often students are unaware of social action strategies and their success. In particular, I frequently wonder whether my students born and raised in Texas, a "right to work" state, have a particularly impoverished sense of social action strategies because of anti–labor/union state policies. They have had no role models for union membership, contract negotiations, and strikes. Consequently, instructors may teach them about specific successful strategies used in social action and collective movements. Instructors first may communicate common strategies (e.g., pickets, boycotts, strikes, marches, coalition building). Then instructors may discuss examples of when a specific strategy effected positive social change. For example, professor and activist Andrea Smith discusses the ways White fishers and Chippewa tribe members formed a coalition to combat mining by Exxon (Deep Blue, 2003). Not only does this provide an example of social action, it also provides an example of an unlikely but successful coalition. Choosing examples familiar to the students (at the time this chapter was written, these included Black Lives Matter, Occupy Wall Street, and Wendy Davis's filibuster of a Texas anti-abortion bill) reveals ways of drawing national attention to important social issues to spark national conversation. The response of the Parkland teenagers after the shooting at Marjory Stoneman Douglas High School is an example of ways in which media attention and clear, actionable demands may foster change as Florida Governor Rick Scott shortly thereafter signed new gun legislation into law. Moreover, instructors should be mindful not only to inform students of time-honored methods and strategies but also to incorporate learning about forms of digital social action that may resonate with contemporary students such as crowdsourcing tasks, creating online petitions, and organizing events via social media. For example, any movement with a hashtag owes some of its success to the strategic use of social media (e.g., #MeToo/#timesup; see Pickering, Chapter 9, this volume).

Have Students Communicate About Social Justice

Another strategy is for students to channel their energies into disseminating what they have learned about social justice. One way they can do this is to collaborate on creating a webpage or a public service announcement. An example that comes to mind are the many universities that have involved undergraduate history students in the research investigating their respective institutions' connections to slavery. Such efforts could be interdisciplinary. Communications and public relations students could be involved in the look and text of the webpage. Computer science students could be involved in any complex programming of it. In addition, some students could create mini TED-like talks or public service announcements to embed as videos on the webpage. These videos could include not only content about inequality but also strategies for countering it.

Another possible assignment would be for students to create a board game to teach their peers about social justice. Students with computer science backgrounds could create an app to run the game. Successful games could become part of student affairs programming in dorms. Members of marginalized groups may find support through these online activities, particularly when their identities are not readily obvious (McKenna & Bargh, 1998). Members of privileged groups may have a particular role as allies communicating about injustice as research finds that when members of disadvantaged groups address injustice among members of privileged groups, they may be dismissed as self-interested complainers (Kaiser & Miller, 2003).

Involve Students in Social Justice Action

An instructor may also make participation in social justice action an option for fulfilling a class assignment. The students may further be empowered by being able to determine what the action is, who it benefits, and what issue it addresses, for example. They could coordinate their efforts with a campus organization to promote social justice on campus, off campus, or both. They may also attempt to build collaborations and coalitions across student groups for certain initiatives and events. To counter the view that meaningful social action requires years of experience, training, networking, and coalition building, instructors can make students aware that social justice action may take many forms that they can readily implement, such as writing a letter or posting flyers. Moreover, training in recognizing and addressing injustice can help build students' confidence. Service learning projects may help students effect positive change (Seider et al., 2011). For example, an important theme in my Health Psychology class is that income inequality is a major factor in health disparities. The students have a group assignment in which they prepare a health intervention for a community group. I strongly encourage them to partner with the local public housing authority for this project.

CONCLUDING WORDS

Although it is incumbent upon us as instructors to convey research on structural inequality, it is equally important to cultivate a classroom experience that attempts to guard against students' despair and ideally fosters their hope and action. Teaching about inequality is not for the faint of heart. I do not say this flippantly. All instructors should regularly engage in self-reflection about not just our intellectual competence but also our emotional competence to teach what we teach. Going into a classroom of diverse students ill-prepared and emotionally ill-equipped to teach about privilege, prejudice, and inequality could end up doing more harm than good. Yet, for those who do this work, the rewards are great. Every class is an opportunity to engage in education that helps students make the world a more just and equitable place.

RESOURCES

Adams, M., Bell, L. A., & Griffin, P. (Eds.). (1997). *Teaching for diversity and social justice*. Routledge.
    Appendices 7E and 7F and the fourth module of Chapters 6–11 all have resources for encouraging social action in students. Each chapter addresses a different form of oppression and provides a variety of classroom exercises.

Dirt! The Movie. (2010, May 11). *I will be a hummingbird—Wangari Maathai (English)* [Film clip]. YouTube. https://www.youtube.com/watch?v=IGMW6YWjMxw

Inspirational clip on small actions adding up featuring the late Wangari Maathai. Instructors may use this clip from *Dirt! The Movie* to bolster students' sense of hope that their actions have impact.

Raquib, J. (2015, November). *The secret to effective nonviolent resistance* [Video]. TED Conferences. https://www.ted.com/talks/jamila_raqib_the_secret_to_effective_nonviolent_resistance?utm_campaign=tedspread&utm_medium=referral&utm_source=tedcomshare

Raquib, a protégé of Gene Sharp, discusses nonviolent collective action. If people are looking for a video rather than or in addition to readings, this TED Talk addresses Gene Sharp's perspective on nonviolent action.

Sharp, G. (1973). *198 methods of nonviolent action*. Albert Einstein Institution. https://www.aeinstein.org/wp-content/uploads/2014/12/198-Methods.pdf. (Originally from Sharp, G. [1973]. *The politics of nonviolent action, Part Two: The methods of nonviolent action*. Porter Sargent Publishers)

Lists specific nonviolent strategies. Often people think of the most obvious forms of nonviolent conflict like protests and boycotts. This list provides a wealth of examples that people often overlook. It may give students ideas on ways to promote change.

Sharp, G. (2008). Nonviolent action. In L. R. Kurtz (Ed.), *Encyclopedia of violence, peace, and conflict* (2nd ed, pp. 1373–1380). Elsevier Science & Technology.

Provides an overview of nonviolent action for social change. Students at times think that pacifism is synonymous with passivity. This chapter describes ways in which nonviolent action is a form of active conflict.

REFERENCES

Adams, M., & Marchesani, L. (1997). Multiple issues course overview. In M. Adams, L. A. Bell, & P. Griffin (Eds.), *Teaching for diversity and social justice* (pp. 261–271). Routledge.

Bandura, A. (2006). Toward a psychology of human agency. *Perspectives on Psychological Science, 1*(2), 164–180. https://doi.org/10.1111/j.1745-6916.2006.00011.x

Banks, R. R., Eberhardt, J. L., & Ross, L. (2006). Discrimination and implicit bias in a racially unequal society. *California Law Review, 94*(4), 1169–1190. https://doi.org/10.2307/20439061

Crocker, J., & Major, B. (1989). Social stigma and self-esteem: The self-protective properties of stigma. *Psychological Review, 96*(4), 608–630. https://doi.org/10.1037/0033-295X.96.4.608

Deep Blue. (2003, June 24). *Interview with Andrea Smith* [Video]. University of Michigan Library. https://deepblue.lib.umich.edu/handle/2027.42/55717

Dirt! The movie. (2010, May 11). *I will be a hummingbird—Wangari Maathai (English)* [Film clip]. YouTube. https://www.youtube.com/watch?v=IGMW6YWjMxw

Greenaway, K. H., Cichocka, A., Veelen, R., Likki, T., & Branscombe, N. R. (2016). Feeling hopeful inspires support for social change. *Political Psychology, 37*(1), 89–107. https://doi.org/10.1111/pops.12225

Gurin, P., Nagda, B. A., & Lopez, G. E. (2004). The benefits of diversity in education for democratic citizenship. *Journal of Social Issues, 60*(1), 17–34. https://doi.org/10.1111/j.0022-4537.2004.00097.x

Kaiser, C. R., & Miller, C. T. (2003). Derogating the victim: The interpersonal consequences of blaming events on discrimination. *Group Processes & Intergroup Relations, 6*(3), 227–237. https://doi.org/10.1177/13684302030063001

Kraus, M., Onyeador, I., Daumeyer, N., Rucker, J., & Richeson, J. (2019). The misperception of racial economic inequality. *Perspectives on Psychological Science, 14*(6), 899–921. https://doi.org/10.1177/1745691619863049

Langlois, J. H., Kalakanis, L., Rubenstein, A. J., Larson, A., Hallam, M., & Smoot, M. (2000). Maxims or myths of beauty? A meta-analytic and theoretical review. *Psychological Bulletin, 126*(3), 390–423. https://doi.org/10.1037/0033-2909.126.3.390

Lopez, G. E., Gurin, P., & Nagda, B. A. (1998). Education and understanding structural causes for group inequalities. *Political Psychology, 19*(2), 305–329. https://doi.org/10.1111/0162-895X.00106

McKenna, K. A., & Bargh, J. A. (1998). Coming out in the age of the internet: Identity "demarginalization" through virtual group participation. *Journal of Personality and Social Psychology, 75*(3), 681–694. https://doi.org/10.1037/0022-3514.75.3.681

Miller, J. G. (1984). Culture and development of everyday social explanation. *Journal of Personality and Social Psychology, 46*(5), 961–978. https://doi.org/10.1037/0022-3514.46.5.961

Myers, D. G., & Diener, E. (1995). Who is happy? *Psychological Science, 6*(1), 10–19. https://doi.org/10.1111/j.1467-9280.1995.tb00298.x

Okonofua, J. A., & Eberhardt, J. L. (2015). Two strikes: Race and the disciplining of young students. *Psychological Science, 26*(5), 617–624. https://doi.org/10.1177/0956797615570365

Rozin, P., Lowery, L., Imada, S., & Haidt, J. (1999). The CAD triad hypothesis: A mapping between three moral emotions (contempt, anger, disgust) and three moral codes (community, autonomy, divinity). *Journal of Personality and Social Psychology, 76*(4), 574–586. https://doi.org/10.1037/0022-3514.76.4.574

Schmitt, M. T., Branscombe, N. R., Postmes, T., & Garcia, A. (2014). The consequences of perceived discrimination for psychological well-being: A meta-analytic review. *Psychological Bulletin, 140*(4), 921–948. https://doi.org/10.1037/a0035754

Seider, S. C., Rabinowicz, S. A., & Gillmor, S. C. (2011). Changing American college students' conceptions of poverty through community service learning. *Analyses of Social Issues and Public Policy (ASAP), 11*(1), 105–126. https://doi.org/10.1111/j.1530-2415.2010.01224.x

Seligman, M. E., Abramson, L. Y., Semmel, A., & von Baeyer, C. (1979). Depressive attributional style. *Journal of Abnormal Psychology, 88*(3), 242–247. https://doi.org/10.1037/0021-843X.88.3.242

Stewart, T. L., Latu, I. M., Branscombe, N. R., & Denney, H. T. (2010). Yes we can! Prejudice reduction through seeing (inequality) and believing (in social change). *Psychological Science, 21*(11), 1557–1562. https://doi.org/10.1177/0956797610385354

Tatum, B. (1992). Talking about race, learning about racism: The application of racial identity development theory in the classroom. *Harvard Educational Review, 62*(1), 1–25. https://doi.org/10.17763/haer.62.1.146k5v980r703023

van Zomeren, M., Postmes, T., & Spears, R. (2008). Toward an integrative social identity model of collective action: A quantitative research synthesis of three socio-psychological perspectives. *Psychological Bulletin*, *134*(4), 504–535. https://doi.org/10.1037/0033-2909.134.4.504

Woods, L. L., II. (2012). The Federal Home Loan Bank Board, redlining, and the national proliferation of racial lending discrimination, 1921–1950. *Journal of Urban History*, *38*(6), 1036–1059. https://doi.org/10.1177/0096144211435126

Young, G. (2003). Dealing with difficult classroom dialogue. In P. Bronstein & K. Quina (Eds.), *Teaching gender and multicultural awareness: Resources for the psychology classroom* (pp. 347–360). American Psychological Association. https://doi.org/10.1037/10570-025

9

EMOTIONALLY CHARGED NEWS IN THE CLASSROOM

RYAN M. PICKERING

Discussing emotionally charged news in the classroom can be difficult and feel overwhelming. Self-reflection and validating students' emotional responses are important steps to responding to these events, as well as considering the context and intersections of identity. I discuss the pros and cons of three main approaches to responding to events in the news. I underline the importance of responding to emotionally charged events *in some way* and discuss research that suggests that almost all responses to emotionally charged news events in the classroom are better than no response at all.

RESPONDING TO EVENTS IN THE NEWS

On Saturday, October 27, 2018, eleven members of the Tree of Life synagogue in Pittsburgh, Pennsylvania—less than 100 miles away from my institution—were murdered by a White man who reportedly believed that Jewish people should be blamed (and punished) for somehow funding the "migrant caravan" from South America headed toward the border of the

---

https://doi.org/10.1037/0000216-009
Navigating Difficult Moments in Teaching Diversity and Social Justice, M. E. Kite, K. A. Case, and W. R. Williams (Editors)
Copyright © 2021 by the American Psychological Association. All rights reserved.

United States. On Sunday, October 28th, a White man tried to enter a Black church in Louisville, Kentucky, and after he was unsuccessful, he entered a grocery store and murdered Vickie Jones and Maurice Stallard, both Black people. On Monday, October 29th, I taught my Psychology of Prejudice class. From Saturday afternoon until class on Monday, I knew I had to do three things: process this information myself; decide whether I should address these events in class; and, if so, decide how I would do that.

On October 29th, I sat down and looked around my classroom. I saw the sadness in some of my students' eyes, in others I saw anxiety, and in others I saw blissful ignorance. Some people in the room had absolutely no awareness of the events. I told the class that we would be discussing the incidents that occurred that weekend and summarized the events for students out of the loop. I let the class know that I was still processing the events myself, but that I felt it was important to discuss them. At that point, I recognized there were some people prepared and willing to speak, and some who were not. Slowly, someone raised a hand and started to share. A Jewish student from Israel began talking about the historic victimization of his people and how much the event had affected him. Another student said that a friend's grandparent was one of the Tree of Life victims and that they had never really been this close to this type of tragedy. Another student commented that a family member said something like, "at least they were older people" who had been murdered, and that statement really bothered the student. That started a conversation about how some people deal with loss and grief by trying to find silver linings and how unhelpful that can sometimes feel.

Another student brought up how common these types of shootings seemed to her, and that she felt expected to process these types of events quickly and silently. This student was particularly concerned about how "shopping while Black" (a concept we had discussed earlier in class) had ended the lives of Vickie Jones and Maurice Stallard. This comment led to a conversation about historical trauma and collective victimhood, emotional expression in the Black community, the common and constant violence against people of color, and the difference in media coverage and responses between the two events that had occurred a day apart. I then directed the conversation to a discussion about blunted physiological response that results from repeated exposure to stressors and why this type of response might be helpful and unhelpful.

As the facilitator, I felt uncomfortable the entire time. Initially, I felt like I was carefully monitoring the emotions of everyone in the room (including myself). I personally have received negative feedback from both students and colleagues about my expressiveness, implying that my emotional reactivity was unprofessional. Putnam and Mumby (1993) found that strong, negative emotions are often viewed as inappropriate and undesirable within the work context and are linked to irrationality. This self-monitoring of physical expressiveness is related to negative stereotypes about three of my stigmatized social identities, discussed below, and often creates dissonance for me in emotionally heightened situations. Beyond that, I felt frustrated by my uncertainty. Is this what I should be doing? Is this right? Should I have cancelled class? As faculty, we are often untrained in responding to traumatic or emotionally charged current events, and that can lead us to feel unprepared for or even actively avoid addressing them. This chapter addresses the complexity of facilitating difficult conversations in response to events in the news.

FACULTY REFLECTION

Avoiding local, national, and world news is often difficult, and perhaps irresponsible, when teaching courses centered on social justice and diversity. With social media available at our fingertips through instant alerts and updates, it may even be *impossible* to avoid news media. Violence and conflict often involve issues related to diversity and social justice including war, genocide, immigration, sexual violence, income inequality, drug abuse, and police brutality. How news media reports these events can also connect to diversity and social justice courses. For example, when teaching about system justifying beliefs, I often assign an article by Napier et al. (2006) about the aftermath of Hurricane Katrina, which included racist coded language from news media. In fact, educators often cite discussing current events as an important teaching strategy for courses related to diversity and social justice (e.g., hooks, 2003; Rivera, 2017).

Some news events are more difficult to discuss than others because of their proximity, magnitude, direct impact, or (student and/or faculty) identification with victims of the tragedy (Huston & DiPietro, 2007). Some events can feel particularly violent, random, traumatizing, or "too big" to tackle in the classroom. These types of events lead to strong cognitive and emotional responses from students, even if they are not directly impacted (Honos-Webb et al., 2006; Liverant et al., 2004; Silver et al., 2002). These reactions can range from shock, fear, horror, and anger to anxiety, mourning, depression, and hopelessness. Discussions about these events within the classroom can be emotionally taxing for everyone in the room and can create a situation of vulnerability and anxiety for instructors.

I believe that having these conversations in our classes is imperative, not only to help students understand the world around them but also to help them cope with trauma in order to facilitate future learning (Schonfeld & Kline, 1994). Unfortunately, many professors are often uncomfortable with and have very little training in discussing emotionally charged current events (Kardia et al., 2002; Rivera, 2017). Faculty may also be under the impression that, when discussing current events, they need to be neutral and suppress emotional displays (Bell et al., 2007). Therefore, being confronted with the responsibility of leading these types of conversations can feel overwhelming.

After these types of events, feeling prepared emotionally, intellectually, and pedagogically can be challenging. Faculty members are expected to process traumatic events quickly, which may add to the anxiety and uncertainty in preparing for difficult dialogues (Sue et al., 2009). Students look to us for guidance and answers, and it can be difficult to admit that we may not have any. College faculty are often expected to be experts, so it can be uncomfortable for us to expose our own uncertainty and struggles surrounding these events (Weinstein & Obear, 1992). Emotional vulnerability can be difficult for a multitude of reasons (some related to our identities and classroom power dynamics, discussed below). Yet, as Bell et al. (2007) argued, "we have to give ourselves permission to be vulnerable and confused" (p. 391).

CONSIDERATIONS OF CONTEXT AND INTERSECTIONALITY

In many courses, bringing in real-world examples and using media and news sources to teach current events may seem like a no-brainer. Pedagogically, it helps students relate the course material to their lives and can help unpack complicated theories or experiences. One might think that "the news" might be a useful resource in all situations and for all instructors. Unfortunately, when it comes to topics related to diversity and social justice, this is not always the case. Some events may be extremely emotional and potentially triggering or retraumatizing for those with posttraumatic stress disorder. Some events may feel inexplicable or unexplainable, and faculty may feel pressure (and literally be asked) to explain why someone would do such a thing. Attempts to explain events through discussions about toxic masculinity or white supremacy may be met with shock, confusion, or anger. Students may not be prepared to have these discussions in all classroom settings or from all instructors. These responses may also be exacerbated by news media and political figures working (consciously or unconsciously) to activate fear-based stereotypes and emotional responses.

All this considered, creating a safe classroom climate before addressing some events in the news is important pedagogically (see Goldstein, Chapter 2, this volume). Otherwise, students may be unwilling to share their experiences, perspectives, and emotional reactions and there may even be social costs to doing so (e.g., coming out of the closet in the classroom while discussing issues related to LGBTQ+ rights). If faculty do not believe their classroom is at the point where the conversation will be confidential, productive, or respectful (perhaps the event happens before the first day of class), it may be important to spend the first part of class working together to form the groundwork for effective classroom discussions and making sure rules are mutually understood. We must also recognize the complex diversity of experiences and ideologies within the classroom when reporting or discussing current events, and we realize that the make-up of each class will be different.

Intersectionality of Personal Identity

Personal experiences as members of marginalized groups can be helpful in teaching courses around diversity and social justice. Members from marginalized groups can often draw from personal experiences and provide real-life examples to help students grasp difficult or complex topics. Personal experiences with grief or trauma may increase feelings of preparedness in discussing emotionally charged events; however, emotional vulnerability and authenticity can be difficult for faculty from marginalized groups, particularly when surrounded by nonmarginalized outgroup members. Faculty from marginalized communities often cope with institutional and student devaluation of their professional status (Bell et al., 2007). Intersections of identity can amplify these concerns. Not only is our authority and legitimacy as faculty at risk, we may even be accused of pushing an agenda or "being political" by discussing current events in the classroom. Institutions also profess the importance of objectivity, civility, and professional distance which may conflict with the types of discussions described above.

There are often negative stereotypes around emotional expression and group membership to consider when teaching about emotionally charged topics. Some of these stereotypes are related to the expectations that come along with the social role of "college professor." We may think we need to act in certain ways because that is "what one does" in the classroom. Other stereotypes may be cultural (e.g., emotional expression among European

American vs. Eastern Asian cultures; Tsai et al., 2006). These stereotypes can activate concerns about perceptions of weakness, fragility, lack of control, being warm and nurturing, or being "overly sensitive." As a fat, gay man from a low-income background, I am aware of negative stereotypes around lack of emotional self-control, middle-class norms related to emotion expression and professionalism, and heteronormative expectations of emotion suppression in men. Therefore, stereotype threat related to losing control of my emotions or being "flamboyant" and emotionally expressive may impact my performance as an effective facilitator (see Rios et al., Chapter 5, this volume). I have experienced coded language around being "too sensitive" or "too expressive" from students, colleagues, and an administrator. Self-monitoring expressiveness and control over my emotionality are therefore important parts of my experience as a faculty member and teaching advice related to authenticity and emotional vulnerability can feel invalidating and inconsiderate.

As Bell and colleagues (2007) contended, "Self-knowledge can be helpful preparation for engaging with student discomfort with these issues and enable us to respond thoughtfully to participants even when we ourselves feel exposed or uncertain" (p. 383). Reflection on how my intersectional identities impact the way I teach these events, as well as which topics feel more comfortable and which I may avoid or fear discussing, is therefore imperative. For example, as an atheist, I am often uncomfortable discussing the research findings about the impact of religion on prejudice and social justice. Being aware of my own discomfort, and communicating it with students, helps me feel more honest and conveys that working on and through prejudice is a complex and ongoing process for everyone, even the people teaching courses on prejudice. I am also able to discuss just about any topic in the classroom, including sexual orientation and gender expression, religion, critiques of government, etc., which is a privilege not enjoyed by all faculty in all countries.

Recognizing my privileged identities is important, particularly as someone who tends to look like the perpetrators of hate crimes in the United States and the insensitive tourist abroad (White, able-bodied, cis, American male). Because most of my stigmatized identities are concealable, I am also often perceived as upper-class and straight. These identities impact my behavior in the classroom as well as perceptions of authority from students. This allows me to discuss events in the classroom, and perhaps be more critical of White people, with less fear of retribution or accusations of bias or self-interest. Interestingly, the intersections of certain group stereotypes may actually improve my evaluations from students. Through contrast effects, male professors stereotyped as "nurturing" have been more positively evaluated compared with similarly stereotyped female professors (Meltzer & McNulty, 2011). These identities have also limited my perspective and recognizing those limitations can be difficult. For example, I was recently made aware of the lack of accessibility of classroom podiums, that a podium cannot easily be used by someone in a wheelchair, and what that inaccessibility might communicate to students, job candidates, and guest speakers. As an American, I have also not experienced the political violence or turmoil felt in other countries and feel relatively safe expressing myself in most situations due to freedom of speech assumptions.

Interaction of Faculty and Student Identities

Because of the impact of perceived power and self-efficacy in the classroom (King, 2018), I begin classes on diversity and social justice with an assignment on positionality in which students position themselves within society, the college, and the classroom. I include questions about perceived positionality of other students and of me. Students should realize that some individuals perceive a power imbalance in the classroom and others do not. This perspective taking helps frame how learning outcomes may be different for everyone in the classroom, and how participation may be more difficult for some if they feel they rate themselves as lower in power than their peers.

People process information in different ways, and for some it may be important to distance themselves from or avoid acknowledging reality in public spaces or around others. They may have a difficult time being perceived as vulnerable, discussing their feelings, or admitting them out loud. This is, in some ways, related to social/cultural norms that devalue or police emotional expression and vulnerability (e.g., men, people of color) in certain spaces. We must therefore recognize that someone may appear fine, they may even appear nonchalant, but still be deeply impacted by the discussion at hand. As facilitators, our attention might be drawn to particular students, for whatever reason, and we may feel the need to "get their perspective." Outing, singling out, staring at, and expecting knowledge/examples from individuals from marginalized communities is inappropriate, disrespectful, and potentially exploitative. I still remember the extremely negative experience of being outed in a college classroom by the instructor after an emotionally charged event.

I would also caution instructors from using phrases like "we're all human" or "we're all equally impacted by this." The impact of these events is not equal. We should therefore consider intersections of group memberships, individual experiences, structural power, and social, cultural, and historical context when addressing these issues (Case, 2017). Research shows that people will respond more positively when outgroup members acknowledge the distinct suffering related to sharing an identity with a victimized group followed by communicating some level of shared emotional responses (for a conversation on inclusive victim consciousness, see Vollhardt, 2015). Intersectionality of our identities and our positionality within different contexts creates complexity in our responses to events, and we must give permission (to ourselves and to our students) to process them however we can (in and out of the classroom).

BEST PRACTICES

There is no perfect formula for responding to emotionally charged current events, particularly after considering the complexity outlined above. Previous research on difficult dialogues describes the importance of validating students' emotional responses (Sue, 2015) and the importance of being self-aware, flexible, and responsive within the classroom. Successful facilitation of these types of conversations may also take practice, experience, and self-reflection with particular attention paid to how we respond in situations of tension or conflict (Bell et al., 2007). A qualitative study by Clair et al. (2002) conducted directly after the September 11th terrorist attacks outlined three self-reported approaches used by instructors after this event: limited acknowledgment, integrative, and events-processing responses.

A limited acknowledgment response, where the facilitator spends a limited amount of time acknowledging the event before moving forward with the planned course material, was utilized when

- the facilitator did not feel they had the resources to have a full discussion,
- they felt unprepared to respond to students' emotional reactions, or
- they perceived their class as a helpful distraction from current events, which some students have reported as important after a traumatic event (Amann, 2003).

Overall, the limited acknowledgment approach is not ideal, and students have rated this approach as unhelpful (Huston & DiPietro, 2007). Limited acknowledgment can also communicate lack of preparedness, skill, or compassion. Perceived indifference may even lead to opposition and anger in response to instructors who do not allow time for discussion.

Within the integrative response approach (Clair et al., 2002), facilitators analyze events in terms of concepts or theory central to course content. In this way, the current event is treated as a real-life example or illustration of course material. This approach allows "intellectual processing" of traumatic events and may help students understand something they perceive as distant, unfamiliar, or illogical. The integrative response can be helpful for coping in some contexts (e.g., a similar event was predicted or discussed in a previous class, the course topic is related to the event in question, students seem to have some psychological distance from the event). Domestic terrorism, for example, can often activate conversations about white supremacy, fragile masculinity, perceived threat, ingroups/outgroups, and other relevant scholarship. Students have also explicitly requested intellectual processing in my classes by asking questions like, "Why would anyone do this?" or "How did no one see this coming?"

Yet, this approach may backfire if the event itself is unrelated to course material (the connections may feel forced), the event cannot easily be intellectualized, or the intellectualization is unnecessary and/or offensive (e.g., telling students a gunman was mentally ill in order to "explain away" violent behavior). This approach can also feel exploitative of trauma and emotionally detached, clinical, and/or insensitive. For example, one professor in the Clair et al. (2002) study wrote that, after September 11th, they spent their next class exploring the potential economic impact for "production operation (and) cross-national production" (p. 44). Discussions around failed architecture, how the event might financially affect the airline industry, or a history lesson on religious fundamentalism may be useful lessons based on real-life events, but students in some contexts may perceive the faculty member facilitating these discussions as unemotional, robotic, or cruel.

Clair et al. (2002) described the events-processing response as allowing time and space for students to process their emotions and reactions to the event. Faculty often leave this type of approach open and unstructured. In some cases, faculty reported allowing students to guide the conversation and work through their emotions together, with some potential for them to make connections to course concepts on their own (with no expectation that they do so). In this context, the professor acts as an (a) inactive observer of this process, or (b) empathic moderator and validator of students' emotions.

Although this approach may seem the most responsive to students' emotional needs, Clair et al. (2002) argued "students may be more harmed in classrooms where professors attempt to debrief trauma but lack the skills to do so" (p. 51). Not only does the facilitator run the risk of being perceived as unskilled, distant, or emotionally untouched by the event, but the conversation may be dominated by specific students and create unintentional and uncomfortable power dynamics within the classroom. This may even lead to or passively allow students to manage difficult dialogues themselves, which is both ineffective and unethical. Our students are not trained facilitators and asking them to run the classroom (verbally or non-verbally), particularly when their emotions are heightened, is irresponsible (see Warner, Chapter 16, this volume).

In my experience, the best approach to take with the class is to give them options and let the students decide what would be most helpful. This gives them some control in the direction of the classroom and helps you as the facilitator to get a read of the room. Most often for me, the discussion becomes a blend of the events-processing and integrative response. I also usually spend no more than one class period discussing the event. This allows for validation of emotions and a productive conversation with the promise that the class will move on soon for those who do not process grief out loud or who need structure and distraction from current events.

Faculty often report confusion about their role in discussing traumatic news events and those who feel confused are less likely to discuss the event in class (DiPietro, 2003). Whatever course of action one chooses, one should respond *in some way*. A study of 13 types of classroom responses to a tragic event found that students rate almost any response, from a moment of silence to fully incorporating the event into the course, as helpful. There was one exception; acknowledging the event happened and then moving on (Huston & DiPietro, 2007). This suggests that a faculty response does not need to be personal, time-intensive, or complicated; it all depends on the context and careful thought of the benefits and consequences of choosing one response over another.

If the facilitator does not feel prepared to use any of these approaches with their students, because they are too emotionally impacted by the event, or because of concerns around their own mental and emotional health, it may be the best course of action to cancel class in order to prepare. The Derek Bok Center for Teaching and Learning (2018) lists self-reflection and attention to your own emotional needs as the very first step in navigating difficult moments in the classroom. Students tend to be very aware of the comfort level of their instructor during difficult dialogues and this may directly influence their levels of participation in the conversation (Sue et al., 2010). The instructor should therefore feel emotionally prepared to facilitate this type of conversation when entering the classroom. It may be useful to send an email to the students in the class ahead of time so that everyone has shared expectations. The email prior to meeting may also remove some of the anticipatory stress and ambiguity that follows these types of events. When a student of mine died suddenly in a car accident, I had a few days to compose myself and prepare the other students for class. The original email confirmed that we would still be meeting, but that we would be discussing the event and remembering the student by wearing bright colors (which she was known for in our class). There were a number of follow-up emails from students perhaps due to my initial message giving them permission to open up about their own reactions. We were all impacted tremendously by her death, but we were able to come together and grieve, and I remember the power in that.

The facilitator may also feel the need to cancel class or postpone discussion if the event has just occurred. For example, a student of color was (allegedly) wrongfully detained by a security guard the night before one of my classes. The students were buzzing when I walked in and ready to share with me the details, but I didn't feel I could process it in the moment. I told them that I would teach class normally and then take time to research and understand the situation outside of class, and that we would talk about it next time. Current events cannot be planned around our schedules and the facilitator should be knowledgeable about and sensitive to different perspectives around complex events *before* the dialogue. This also underlines the importance of being connected to current events and of awareness of media bias and literacy (Scharrer & Ramasubramanian, 2015).

However you choose to address emotionally charged events in the news, you should be clear that you are not asking students to "get over it and move on" and that you acknowledge the complexity and difficulty of processing trauma. Acknowledge that the process is different for everyone and that their response is valid. Acknowledge the importance of teaching social justice courses. I try to remind students that, in some small way, my personal hope is that teaching courses about social justice might reduce the likelihood of these events happening in the future. As hooks (2003) wrote, "When teachers teach with love, combining care, commitment, knowledge, responsibility, respect, and trust, we are often able to enter the classroom and go straight to the heart of the matter, which is knowing what to do on any given day to create the best climate for learning" (p. 134). Although knowing what to do can be difficult on hard days, there are ways to prepare ourselves for these devastatingly predictable events.

RESOURCES

Cornell, D., Heaps, R. A., Martin, J., O'Neill, H. K., Settle, K., Sheras, P., & Koch-Sheras, P. (n.d.). *Tips for college and university students: Managing your distress in the aftermath of the Virginia Tech shootings*. American Psychological Association. https://www.midwestern.edu/Documents/IL%20Student%20Services/Aftermath%20of%20Shooting.pdf

This three-page factsheet by members of APA's Division 17 (Society of Counseling Psychology) provides strategies for students when responding to a traumatic event, specifically the school shooting at Virginia Tech.

Faculty Development and Instructional Design Center. (n.d.). *Teaching in times of crisis*. Northern Illinois University. https://www.niu.edu/facdev/_pdf/teaching.pdf

This three-page factsheet provides tips, strategies, and resources for faculty and staff when responding to tragic events.

Fasching-Varner, K. J., Reynolds, R. E., Albert, K. A., & Martin, L. L. (Eds.). (2014). *Trayvon Martin, race, and American justice: Writing wrong*. Sense Publishers.

This edited volume contains a number of short chapters about the state of race in the United States in the 21st century. This interdisciplinary volume may help to start difficult conversations in the classroom about the killing of unarmed Black people (including children) and about the impact of race and the intersection of race and gender in the United States.

Mastro, D., & Tukachinsky, R. (Eds.). (2015). Media representations of race and ethnicity: Implications for identity, intergroup relations, and public policy. *Journal of Social Issues, 71*(1), 1–217.

This volume of the *Journal of Social Issues* focuses on the portrayals of race and ethnicity in the media, the impact of these portrayals on public policy, and the importance of media literacy education in courses related to social justice and diversity.

Siegel, D. (1994). *Campuses respond to violent tragedy*. Oryx Press.

This book offers advice and insight for campus communities on responding to violent tragedy including real-world examples of successes and failures.

Society for the Psychological Study of Social Issues. (n.d.). *A call to action in the face of tragedy: SPSSI responds to the Pulse nightclub tragedy*. https://www.spssi.org/index.cfm?fuseaction=page.viewPage&pageID=2070&nodeID=1

This website includes a syllabus centered on the Pulse nightclub tragedy in Orlando (including sections on the LGBTQ community, intersectionality, terrorism, gun violence, and Islamophobia) which educators may use for a range of courses. This website also includes a link to a special virtual issue by SPSSI called *Toward an Understanding of the Orlando Massacre*, which includes nine articles related to LGBTQ issues, gun violence, and terrorism.

REFERENCES

Amann, T. L. (2003, March). Adult learners' perceptions of teaching and learning during times of crisis. *Proceedings of the Pennsylvania Adult and Continuing Education Research Conference*, 60–66. https://files.eric.ed.gov/fulltext/ED475683.pdf#page=69

Bell, L. A., Love, B. J., Washington, S., & Weinstein, G. (2007). Knowing ourselves as social justice educators. In M. Adams, L. A. Bell, & P. Griffin (Eds.), *Teaching for diversity and social justice* (pp. 381–393). Routledge.

Case, K. (2017). *Intersectional pedagogy: Complicating identity and social justice*. Routledge.

Clair, J., Maclean, T., & Greenberg, D. (2002). Teaching through traumatic events: Uncovering the choices of management educators as they responded to September 11th. *Academy of Management Learning & Education, 1*(1), 38–54. https://doi.org/10.5465/amle.2002.7373603

Derek Bok Center for Teaching and Learning. (2018). *Inclusive moves*. Harvard University Press. Retrieved from https://bokcenter.harvard.edu/inclusive-moves

DiPietro, M. (2003). The day after: Faculty behavior in post-September 11, 2001 classes. *To Improve the Academy, 21*, 21–39. https://doi.org/10.1002/j.2334-4822.2003.tb00379.x

Honos-Webb, L., Sunwolf, Hart, S., & Scalise, J. T. (2006). How to help after national catastrophes: Findings following 9/11. *The Humanistic Psychologist, 34*(1), 75–97. https://doi.org/10.1207/s15473333thp3401_7

hooks, b. (2003). *Teaching community: A pedagogy of hope*. Routledge.

Huston, T. A., & DiPietro, M. (2007). In the eye of the storm: Students' perceptions of helpful faculty actions following a collective tragedy. *To Improve the Academy, 21*, 207–224. https://doi.org/10.1002/j.2334-4822.2007.tb00483.x

Kardia, D., Bierwert, C., Cook, C. E., Miller, A. T., & Kaplan, M. (2002). Discussing the unfathomable classroom-based responses to tragedy. *Change: The Magazine of Higher Learning, 34*(1), 18–22. https://doi.org/10.1080/00091380209601831

King, E. (2018). Understanding classroom silence: How students' perceptions of power influence participation in discussion-based composition classrooms. *Teaching English in the Two-Year College, 45*(3), 284–305.

Liverant, G. I., Hofmann, S. G., & Litz, B. T. (2004). Coping and anxiety in college students after the September 11th terrorist attacks. *Anxiety, Stress, and Coping, 17*(2), 127–139. https://doi.org/10.1080/0003379042000221412

Meltzer, A. L., & McNulty, J. K. (2011). Contrast effects of stereotypes: "Nurturing" male professors are evaluated more positively than "nurturing" female professors. *Journal of Men's Studies, 19*(1), 57–64. https://doi.org/10.3149/jms.1901.57

Napier, J. L., Mandisodza, A. N., Andersen, S. M., & Jost, J. T. (2006). System justification in responding to the poor and displaced in the aftermath of Hurricane Katrina. *Analyses of Social Issues and Public Policy, 6*(1), 57–73. https://doi.org/10.1111/j.1530-2415.2006.00102.x

Putnam, L. L., & Mumby, D. K. (1993). Organizations, emotions and the myth of rationality. In S. Fineman (Ed.), *Emotion in organizations* (pp. 36–57). Sage.

Rivera, D. P. (2017). Revealing hidden intersections of gender identity, sexual orientation, race, and ethnicity: Teaching about multiple oppressed identities. In K. Case (Ed.), *Intersectional pedagogy: Complicating identity and social justice* (pp. 173–193). Routledge.

Scharrer, E., & Ramasubramanian, S. (2015). Intervening in the media's influence on stereotypes of race and ethnicity: The role of media literacy education. *Journal of Social Issues, 71*(1), 171–185. https://doi.org/10.1111/josi.12103

Schonfeld, D. J., & Kline, M. (1994). School-based crisis-intervention: An organizational model. *Crisis Intervention and Time-limited Treatment, 1*(2), 155–166.

Silver, R. C., Holman, E. A., McIntosh, D. N., Poulin, M., & Gil-Rivas, V. (2002). Nationwide longitudinal study of psychological responses to September 11. *JAMA, 288*, 1235–1244. https://doi.org/10.1001/jama.288.10.1235

Sue, D. W. (2015). *Race talk and the conspiracy of silence: Understanding and facilitating difficult dialogues on race*. John Wiley & Sons.

Sue, D. W., Rivera, D. P., Capodilupo, C. M., Lin, A. I., & Torino, G. C. (2010). Racial dialogues and White trainee fears: Implications for education and training. *Cultural Diversity and Ethnic Minority Psychology, 16*(2), 206–214. https://doi.org/10.1037/a0016112

Sue, D. W., Torino, G. C., Capodilupo, C. M., Rivera, D. P., & Lin, A. I. (2009). How White faculty perceive and react to difficult dialogues on race: Implications for education and training. *The Counseling Psychologist, 37*(8), 1090–1115. https://doi.org/10.1177/0011000009340443

Tsai, J. L., Levenson, R. W., & McCoy, K. (2006). Cultural and temperamental variation in emotional response. *Emotion, 6*(3), 484–497. https://doi.org/10.1037/1528-3542.6.3.484

Vollhardt, J. R. (2015). Inclusive victim consciousness in advocacy, social movements, and intergroup relations: Promises and pitfalls. *Social Issues and Policy Review, 9*, 89–120. https://doi.org/10.1111/sipr.12011

Weinstein, G., & Obear, K. (1992). Bias issues in the classroom: Encounters with the teaching self. *New Directions for Teaching and Learning, 52*, 39–50. https://doi.org/10.1002/tl.37219925205

10
RAISING THE CONSCIOUSNESS OF STUDENTS HOLDING INGROUP STEREOTYPES

LISA M. BROWN AND WENDY R. WILLIAMS

I work hard, but other low-income people are just lazy.

–A low-income individual

Women are nurturing and good with children.

–A woman

People are born gay. Why would anyone choose to be gay?

–A gay man

Young people are tech-savvy, but I'm a nonconformist.

–An 18-year-old

Black people are not good with money.

–A Black person

Obese individuals just lack willpower.

–An obese student

---

https://doi.org/10.1037/0000216-010
Navigating Difficult Moments in Teaching Diversity and Social Justice, M. E. Kite, K. A. Case, and W. R. Williams (Editors)
Copyright © 2021 by the American Psychological Association. All rights reserved.

There is a long history of research on marginalized groups resisting stereotypes, prejudice, and discrimination and engaging in collective action to bring about positive social change (see Brown, Chapter 8, this volume). Nevertheless, there are instances when members of marginalized groups accept and even perpetuate the status quo, including endorsement of ingroup stereotypes. Although faculty may expect students from privileged groups to endorse stereotypes of marginalized outgroups, we can be taken by surprise when students from marginalized groups endorse and communicate stereotypes about their own groups because we expect them to be aware of the problems with stereotypes.

In these moments, it can be hard not to respond with either incredulity ("What are you talking about?!") or disdain ("That is messed up—how can YOU believe that?!")—responses both authors of this chapter have sometimes felt but have been able to suppress. Yet our *actual* actions within the classroom have occasionally left us feeling like we missed the mark, that our challenges to these stereotypes changed neither the speaker's beliefs nor the minds of the rest of the class, as we fumbled our way to a (not awful, but not great) response. In these less-than-skillful moments, these students' verbal or nonverbal behaviors signal that their ingroup stereotypes remain intact, whether through active disagreement (e.g., their words continuing to reiterate their position) or disengagement (e.g., their body language indicating they have stopped listening). Worse still, we have left classes fearing that students from other groups, who may have been silent in the discussion but who may hold the same stereotype, have had their stereotype reaffirmed because we were not adroit enough in our disconfirmation of the stereotype.

FACULTY REFLECTION

In talking with peers and writing this chapter, we realized that the difference between the "nailed it!" and "ain't nobody changed their mind" moments was when we were able to accurately determine the reason behind *why* the student was expressing the stereotype about their ingroup. Conversely, a mismatch between our response and the speaker's motivation was more likely to predict outcomes like student disbelief, disengagement, or resistance. As a result, quick determination of the kind of ingroup stereotyping present is essential to handling these moments as they occur.

Consistent with the paraphrased quotes at the start of the chapter (all themes we have encountered while teaching), we think ingroup stereotyping in the classroom is most likely to take one of the following three forms:

- First, students endorse the most well-known stereotypes of their own group (e.g., low-income students stating that low-income people are lazy or obese students saying that obese people just lack willpower).
- Second, students overgeneralize views of their own group that may be accurate, but not for all group members (e.g., a young person claiming that generally young people are tech-savvy; a gay male student tacitly suggesting there is little to no fluidity in sexual orientation, when research suggests that for females, there may be some).
- Third, students state ingroup stereotypes to the professor who is a member of the same ingroup expecting the professor's support (e.g., a Black student complaining about Black people's mismanagement of money to a Black professor as if they both share this insider's opinion, a female student stating that women are nurturing and good with children to a female professor).

When these moments occur, it is also helpful to determine if the speaker is endorsing a positive stereotype (e.g., women are nurturing) or a negative one (e.g., low-income people are lazy) and whether the speaker is self-stereotyping by including themselves within the group (e.g., "I am obese and need more willpower") or holding themselves separate from the ingroup stereotype (e.g., "young people are tech savvy, but I'm a nonconformist").

Although the following sections in this chapter rely more heavily on theory than other chapters in this volume, we offer the following theories and typologies in Table 10.1 (explained in more detail in the following paragraphs) because we believe they effectively and quickly help faculty and students examine these moments without demonizing students who express these opinions.

Cognitive Fallacies Inherent in All Stereotypes

To tackle ingroup stereotyping dilemmas, faculty must first get both ingroup and outgroup students to understand cognitive fallacies that underlie all stereotypes. Here, helping students understand two facets about stereotypes is key. First, stereotyped and nonstereotyped groups overlap on any given trait or behavior. Second, within-group variability exists on every stereotyped trait or behavior that usually exceeds between-group differences. If the stereotype about one group can be applied to members of another group (i.e., the distribution of the traits or behaviors overlap), it illustrates its lack of utility for defining the stereotyped group. Similarly, if the stereotype does not apply to all members of the group (i.e., it is overgeneralized to members

TABLE 10.1. Cognitive and Motivational Underpinnings of Ingroup Stereotypes

Cognitive underpinnings of ingroup stereotypes		
Cognitive fallacies inherent in stereotypes	**Example**	**Cognitive strategies for instructors to use**
Distributions are separate	"As women, we never get the respect men get"	Overlapping distributions
Groups are homogenous	"All heterosexuals have the same experience"	Within group variability

Motivational underpinnings of ingroup stereotypes		
	Example	**Possible underlying motivation needs**
Positive stereotypes		
Self-stereotype	"Women, like me, are nurturing and good with children"	Self-enhancement Optimal distinctiveness
Exclude self	"Young people are tech-savvy, but I'm a nonconformist"	Individualism
Negative stereotypes		
Self-stereotype	"Obese people, like me, just lack willpower"	Optimal distinctiveness System justification
Exclude self	"Low-income people are lazy, but not me"	Self-enhancement Individualism System justification
Students' desire for affiliation with ingroup faculty	"Black people mismanage money, but not us"	Self-enhancement Individualism Optimal distinctiveness

despite not applying to all of them), it reinforces that the stereotyped group is heterogeneous, and thus the stereotype does not accurately define the group. To help students understand overlapping distributions and within-group variability, we often turn to our own experiences.

Overlapping Group Distributions

Research finds that men typically receive more deference and respect than women, often because they are perceived as authorities. Yet I (Lisa) have conveyed ways I received more respect from students in class than two female colleagues also in their first year of teaching likely because my voice was deeper than theirs and the way I moved around the classroom communicated athleticism—all cues associated with the perception of masculinity and power (Hall et al., 2005). This example may help students realize ways in which distributions of femininity and masculinity between female and male faculty overlap. I (Wendy) use a different example; I convey the ways the experiences of low-income college students overlap with those of high-income students by contrasting my education as a low-income student at a college that provided little financial support to the experiences of my low-income students at a college that provides extensive financial support. My students can see ways in which low-income students at their undergraduate institution are getting the same opportunities that wealthy students got at my undergraduate institution. Thus, examples of overlapping distributions between groups help students recognize the cognitive fallacy that groups are very different from each other.

Within-Group Variability
To illustrate that within-group differences are usually greater than between-group differences, I (Lisa) frequently harken to differences between the experiences of the side of my family raised in the urban North versus the side raised in the rural South of the United States. When I offer this personal example, I frequently follow it up with ways a man, a low-income person, an LGBTQIA+ person, an immigrant, or a darker or lighter skinned person may have different experiences despite the fact that we are all Black, reminding students that there is not one Black experience. I (Wendy) often make a similar point for sexual orientation to show that there is not one heterosexual experience. Because disabled women are seen as asexual and their agency over their bodies denied (Ferri & Gregg, 1998), being able-bodied, I am allowed to own my heterosexuality without question, whereas people often dismiss the sexuality of my disabled sister. Noting that there is not one experience for all members of a group helps students understand within-group variability.

Possible Underlying Motivational Needs for Ingroup Stereotyping

Pointing out the cognitive fallacies in ingroup stereotyping we have described is often a necessary first step; however, just understanding overlapping distributions and within-group variability alone does not help us parse *why* ingroup members will either ingroup stereotype or self-stereotype. To fully unpack ingroup stereotyping, faculty must go beyond cognitive fallacies to help illuminate common human motivations for endorsing ingroup stereotypes.

Self-Enhancement and Individualism
Contemporary research findings generally counter outmoded self-hatred theories that suggest that members of negatively stereotyped groups passively internalize those stereotypes (Crocker & Major, 1989). This is in part because,

at least in Western cultures, people commonly have a self-enhancing motivation to feel and think positively about themselves as well as an individualistic motivation to see themselves as autonomous individuals separate from others (Markus & Kitayama, 1991). Typically, when people endorse stereotypes of their own groups as also true of themselves (i.e., self-stereotype), the stereotypes are positive. In the short term, this is self-enhancing (Bell & Burkley, 2014). Selective self-stereotyping occurs when people claim that certain (usually positive) group stereotypes apply to themselves while certain other (usually negative) group stereotypes apply to other members of the group but not themselves (Biernat, Vescio, & Green, 1996). Both of these tendencies should make individuals feel better about themselves personally, fulfilling the need for self-enhancement. In contrast, individuals who exclude themselves from a stereotype about their group, regardless of whether it is positive or negative stereotype, may be seeking to emphasize their individualism. In both cases, individuals are asserting their separateness from the group. Putting these motives together, perceiving that one does not have a negative, stereotypical characteristic (i.e., "I'm not like other members of my group because I do not do this *negative* thing—I'm low-income, but I'm not lazy") may satisfy both the need for self-enhancement and the need for individualism.

Yet, given these two motivations (individualism and self-enhancement), some forms of ingroup stereotyping, and its subcategory self-stereotyping, are counterintuitive because they may include negative stereotypes (undermining self-enhancement) and diminish individuality in saying the self is like the group (undermining individualism). We find two additional theories are particularly relevant to explain these situations: optimal distinctiveness theory and system justification theory.

Optimal Distinctiveness

Optimal distinctiveness theory suggests that people have a need to be both similar to (i.e., need for assimilation) and different from (i.e., need for differentiation) others (Brewer, 1991). One way the need for assimilation may be satisfied is by perceiving oneself as similar to ingroup members, while one way the need for differentiation may be satisfied is by perceiving oneself (and one's group) as different from an outgroup. Thus, optimal distinctiveness offers a second reason why individuals would positively self-stereotype. Perceiving that one has a positive, stereotypical characteristic (i.e., "I'm like all members of my group because I do this *positive* thing— As a woman, I'm good with kids and so are other women") may satisfy both the need for self-enhancement and the need for optimal distinctiveness. At the same time, optimal distinctiveness may also provide a reason why individuals may negatively self-stereotype (e.g., an obese person supporting that obese people, themselves included, need more willpower). Although not self-enhancing, optimal distinctiveness for these individuals could serve both the need for assimilation and differentiation (i.e., it brings me closer to my group, while keeping me different from other groups).

System Justification Theory

An additional motivation that may be relevant when members of disadvantaged groups endorse *negative* ingroup stereotypes, including self-stereotyping, is system justification. System justification theory suggests that people support and rationalize the status quo out of needs for security, predictability, and order (Jost et al., 2004). Members of subordinate groups may be susceptible to system justification despite it being against their individual and collective interests (McCoy & Major, 2007). For instance, they may claim that low-income people are lazy, obese people need more willpower, or Black people mismanage money as a way of justifying that the status quo is fair and that those individuals deserve the negative consequences of their individual choices.

Addressing Well-Known Stereotypes

As we have outlined, we find three forms of ingroup stereotyping to be most common in the classroom. The most frequent is when students endorse a well-known stereotype about their group. In these situations, locating the stereotype on the second typology and discussing the motivation for endorsement can be illuminating to both ingroup and outgroup members. This is particularly true if the topic is paired with other situations in which we engage in these motives outside of the context of stereotypes. For example, we engage in self-enhancement when we choose online profile pictures that minimize our flaws. We engage in individualism in the kinds of clothing we wear. We engage in optimal distinctiveness when we wear apparel displaying our connection to a place of origin. We engage in system justification when we blame victims of domestic violence for their abuse. Normalizing these same human motivations outside the context of stereotypes can minimize students feeling attacked or criticized for their endorsement of an ingroup stereotype.

CONSIDERATIONS OF CONTEXT AND INTERSECTIONALITY

We recognize ways in which our group memberships and personal identities affect our pedagogy and students' responses to us in relatively obvious, but also subtle, ways. I (Lisa) identify as a Black woman with tomboyish-side-of-feminine gender presentation, and I (Wendy) identify as a White woman with feminine gender presentation, making race/ethnicity, gender, and gender presentation visible in the classroom. In contrast, our identities with regard to religion (Christian—Lisa; Agnostic—Wendy), sexual orientation (heterosexual—Lisa and Wendy), social class as children (lower middle-class—Lisa; middle-class and low-income—Wendy), level of education (PhD—Lisa and Wendy), and ability (nondisabled and athletic—Lisa and Wendy) affect our pedagogy and students' responses to us in more subtle, and arguably more complicated, ways because these identities and group memberships are often invisible until we make them visible. Yet we can effectively utilize the interplay of intersectional social locations within ourselves, as well as between ourselves and our students, as pedagogical tools in situations in which we want to use illustrative anecdotes to reinforce lessons on stereotypes. Communicating the variations among our groups by pointing out intersectionality of identities should encourage students to think more critically and complexly—and thus less stereotypically—about their own groups, as noted earlier in the ways we address both overlapping distributions and within variations.

Interaction of Faculty and Student Identities

Certain tensions can occur when the instructor does not belong to the group to which the student belongs. The student can legitimately claim to have insider's knowledge and experience. Yet the student's experience may have created a particular lens (see Goldstein, Chapter 15, this volume). The instructor's job can be to get students to realize that the lens they are looking through has the wrong focus. That is, they have zoomed out thinking their experience is generalizable, instead of zooming in and realizing that their experience is particular to them.

Addressing Overgeneralization of Stereotypes

Regarding the common classroom example of overgeneralization of an ingroup stereotype, illuminating both cognitive and motivational strategies may be helpful. Believing "this is true of all of us" could satisfy the need for assimilation, particularly among those who identify strongly with the group. For these individuals, the need for assimilation may at times outweigh the need for self-enhancement. For example, when a gay male student displayed exasperation with a student's anonymous question around sexual orientation being fluid, I (Lisa) carefully pushed back ("Well, it's complicated") with research finding that sexual orientation becomes less flexible for males earlier in life than it does for females (Baumeister, 2000). As an outgroup member, this was particularly delicate. While not delegitimizing his experience,

I educated the class about these gender differences in the experience of sexual attraction and sexual orientation. In this way, by highlighting within-group differences consistently found in the research, I did not allow the student to generalize his experience in a group to all members by ignoring issues of intersectionality. I forced him to "zoom in" to see complex within-group differences, rather than "zoom out" to overgeneralize his specific personal experience to all others in the group.[1]

Addressing Students' Need for Assimilation Through Affiliation With the Ingroup Faculty Member

As relates to the salience of both students' and instructors' multiple identities in the classroom, we personally find the classroom situations when students who share an identity with us say something stereotypical about our shared group and then look to us as if we agree with this insider's knowledge to be the most complicated of occasions. The student's comment implicates and threatens the instructor's professional identity as a person who teaches about diversity, inclusion, and social justice in three ways (Shapiro & Neuberg, 2007), leaving faculty members to ask themselves: (a) "Do other students now think that stereotype describes me because I share a demographic identity with the student?" (b) "If other students recognize it is a stereotype, does it undermine my social justice credibility as a professor if I do not challenge it?" and (c) "If I refute this ingroup student who made

---

[1] In addition, it was important to point out that while biological explanations of sexual orientation are associated with reducing prejudice, they do not necessarily lead to full inclusion in society. (Although such beliefs are not ingroup stereotypes, they are nevertheless ideologies about groups that may undergird certain stereotypes.) Tolerating a group out of pity because they presumably do not have choice in their "problematic" behavior may not be blatantly prejudiced, but it certainly is not nonprejudiced. In this specific case, Lisa pointed out that (a) studies show that believing sexual orientation is biologically determined is associated with less prejudice than believing it is a choice (e.g., Aguero et al., 1984; Biernat, Vescio, Theno, & Crandall, 1996; Hegarty & Pratto, 2001) and (b) while liberals tend to endorse biological explanations and conservatives tend to endorse personal choice for political rather than scientific reasons (Garretson & Suhay, 2016; Suhay & Jayaratne, 2013), that (c) in a free society one should be able to choose one's sexual orientation and not be discriminated against, devalued, or discredited because of that choice (Jakobsen & Pellegrini, 2004). We detail this incident to make clear that even when certain members of a marginalized group engage in progressive social clubs and causes, they may still use the most common political framing of things (i.e., sexual orientation is not fluid and is not a choice) rather than those that are truly most egalitarian (i.e., sexual orientation is fluid for some, and in a free society people should be able to choose their sexual orientation without prejudice). It is our job to point that out, even when students are members of marginalized groups to which we do not belong.

the comment, do I appear to be a disloyal member of the group?" (see also Rios et al., Chapter 5, this volume). Strategies to defend these identity threats may at times align with each other but may often be incompatible. Although we do not think there is one strategy that neatly resolves these three identity threats, we believe the identity to prioritize in a classroom focused on social justice is that of a competent and credible educator.[2]

Yet the first few times this happened, it was hard for us to not feel personally implicated. I (Lisa) have experienced this with students who were Black, female, or Christian, and I (Wendy) have had similar experiences with students who were White-Appalachian, female, or low income. Moreover, it was even more challenging to stay focused on the underlying cognitive or motivational reasons why the student made the statement. For example, I (Wendy) remember the first time that a low-income student turned to me in a discussion on the American Dream ideology and claimed that "anyone who works hard can get ahead." Because the students had just read my personal "Social Class Autobiography" (Williams, 2014), which includes information about my family's drop in social class to low income while I was in high school, the student was clearly using me as an example of someone who overcame difficult circumstances. It was hard to suppress my first response of defensiveness, never mind to ignore that my face immediately flushed and a sweat broke out on my brow. In that case, I know I fumbled some answer about not using one case study to represent the group, but it was a less than skillful response. I am certain the student remained unconvinced. Not only am I now better prepared to discuss overlapping distributions and within-group variability, I recognize that this kind of moment may also reflect a different motivation: need for assimilation through affiliation. In retrospect, I believe the student was attempting to connect with me by seeing me as an ingroup role model for their overcoming their own difficult circumstance, rather than as simply an endorsement of an ingroup stereotype.

Similarly, being in class with me (Lisa) may be a rare experience for Black students as I am the only Black, tenure-track faculty member born in the

---

[2] Regarding credibility in the classroom, students perceive White instructors to be less credible when teaching about racial inequality while they perceive Black instructors to be more biased (Littleford & Jones, 2017; Littleford et al., 2010). White students evaluate both Black and White instructors lower when they teach about white privilege versus social learning theory (Boatright-Horowitz & Soeung, 2009). Generally, students evaluate instructors of color lower than White instructors on course evaluations (Hamermesh & Parker, 2005; Reid, 2010) and are more critical of gay male instructors than heterosexual male instructors (Russ et al., 2002). Women of color may particularly experience hostility in the classroom (Pittman, 2010; Rios et al., Chapter 5, this volume).

United States currently on my campus. Thus, I may serve as a social support, a role model, and a source of group pride (Zirkel, 2002). Calling out a student who has that type of regard for me could be particularly damaging to our student–faculty relationship. Another layer of complication is that, despite our role as faculty members, we may feel some sense of group solidarity with the student and may feel pressure to abide by the unspoken rule of not making an ingroup member look bad in front of outgroup members (Packer, 2014). Both of these layers discourage addressing the ingroup stereotype directly. Yet if I say nothing, the stereotype goes unchallenged for both ingroup and outgroup members. Moreover, leaving it unaddressed may even strengthen beliefs because students can point to ingroup members who have not disconfirmed the stereotype. Thus, I typically push back.

BEST PRACTICES

Overcoming ingroup stereotyping is complicated by the fact that there may be both cognitive and motivational reasons for espousing the beliefs. Yet we believe that the typologies outlined in Table 10.1 can be useful to professors seeking to help students break down ingroup stereotyping. Encouraging students to explore their own and others' thoughts and motivations in these situations allows students to see that we all can fall prey to stereotyping from time to time, rather than judging those who either self-stereotype or ingroup stereotype.

The Irrelevance of Standard Prejudice Reduction Techniques

Ironically, the best-known strategy for prejudice and stereotype reduction is potentially irrelevant when discussing *ingroup* stereotyping. Contact theory—that is, increased contact between groups leading to reductions in prejudice and stereotyping (Pettigrew & Tropp, 2006)—is not helpful because most people have an abundance of contact with ingroup members. As an illustration of this, contact is not likely an effective way of reducing women's stereotypes of women because most have had contact with other women. Additional strategies for improving intergroup relations involve reducing the discrepancy between the negative bias against an outgroup and the positive bias toward one's ingroup (e.g., imagined contact theory, Crisp & Turner, 2009; implicit bias reduction, Devine et al., 2012; common group identity theory, Dovidio et al., 2007; and extended contact theory, Wright et al., 1997). Yet typically people's views of and feelings towards their ingroups are at worst ambivalent and, as mentioned above, typically positive—even when they are stereotypical. Consequently, one must use other processes to tackle ingroup stereotyping among students.

Addressing Overlapping Distributions and Overgeneralized Stereotypes

As described earlier in the chapter, it is important to have already laid the groundwork that any statements either that traits and behaviors of one group are not found in all groups or that all members of any group are all alike are false and empirically unsubstantiated premises. Fact-based quizzes that ask students whether certain stereotypes are true (and then give the data to show they are not true) can help to set this groundwork by illustrating that there is less difference between groups and more variability within groups than people generally acknowledge. This pedagogical strategy is consistent with research indicating that exposure to a collection of varied members of an outgroup increases the perceived variability and willingness to help that group, as well as reduces prejudice towards, and negative stereotypes about, that outgroup (Er-rafiy & Brauer, 2013). An instructor can always return to this strategy throughout the class ("Really? *All* members of your group do X? You know *every* member of your group?"). In doing so, students frequently realize that their generalization was in fact too broad ("Well, OK, not *every*"). The goal is to challenge students' stereotypical thinking and conclusions as faulty, not to deny their personal experiences.

When students overgeneralize a group stereotype to themselves and all ingroup members, as mentioned earlier, it is typically a neutral or positive characteristic. We suggest caution, however, in shifting students' overgeneralized ingroup stereotypes. Previous research finds that being exposed to both positive and negative information about a group leads to reducing prejudice more than exposure to only positive information because receiving only positive information may lead to reactance (Brauer et al., 2012). Thus, it is important not to deny that a group may have negative traits but rather to put those traits into context (e.g., illuminating structural causes for why Native peoples in the United States have lower levels of educational attainment, or why obesity is not simply a matter of willpower). In a similar vein, evoking negative self-directed affect is better at reducing implicit bias than counterstereotyping training (Burns et al., 2017). In other words, simply telling the students they are wrong will often backfire; rather, getting students to recognize the discrepancy between their desire to be nonprejudiced and their endorsement of a stereotype may be more effective. Moreover, it may be particularly necessary when trying to dismantle ingroup stereotyping to compensate for the motivational needs self-stereotyping satisfies. For example, instructors may need to remind students of their similarity to ingroup members and their difference from outgroup members in ways that do not reify stereotypes (e.g., mentioning that people often ask sexual minorities but not heterosexuals to explain their sexual orientation).

Addressing Negative Stereotypes

If the ingroup stereotype is a negative characteristic, students may distance themselves from those they think have it. As mentioned above, this distancing satisfies both the needs for self-enhancement and individualism. It may also satisfy the need to justify the system. To challenge this, instructors can use information that is critical of assumptions about the fairness of the status quo. For example, views that certain groups make bad financial choices may be countered with historical examples of government policies and their economic consequences. More specifically, the belief that individual choices lead to poverty can be countered with explanations of structural impediments like local distribution of taxes and forced residential segregation through redlining that affected access to quality schooling and safe neighborhoods as well as the ability to acquire assets like property to pass on to descendants (Woods, 2012). This strategy is consistent with research findings that students increase structural explanations for events (Lopez et al., 1998) and decrease individualistic explanations for events (i.e., the Protestant work ethic; Cole et al., 2011) after taking a course on diversity. Yet there are certain cautions about trying to lessen system justification. For example, criticizing the system can backfire and lead to more support of the system (Liviatan & Jost, 2014).

To address students' system justification, faculty may want to utilize activities, games, and simulations which allow students to temporarily experience structural barriers for themselves. For example, we have found "Play Spent," "Sociopoly," and "The Game of Social Life" effective in teaching students about ways the system is often "rigged" against individual choices (see Resources for more information). Because the games purposefully disadvantage certain students, the students can see how often their personal choices are irrelevant to their ultimate success. Instead, they see the ways that structures, like the sometimes invisible rules of the game, are more responsible for their outcomes. Instructors can incorporate games like these either early in a semester or in response to events within the class.

Connecting With Students Outside of Class

Faculty may want to connect with students who endorse ingroup stereotypes outside of class. In addition to affirming the student's need for assimilation by affiliating with certain faculty, a one-on-one conversation can allow a faculty member to more clearly articulate why they chose the strategy they did during a class discussion. For example, faculty may explain privately why they chose to challenge an ingroup stereotype despite the cost of making a member of the ingroup look bad. They can also use the opportunity to check in with students on a personal level to gauge understanding and comfort after the conversation. This can be done by asking the student to stay after class for a few minutes or to come to office hours so that they can discuss the topic further. Because students may feel shut down by having their views challenged and this feeling can continue to harm future classroom interactions (see Kite et al., Chapter 4, this volume), a one-on-one follow-up conversation can help dispel any remaining misunderstandings about reasons ingroup stereotypes are problematic. To be clear, we do not believe this practice replaces in-class conversations but instead that one-on-one conversations can ameliorate any remaining negative feelings after a class discussion in which ingroup stereotypes occur. At the same time, one-on-one conversations can build rapport with the instructor so that trust is built over time to continue to tackle difficult topics if they arise again.

RESOURCES

Bramesfeld, K. D. (2015, February 23). *The Game of Social Life: A multidimensional poverty simulation*. American Sociology Association Teaching Resources and Innovations Library for Sociology. http://trails.asanet.org/Pages/Resource.aspx?ResourceID=12868

    The Game of Social Life allows students to see the structural barriers to an issue that they frequently see as individual: poverty. It also highlights the intersectional nature of who is living in poverty and the cumulative privilege of certain characteristics, including access to education, occupational status, and health.

Jessup, M. M. (2001). Sociopoly: Life on the boardwalk. *Teaching Sociology, 29*(1), 102–109. https://doi.org/10.2307/1318787

    Sociopoly takes the game of Monopoly and changes the rules so that certain players start off with more resources than others. The game is then played according to this rigged system. By changing the rules of a game that many students have played before and in which winning is usually understood as a result skill and luck and replacing it with a visible rigid hierarchy, students are able to see the ways what appear to be individual choices are situated in structural (rigged) systems.

Jones, J., Overbey, M. M., Goodman, A., Mukhopadhyay, C., Moses, Y., & Beckrich, A. (2007). *Race: A teacher's guide for high school*. American Anthropological Association. http://understandingrace.org/resources/pdf/racehighschoolteachersguide.pdf

    Created for high school students, this teacher's guide translates well for lower level undergraduate courses, including activities that illuminate biological, cultural, and historical variations in race and suggestions for activities and quizzes to illustrate overlapping distributions and variability within groups.

Teaching Tolerance. (1991–2020). *Classroom resources.* Teaching Tolerance. https://www.tolerance.org/classroom-resources
   This website's section on classroom resources includes a variety of materials for antibias education, from general teaching tips to specific activities like films and action projects. Although often aimed at younger students, many activities can be adapted for college classrooms around challenging ingroup and outgroup stereotypes.

Urban Ministries of Durham. (2011, February). *Play Spent.* http://playspent.org/
   This online game has students imagine that they are newly unemployed, without a home and with resources of only $1,000. Students then make a series of choices to survive the month without going broke. Although possible to do, students quickly realize they must either compromise their values, sense of self, or the law to do so.

REFERENCES

Aguero, J. E., Bloch, L., & Byrne, D. (1984). The relationships among sexual beliefs, attitudes, experience, and homophobia. *Journal of Homosexuality, 10*(1–2), 95–107. https://doi.org/10.1300/J082v10n01_07

Baumeister, R. F. (2000). Gender differences in erotic plasticity: The female sex drive as socially flexible and responsive. *Psychological Bulletin, 126*(3), 347–374. https://doi.org/10.1037/0033-2909.126.3.347

Bell, A. C., & Burkley, M. (2014). "Women like me are bad at math": The psychological functions of negative self-stereotyping. *Social and Personality Psychology Compass, 8*(12), 708–720. https://doi.org/10.1111/spc3.12145

Biernat, M., Vescio, T. K., & Green, M. L. (1996). Selective self-stereotyping. *Journal of Personality and Social Psychology, 71*(6), 1194–1209. https://doi.org/10.1037/0022-3514.71.6.1194

Biernat, M., Vescio, T. K., Theno, S. A., & Crandall, C. S. (1996). Values and prejudice: Toward understanding the impact of American values on outgroup attitudes. In C. Seligman, J. M. Olson, & M. P. Zanna (Eds.), *The psychology of values: The Ontario symposium* (Vol. 8, pp. 153–189). Lawrence Erlbaum Associates.

Boatright-Horowitz, S. L., & Soeung, S. (2009). Teaching White privilege to White students can mean saying good-bye to positive student evaluations. *American Psychologist, 64*(6), 574–575. https://doi.org/10.1037/a0016593

Brauer, M., Er-rafiy, A., Kawakami, K., & Phills, C. E. (2012). Describing a group in positive terms reduces prejudice less effectively than describing it in positive and negative terms. *Journal of Experimental Social Psychology, 48*(3), 757–761. https://doi.org/10.1016/j.jesp.2011.11.002

Brewer, M. B. (1991). The social self: On being the same and different at the same time. *Personality and Social Psychology Bulletin, 17*(5), 475–482. https://doi.org/10.1177/0146167291175001

Burns, M. D., Monteith, M. J., & Parker, L. R. (2017). Training away bias: The differential effects of counterstereotype training and self-regulation on stereotype activation and application. *Journal of Experimental Social Psychology, 73*, 97–110. https://doi.org/10.1016/j.jesp.2017.06.003

Cole, E. R., Case, K. A., Rios, D., & Curtin, N. (2011). Understanding what students bring to the classroom: Moderators of the effects of diversity courses on student attitudes. *Cultural Diversity & Ethnic Minority Psychology, 17*(4), 397–405. https://doi.org/10.1037/a0025433

Crisp, R. J., & Turner, R. N. (2009). Can imagined interactions produce positive perceptions? Reducing prejudice through simulated social contact. *American Psychologist, 64*(4), 231–240. https://doi.org/10.1037/a0014718

Crocker, J., & Major, B. (1989). Social stigma and self-esteem: The self-protective properties of stigma. *Psychological Review, 96*(4), 608–630. https://doi.org/10.1037/0033-295X.96.4.608

Devine, P. G., Forscher, P. S., Austin, A. J., & Cox, W. T. (2012). Long-term reduction in implicit race bias: A prejudice habit-breaking intervention. *Journal of Experimental Social Psychology, 48*(6), 1267–1278. https://doi.org/10.1016/j.jesp.2012.06.003

Dovidio, J. F., Gaertner, S. L., & Saguy, T. (2007). Another view of "we": Majority and minority group perspectives on a common ingroup identity. *European Review of Social Psychology, 18*(1), 296–330. https://doi.org/10.1080/10463280701726132

Er-rafiy, A., & Brauer, M. (2013). Modifying perceived variability: Four laboratory and field experiments show the effectiveness of a ready-to-be-used prejudice intervention. *Journal of Applied Social Psychology, 43*(4), 840–853. https://doi.org/10.1111/jasp.12010

Ferri, B. A., & Gregg, N. (1998). Women with disabilities: Missing voices. *Women's Studies International Forum, 21*(4), 429–439. https://doi.org/10.1016/S0277-5395(98)00038-7

Garretson, J., & Suhay, E. (2016). Scientific communication about biological influences on homosexuality and the politics of gay rights. *Political Research Quarterly, 69*(1), 17–29. https://doi.org/10.1177/1065912915620050

Hall, J. A., Coats, E. J., & LeBeau, L. S. (2005). Nonverbal behavior and the vertical dimension of social relations: A meta-analysis. *Psychological Bulletin, 131*(6), 898–924. https://doi.org/10.1037/0033-2909.131.6.898

Hamermesh, D. S., & Parker, A. (2005). Beauty in the classroom: Instructors' pulchritude and putative pedagogical productivity. *Economics of Education Review, 24*(4), 369–376. https://doi.org/10.1016/j.econedurev.2004.07.013

Hegarty, P., & Pratto, F. (2001). Sexual orientation beliefs: Their relationship to anti-gay attitudes and biological determinist arguments. *Journal of Homosexuality, 41*(1), 121–135. https://doi.org/10.1300/J082v41n01_04

Jakobsen, J. R., & Pellegrini, A. (2004). *Love the sin: Sexual regulation and the limits of religious tolerance*. Beacon Press.

Jost, J. T., Banaji, M. R., & Nosek, B. A. (2004). A decade of System Justification Theory: Accumulated evidence of conscious and unconscious bolstering of the status quo. *Political Psychology, 25*(6), 881–919. https://doi.org/10.1111/j.1467-9221.2004.00402.x

Littleford, L. N., & Jones, J. A. (2017). Framing and source effects on White college students' reactions to racial inequity information. *Cultural Diversity & Ethnic Minority Psychology, 23*(1), 143–153. https://doi.org/10.1037/cdp0000102

Littleford, L. N., Ong, K. S., Tseng, A., Milliken, J. C., & Humy, S. L. (2010). Perceptions of European American and African American instructors teaching race-focused courses. *Journal of Diversity in Higher Education, 3*(4), 230–244. https://doi.org/10.1037/a0020950

Liviatan, I., & Jost, J. T. (2014). A social-cognitive analysis of system justification goal striving. *Social Cognition, 32*(2), 95–129. https://doi.org/10.1521/soco.2014.32.2.95

Lopez, G. E., Gurin, P., & Nagda, B. A. (1998). Education and understanding structural causes for group inequalities. *Political Psychology, 19*(2), 305–329. https://doi.org/10.1111/0162-895X.00106

Markus, H. R., & Kitayama, S. (1991). Culture and the self: Implications for cognition, emotion, and motivation. *Psychological Review, 98*(2), 224–253. https://doi.org/10.1037/0033-295X.98.2.224

McCoy, S. K., & Major, B. (2007). Priming meritocracy and the psychological justification of inequality. *Journal of Experimental Social Psychology, 43*(3), 341–351. https://doi.org/10.1016/j.jesp.2006.04.009

Packer, D. J. (2014). On not airing our dirty laundry: Intergroup contexts suppress ingroup criticism among strongly identified group members. *British Journal of Social Psychology, 53*(1), 93–111. https://doi.org/10.1111/bjso.12017

Pettigrew, T. F., & Tropp, L. R. (2006). A meta-analytic test of intergroup contact theory. *Journal of Personality and Social Psychology, 90*(5), 751–783. https://doi.org/10.1037/0022-3514.90.5.751

Pittman, C. T. (2010). Race and gender oppression in the classroom: The experiences of women faculty of color with White male students. *Teaching Sociology, 38*(3), 183–196. https://doi.org/10.1177/0092055X10370120

Reid, L. D. (2010). The role of perceived race and gender in the evaluation of college teaching on RateMyProfessors.com. *Journal of Diversity in Higher Education, 3*(3), 137–152. https://doi.org/10.1037/a0019865

Russ, T. L., Simonds, C. J., & Hunt, S. K. (2002). Coming out in the classroom . . . An occupational hazard? The influence of sexual orientation on teacher credibility and perceived student learning. *Communication Education, 51*(3), 311–324. https://doi.org/10.1080/03634520216516

Shapiro, J. R., & Neuberg, S. L. (2007). From stereotype threat to stereotype threats: Implications of a multi-threat framework for causes, moderators, mediators, consequences, and interventions. *Personality and Social Psychology Review, 11*(2), 107–130. https://doi.org/10.1177/1088868306294790

Suhay, E., & Jayaratne, T. E. (2013). Does biology justify ideology? The politics of genetic attribution. *Public Opinion Quarterly, 77*(2), 497–521. https://doi.org/10.1093/poq/nfs049

Williams, W. R. (2014). No yellow tickets: The stigma of poverty in the school lunch line. In C. Collins, J. Ladd, & F. Yeskel (Eds.), *Class lives: Stories from across our economic divide* (pp. 48–52). Cornell University Press.

Woods, L. L., II. (2012). The Federal Home Loan Bank Board, redlining, and the national proliferation of racial lending discrimination, 1921–1950. *Journal of Urban History, 38*(6), 1036–1059. https://doi.org/10.1177/0096144211435126

Wright, S. C., Aron, A., McLaughlin-Volpe, T., & Ropp, S. A. (1997). The extended contact effect: Knowledge of cross-group friendships and prejudice. *Journal of Personality and Social Psychology, 73*(1), 73–90. https://doi.org/10.1037/0022-3514.73.1.73

Zirkel, S. (2002). Is there a place for me? Role models and academic identity among White students and students of color. *Teachers College Record, 104*(2), 357–376. https://doi.org/10.1111/1467-9620.00166

11 WHITE PRIVILEGE IN THE CLASSROOM

LEAH R. WARNER, LISA S. WAGNER, AND PATRICK R. GRZANKA

A primary insight of critical race scholarship is that race and racism are processes, not just identities, structures, or attitudes (Delgado & Stefancic, 2012). Accordingly, antiracist praxis—including attending to our embodied privilege(s) in the classroom—requires emotional stamina and critical self-reflexivity throughout our careers (DiAngelo, 2011). We offer three scenarios as White, cisgender instructors, each providing our own reflection on difficulties we encountered in addressing our white privilege, or systemic unearned advantage, in the classroom. We then examine themes that cut across the scenarios, particularly in terms of the need for both continued self-reflection and participation in social action.

LISA'S DILEMMA: FACING WHITE PRIVILEGE AND RACISM

I experienced the complex nature of white privilege during my first year of full-time teaching. Having just completed my PhD, I was in the midst of the hectic first years of teaching, simultaneously prepping four courses while

---

https://doi.org/10.1037/0000216-011
Navigating Difficult Moments in Teaching Diversity and Social Justice, M. E. Kite, K. A. Case, and W. R. Williams (Editors)
Copyright © 2021 by the American Psychological Association. All rights reserved.

trying to keep my head above water. One course examined social science research methods within the context of a particular topic, in my case stereotyping and prejudice. In part because I was teaching a research methods course and in part because I disliked discussion-based courses where the loudest voices in the class were the only experiences heard and discussed, I wanted to create a course grounded in empirical evidence about stereotyping and prejudice that examined how privilege is inextricably tied to oppression and then use experiential exercises to help illustrate the emotional impact of these concepts.

At the end of the final class of the semester, as I was quickly packing up so the next class could enter, a White female student approached me. She said she wanted to let me know that she enjoyed the class. She also wanted to caution me to be careful about what I said in class because, given my position as a White professor, students would give more weight to what I said. She was concerned that I might be inadvertently overstating the effects of racism and, because I was White, students would believe me. She said I should be careful to stick only to the facts and not share my beliefs or opinions. I was taken aback by all that she said and did not think to question her further. After class, I repeatedly went over her words and tried to make sense of them. Given that I so carefully grounded the course in research, I knew that I had not conveyed anything that was not backed by solid evidence. And yet she believed that I was espousing things that were not supported by data. I wondered, "What kind of evidence would it take to have a White student like her believe the effects of racism?" She also recognized something that I had not: a White person speaking out about racism may be more readily believed than People of Color. Indeed, people may believe a person with privilege speaking out about prejudice against others more then they believe a member of the oppressed group.

LEAH'S DILEMMA: ADDRESSING (INEVITABLE) DEFENSIVENESS

When I think about situations that influenced my understanding of white privilege in the classroom, particularly as a White female tenured professor interacting with Students of Color, one of the most profound occurred during an informal encounter while I was a faculty cochair of a campus-wide diversity committee. A coalition of student groups called for a meeting of campus leaders to discuss systemic inequality that Black students experience at my college. After the meeting, I initiated a conversation with a Black student so that I could gather information to bring back to the committee. During the interchange, the student did not have confidence in my intent nor in my likelihood of carrying out the students' demands for changing the campus climate. Particularly, he asked whether I had been to Newark (a predominately Black and Latinx city in New Jersey) to get to know and help people there. I responded that I had not been to Newark for that purpose, which he said showed that I did not know what Black students face, and that I therefore did not support Students of Color. I spent the time actively listening and providing affirmative responses, but not a lot of feedback (e.g., nodding, saying "OK," thanking him for sharing). After the conversation, I followed up with one of the student groups, where I gathered more information to bring back to the diversity committee. Our committee integrated their feedback into our recruitment and retention plan and our faculty training program. I personally integrated their feedback into my teaching on racism and increased attention to local issues in my hometown with respect to race.

On the outside, it seemed like my responses to the student were positive: listening, learning, and making changes that would address the campus climate. But on the inside, I found my response troubling. The student revealed to me elements of my own white privilege as he emphasized that I had not learned about, nor engaged in, actions to support lived experiences of some of my students. In response, I found myself feeling very defensive, with thoughts like, "I don't have to go to Newark specifically; I feel misunderstood; the student was taking his anger out on me." I spent more time than I would like to admit thinking about whether or not I could be justifiably defensive in this case.

PATRICK'S DILEMMA: ADMITTING YOU'RE WRONG (WHEN YOU THOUGHT YOU WERE RIGHT)

I find it especially difficult to face the moments in which I feel I am being completely reasonable while also recognizing that my class, race, and gender privileges inform how I interact with students in potentially unfair ways. A few semesters ago, at perhaps the fourth meeting of class, my students were engaged in small group work when I observed one—let's call her Bryanna—without her book out. "Where's your book?" I asked. "I don't have it yet," she answered, unapologetically. I responded frankly and firmly, with something like: "I have spent the past 2 weeks explaining how important it is that you acquire the books *and* how I am here to help if you have any trouble getting them. This is unacceptable; I'll talk to you after class." The student had behaved with apparent disregard to my expectations, much less her own learning, and I was having a "not today" moment. I was irritated.

After class, I approached Bryanna, a traditional college-age Black woman. "So, what's the problem with the books?" I asked, my tone friendly after a lively class discussion of early feminist writing. I honestly don't remember the reason she provided (it was not substantive), but I do remember the unsolicited feedback she gave me: "You did not need to call me out like that publicly. That was completely unnecessary and embarrassing." I was taken aback. She was not attacking me, and she was not trying to embarrass me. She was, however, expressing her experience of me, which is that I barked at her in the middle of a class (about feminism) in the beginning of the semester. I remember saying something like, "OK, I'm sorry. I should have spoken to you one-on-one after class. And you should have gotten the books or talked to me sooner. Let's not do that to each other again." She smiled, and we moved on. Fortunately, we rebounded and actually developed a good relationship that semester, despite my aggressive behavior. I cannot apologize for my expectations that students acquire required course content or reach out to me about alternative arrangements, but my entire approach is informed by my privilege: I am a White man who has always attended or worked in predominantly white institutions—my professional social worlds have always accommodated me. It never occurred to me that a student might not want to start the semester explaining why they cannot acquire $150 of books for *any reason*. Rather than ask students to request special PDFs of readings, I could just provide all readings electronically for the first 3 weeks until students' loan deposits have been made and they have had time to order books. Why didn't I do this? The answer: privilege. Our interaction reflected the residue of my intersectional privilege, which is effectively the alchemy of white supremacy and patriarchy I carry with me everywhere even as I say I wish to leave it behind (Williams, 1991).

FACULTY REFLECTION

Lisa's Reflection

Although many aspects of the student's comments warrant unpacking, three stand out: (a) when in a homogenous racial group (as she and I were), racial affinity can lead to disturbingly racist situations; (b) the power that privilege in general, and white privilege in particular, brings when discussing issues of prejudice; and (c) that leveraging that power to speak out against prejudice may inadvertently reinforce the power structure that created the privilege.

First, the student took advantage of our shared racial background (and perhaps my youth) to give me a warning. She couched it in the form of pedagogical advice, but she was warning me that my words held power and that I could damage the status quo if I continued teaching in this way. Her response was perhaps due to a defensive reaction to course material suggesting she had privilege (DiAngelo, 2011). As I was wholly unprepared for her comments, I missed an opportunity to address her defensive response. Many report that in White-only contexts, it is commonplace for White people to make statements like this student's (Bonilla-Silva, 2014). New faculty may not be prepared for the reality that they need to do so much antiracism work in White-only contexts, even in ones that appear to be supportive of social justice. Being prepared to respond when White students, peers, and senior colleagues give these kinds of warnings couched within "pedagogical advice" is key to productive conversations that might help achieve antiracism goals.

Second, this student thought that because I was White, when I spoke about racism people would automatically believe that what I said was true. Her implication was that when People of Color speak about racism, others would not automatically believe them. Members of privileged groups may be seen as having nothing to gain (and in fact, having privilege to lose) by speaking out about prejudice, so when they do speak out, their voices may carry more weight. Subsequent research supports her beliefs (e.g., Rasinski & Czopp, 2010). For me at the time, this recognition reinforced the importance of and a sense of personal responsibility for speaking out against injustice, especially when I am not the target of the injustice. When instructors fail to include an understanding of the role of privilege in the oppression/privilege system, students may distance themselves from oppression that they do not experience, convincing themselves that it is not really their business to interfere. When students make the connection between their privilege and others' oppression, they can recognize that they are responsible for speaking out against oppression.

This recognition of the power and responsibility that privilege brings leads directly to the third point: using one's privilege to speak out against prejudice may inadvertently serve to reinforce the power structure that creates the privilege. It is very important to be an ally, and yet, by leveraging one's privilege, one is also reinforcing the existing status quo. For example, when Students of Color express how damaging racism is, some students may be dismissive, but when the White instructor makes the same point, these same students may be swayed. Although the message has been successfully received, it was done in a way that reinforces the existing racial power structure. As an instructor, it is especially important to help students recognize their own privilege and the role they play in the oppression/privilege system.

In doing so, instructors can embolden students to become genuine allies to other groups. They can also model how to speak out against oppression and can work to create environments where people from oppressed groups have the power to speak out and be heard. Figuring out how to create these situations where People of Color also possess power to speak against racism so that their voices can be heard is essential.

Leah's Reflection

My reflection on this experience taught me some invaluable lessons that I take with me to this day. Particularly, I reflected on why I was so focused on my own defensiveness, rather than merely focused on taking action to address systemic inequality for Black students at my college. I draw from DiAngelo's (2011) work on white fragility to understand my reaction. White fragility occurs when even a small amount of racial discomfort can lead White people to engage in a variety of defensive responses that portray themselves as victims, such as shutting down, indulgence in one's overwhelming emotions, and actively resisting the discomfort. This enactment, in turn, frames whiteness as morally superior and blames others for their discomfort, effectively reestablishing the "white racial equilibrium" (DiAngelo, 2011, p. 54) of racial power and privilege that is largely obscured from conscious awareness. Thus, rather than an example of weakness, white fragility is actually a performance of invulnerability, an enactment of power in the face of challenges to it (Applebaum, 2017).

Although I previously was aware of white fragility as an academic concept, it took this experience for me to truly understand my own participation in it. I believed I "overcame" previous discomfort about my white privilege and thus failed to see my own continued enactment of white fragility. My perception that I "achieved" critical engagement with my white privilege, coupled with my defensiveness, reflects the tendency for White people to center racialized conversations on themselves (Wise & Case, 2013).

For this scenario, addressing my white fragility meant thinking through the appropriate path for addressing my feelings so as not to reestablish white racial equilibrium. Most importantly, my defensiveness is my burden to bear when facing my privilege. I must recognize that I might feel misunderstood and invalidated as an ally. But it is wrong for me to try to convince others to understand my intentions or seek validation from People of Color that I am not prejudiced. In other words, it is wrong for me to place my burden onto the person who is confronting me or other People of Color, because doing so would turn the attention to me and reestablish my privilege. I need to be appreciative of the significant risks that the student took to confront me and to acknowledge the emotional labor involved in revealing his perspective to me. To that end, I am responsible for taking risks and having more engaged conversations than I did in that moment. My ability to pick and choose when I speak is also a privilege of my social standing at my institution as a tenured professor. Even though I was actively listening, the fact that I said relatively little during the conversation may have understandably frustrated the student. Clearly, I had (and still do have) much to learn about my participation in white privilege. Nevertheless, now I recognize that my white privilege is something I need to continually address, rather than something that I can simply "overcome."

Patrick's Reflection

I could tell you about many other times when I've gotten it completely wrong. I could have told you stories of when I've microaggressed (though there are countless others I'll never know about), inadvertently but predictably triggered someone, made a joke that offended, or spoke with confidence about something or some group I am actually mischaracterizing. But I have come to see those moments are less "difficult" and more obvious. I am practiced in the negotiation of guilt (I wrote my dissertation on white guilt and shame), including how to apologize, get up, learn, move on, be better, and fail again. This is part of committed antiracism. But it is much harder to admit that you are wrong when the situation is more ambiguous, especially when the conflict is less about particular behaviors and more about affect and positionality. I think that White people who have already developed an antiracist identity are often comfortable rehearsing and reciting the moments where their uninterrogated whiteness caused them to do something obviously racist, including at least implicitly the part where they grew as a person and are now so comfortable in their antiracist identity that they write publications about their failures, which they will never repeat (right?). Those stories are important to share, surely, and they can be revelatory for White folks who are at the early stages of their antiracist identity development. But I think we need to stay with the trouble (Haraway, 2016) of the moments that are less obviously terrible but are no less problematic. How can we practice an intersectional antiracism less invested in saviors, guilty subjects, and confessionals, and more in the modest, self-reflexive, generous, and critical readings of actions that are not blatantly racist but are nonetheless inextricable from the white supremacy of American society? What if we took seriously the finite capacities of White people to ever see racism as it is *but/and* build capacities for us to see a way forward when we (White people) find ourselves called out in what might feel like otherwise unremarkable interactions? As aspirational allies, what do we do with the moments that are difficult to predict or the dynamics that catch us completely by surprise?

As each of our reflections reveal, white privilege is pernicious. It appears in ways we do not expect at all career stages—early, when there is a recognition of the need to learn, but also mid- and surely late-career, when we would like to think that we "achieved" critical understanding of whiteness. Our reflections demonstrate that resisting white privilege requires a constant vigilance to prevent us from reproducing its harmful effects. Further, vigilance requires more than a "whack-a-mole" approach, where we simply react to instances after they've occurred. Rather, challenging white privilege requires systematic rethinking our pedagogical approaches to reduce privilege-based ruptures from happening in the first place.

CONSIDERATIONS OF CONTEXT AND INTERSECTIONALITY

Our social locations influence our approaches to each section of this chapter. First, they affect our reflections on our scenarios. When, I (Lisa) thought back to my scenario, I recognized that as a White, cisgender woman, straight professor, my privileged status may give my voice more weight speaking out against prejudice based on race, gender identity, or sexual orientation. But when speaking about issues of sexism, my voice may carry less power. This realization affected my approach to classroom discussions about confronting prejudice in homogenous settings. In my current class, we spend time examining where we each have privilege and experience oppression. We then discuss that when we are not the target of prejudice, it sometimes feels as if it is not our business to step in and say something, especially when there are not any people from that group around to be hurt. When we do recognize our privilege, we may begin to see that not saying something is silently participating in the oppression/privilege cycle. If, instead, we speak out, people may hear our privileged voice, and we may make a difference. For example, students often wonder why they should bother to say anything when Uncle Harry makes yet another racist joke when there are not any people from that racial group around to be hurt. But when instructors connect the privilege/oppression cycle, students can recognize that their voices might be heard, if not by Uncle Harry, perhaps by younger cousins. Indeed, when others disagree with prejudiced comments, bystanders' own prejudice and their tolerance of prejudiced comments decrease (e.g., Blanchard et al., 1994). Students resonate with the idea that just as we want allies to speak out for us when we experience oppression, we are responsible to speak out for others, even if they are not physically present.

Additionally, our social locations influence our recommendations for best practices. For example, I (Leah) am a White professor from a family with a long-standing participation in higher education. Three of my four grandparents held degrees beyond college level; two of them were professors. From a young age, I internalized how to succeed within institutions of higher education. This standpoint means I do not possess a lived experience to guide my understanding of marginalization within a college setting. Therefore, it is especially critical that I attend to people's intersectional lived experiences and familiarize myself with patterns of marginalization within higher education. I (Patrick) confront the embodied complexity of intersectionality every time I enter the classroom as a professor of psychology and women, gender, and sexuality studies who is a White, cisgender, queer man. I (try to) practice intersectional feminist pedagogy (Case, 2017) from a nexus of privilege: masculinity, whiteness, and middle-class status, in particular. Negotiating the classroom as a person whose social identities and professional position imbues me with *authority* (some of which is, of course, unfair and unearned) is an especially fraught dynamic when teaching Psychology of Gender or Introduction to Women, Gender, and Sexuality, both of which necessitate me speaking to others' experiences with all the confidence of a professor but without the lived experience of most of the subjects of my course (see Goldstein, Chapter 15, this volume). Furthermore, since all three of us (Lisa, Leah, and Patrick) are tenured faculty, we possess the privilege of taking risks in the classroom when confronting our privilege. We expose our weaknesses here without concern over our job security, which is a privilege inevitably informed by our whiteness. We can admit our mistakes without worrying whether doing so will negatively affect our job performance evaluations. Thus, we provide our recommendations with the acknowledgment that instructors concerned about job security, such as contingent faculty, may not be afforded the same leeway with their pedagogical approaches.

BEST PRACTICES

The Process of Challenging White Privilege

There are three immediate, rather disheartening reactions that could potentially occur from each of our scenarios. First, all three of us felt bad after experiencing them. Defensiveness, hurt, guilt, and sadness are common reactions to engaging with white privilege. It is also possible to feel a sense of continual defeat, as our scenarios reflected difficult situations across a range of circumstances. And finally, these scenarios engender a sense of relief at the prospect of disengaging with white privilege, which is itself an aspect of privilege (Wise & Case, 2013). In other words, each of our three scenarios could potentially allow our guilt to slip into white fragility, as Leah did when the student confronted her. But despair and misery, disengagement and defensiveness are unlikely to produce racial justice. Where can instructors draw inspiration and hope in opposition to these reactions? Each of our scenarios emphasize the need for instructors to engage in the dialectic of critical self-reflection and positive social action, of turning inward and turning outward at the same time.

Critical self-reflection is not utopian, but rather a pragmatic, continued commitment to rejecting white fragility. In particular, Applebaum (2017) suggested cultivating "critical hope" (Boler, 2004, p. 130), which involves (a) acknowledging one's participation in systemic oppression and (b) assurance that the discomfort from this acknowledgment will provide an opportunity for profound learning—about oneself and about others. Discomfort, rather than something to be reduced or ignored, is foregrounded as a signal for learning. It signals that we do not know something, perhaps something we are motivated to ignore, and it provides us an opportunity to broaden the scope of our understanding of structures of power and domination. Furthermore, critical hope encourages continual openness to change, willingness to risk exposure, and acknowledgment of uncertainty. As Applebaum asserted, "critical hope entails an ethical and political responsibility requiring constant vigilance in the process of change and becoming resulting in the potential for relations in solidarity with others" (p. 872). In other words, rather than reasserting White people's moral innocence or quelling white guilt, critical hope provides individuals with increased stamina for contemplating one's role in perpetuating racism (DiAngelo, 2011) and responsibility for addressing it.

Moving From Reflection to Action

Critical self-reflection alone, however, will not do the work of addressing white privilege. White instructors cannot just look inward, which some suggest is the seductive appeal of white guilt (Grzanka et al., 2020), but must also engage outward in the form of positive social action. In particular, intersectional coalitions can serve as a model for instructors looking to engage in social justice (Crenshaw, 1989; Luna, 2016; Rosenthal, 2016). Intersectional coalitions involve the recognition of intertwined and distinct experiences of oppression based on race, gender, sexuality, and age, among many other factors. These coalitions encourage us to work within and across social locations to fight all forms of oppression. Based on interviews with diverse Women of Color activists, Cole (2008) argued that coalitions better enable community-building, shared experience, and action than more restrictive notions of identity that often deny intersectionality (e.g., reproductive justice; Ross, 2017). Learning from each other's expertise facilitates interactional collaboration with the recognition that systems of oppression impact all people differently. Coalitions, as opposed to identity silos that fixate on a single axis of experience, avoid the reassertion of white privilege by centering the experiences of multiply marginalized groups who are affected by the nexus of oppressive systems (Crenshaw, 1989). Instructors committed to addressing white privilege should seek out social justice efforts that are based on a coalition model, since observing connections across systems of inequality catalyzes activism and increases positive attitudes across social groups (Curtin et al., 2015).

The Need for Tools to Engage in the Process

We are not prepared to offer a rubric for how to manage white privilege as instructors in the classroom, because we are not confident one exists. Instead, we identified dynamics that forced us to reflect upon and change our relationship to our own whiteness, particularly in terms of intersectionality. Academia is a competitive industry, and many professors are drawn to academic work because they were good students. In other words, they were good at getting the "right" answer. Similarly, privilege can lead us to focus on the outcome rather than the process; in the narratives we elaborated in this chapter, the process was infinitely more consequential than getting or being right. As Patrick's story illustrates, he needed to face how he was wrong in order to repair the relationship with his student. As we attempted to stress throughout, *change* is as important as *reflection*, because thinking about whiteness is not the same as doing something about it. In other words, awareness is not action, and cognizance of white privilege is not equivalent to resisting the unearned and unfair advantages of whiteness that all White instructors bring into the classroom. Though there is no checklist or guidebook to disinvesting from white privilege, there are myriad tools (see Case, 2013). For example, Case's (2015) *therapeutic ally-ance*, a model for White practitioners to dismantle racism and privilege, provides concrete teaching strategies to encourage Whites' critical self-reflection and social action.

These involve an examination of various forms of privilege, considering privilege through an intersectional perspective, fostering critical analysis through student reflection of their own privilege, and promoting action to undo white privilege (Case, 2015). Rather than recenter whiteness in the interest of naming and deconstructing it, we think it is more productive to recognize and wrestle with whiteness as the necessary terms of our antiracism: whiteness cannot go away, but white privilege can. Such an approach helps us to both recognize racial privilege and work with others to find novel ways to use privilege against white supremacy and intersecting forms of social inequality.

RESOURCES

Case, K. A. (Ed.). (2013). *Deconstructing privilege: Teaching and learning as allies in the classroom*. Routledge.

Kim Case's edited volume provides a wealth of information from experts on deconstructing privilege, ranging from classroom applications to theory. Readings guide instructors' critical self-reflection and forms of action to facilitate their growth as social justice allies.

DiAngelo, R. (2018). *White fragility: Why it's so hard for White people to talk about racism*. Beacon Press.

Antiracist educator Robin DiAngelo describes the phenomenon of white fragility and examines the defensive moves that White people make when challenged about racial issues. Behaviors stemming from white fragility can end up reinforcing the current racial status quo and stymie any meaningful cross-racial dialogue. Chapter 12 provides direction to move beyond white fragility to constructive dialogue and action.

Landis, K. (Ed.). (2008). *Start talking: A handbook for engaging difficult dialogues in higher education*. University of Alaska, Anchorage; Alaska Pacific University. https://ctle.utah.edu/inclusiveteaching/resources/challenging_situations/Start_Talking_full_book_pdf.pdf

Although faculty have expertise in specific content areas, we often have little training in how to have positive classroom discussions around challenging topics such as race. This handbook promotes the development of civil discourse in the classroom in topic areas that can be difficult. Chapter 3 focuses on classroom discussions around issues of race, class, and culture.

Wise, T. (2005). *White like me: Reflections on race from a privileged son*. Soft Skull Press.

Including stories and personal insights gained from 15 years as an educator, Tim Wise examines white privilege and its costs to everyone. He describes ways White people can challenge their unjust privileges and why it is in their self-interest to do so.

REFERENCES

Applebaum, B. (2017). Comforting discomfort as complicity: White fragility and the pursuit of invulnerability. *Hypatia, 32*(4), 862–875. https://doi.org/10.1111/hypa.12352

Blanchard, F., Crandall, C., Brigham, J., & Vaughn, L. (1994). Condemning and condoning racism: A social context approach to interracial settings. *Journal of Applied Psychology, 79*(6), 993–997. https://doi.org/10.1037/0021-9010.79.6.993

Boler, M. (2004). Teaching for hope: The ethics of shattering world views. In D. Liston & J. Garrison (Eds.), *Teaching, learning, and loving: Reclaiming passion in educational practice* (pp. 117–136). Routledge Falmer. https://doi.org/10.4324/9780203465622_chapter_7

Bonilla-Silva, E. (2014). *Racism without racists: Color-blind racism and the persistence of racial inequality in America* (4th ed.). Rowman & Littlefield.

Case, K. A. (Ed.). (2013). *Deconstructing privilege: Teaching and learning as allies in the classroom*. Routledge.

Case, K. A. (2015). White practitioners in therapeutic ally-ance: An intersectional privilege awareness training model. *Women & Therapy, 38*(3–4), 263–278. https://doi.org/10.1080/02703149.2015.1059209

Case, K. A. (Ed.). (2017). *Intersectional pedagogy: Complicated identity and social justice*. Routledge.

Cole, E. R. (2008). Coalitions as a model for intersectionality: From practice to theory. *Sex Roles, 59*(5–6), 443–453. https://doi.org/10.1007/s11199-008-9419-1

Crenshaw, K. (1989). Demarginalizing the intersection of race and sex: A Black feminist critique of antidiscrimination doctrine. *University of Chicago Legal Forum, 140*(1), 139–167.

Curtin, N., Stewart, A. J., & Cole, E. R. (2015). Challenging the status quo: The role of intersectional awareness in activism for social change and pro-social intergroup attitudes. *Psychology of Women Quarterly, 39*(4), 512–529. https://doi.org/10.1177/0361684315580439

Delgado, D., & Stefancic, J. (2012). *Critical race theory: An introduction* (2nd ed.). NYU Press.

DiAngelo, R. (2011). White fragility. *The International Journal of Critical Pedagogy, 3*(3), 54–70.

Grzanka, P. R., Frantell, K. A., & Fassinger, R. E. (2020). The White Racial Affect Scale (WRAS): Development and initial validation of a scale of white guilt, shame, and negation. *The Counseling Psychologist, 48*(1), 47–77. https://doi.org/10.1177%2F0011000019878808

Haraway, D. J. (2016). *Staying with the trouble: Making kin the Chthulucene*. Duke University Press. https://doi.org/10.1215/9780822373780

Luna, Z. (2016). "Truly a women of color organization:" Negotiating sameness and difference in pursuit of intersectionality. *Gender & Society, 30*(5), 769–790. https://doi.org/10.1177/0891243216649929

Rasinski, H. M., & Czopp, A. M. (2010). The effect of target status on witnesses' reactions to confrontations of bias. *Basic and Applied Social Psychology, 32*(1), 8–16. https://doi.org/10.1080/01973530903539754

Rosenthal, L. (2016). Incorporating intersectionality into psychology: An opportunity to promote social justice and equity. *American Psychologist, 71*(6), 474–485. https://doi.org/10.1037/a0040323

Ross, L. J. (2017). Reproductive justice as intersectional feminist activism. *Souls, 19*(3), 286–314. https://doi.org/10.1080/10999949.2017.1389634

Williams, P. J. (1991). *The alchemy of race and rights: Diary of a law professor*. Harvard University Press.

Wise, T., & Case, K. A. (2013). Pedagogy for the privileged: Addressing inequality and injustice without shame or blame. In K. A. Case (Ed.), *Deconstructing privilege: Teaching and learning as allies in the classroom* (pp. 17–33). Routledge.

12 NAVIGATING DIFFICULT MOMENTS OUTSIDE THE CLASSROOM

WENDY R. WILLIAMS AND F. TYLER SERGENT

Faculty who teach diversity courses often define themselves holistically as social justice advocates. For these faculty, teaching does not stop when they leave the classroom. As a result, they may find themselves in unjust situations on their campuses in which their internal sense of fairness says they must act. At other times, people on campus seek them out for assistance with unfair circumstances because they either know the faculty members' knowledge of diversity issues or their reputations for action. Although these faculty may be prepared to tackle social justice *inside* their classrooms, where they control content and ground rules, they may be caught off-guard when encountering difficult moments on their campus *outside* their classrooms.

Together, the authors of this chapter find ourselves regularly caught off-guard on our campus. At the same time, we have had a measure of success in navigating these moments. In our experiences, we find that these situations often fall into three categories: (1) *students* needing assistance, either as individuals or as an officially (or unofficially) recognized group, (2) *peers* behaving in discriminatory ways that the faculty member personally witnesses or peers seeking help dealing with the discriminatory behavior of other peers, and (3) confronting the unjust behavior of *administrators* or *the institution*.

https://doi.org/10.1037/0000216-012
Navigating Difficult Moments in Teaching Diversity and Social Justice, M. E. Kite, K. A. Case, and W. R. Williams (Editors)
Copyright © 2021 by the American Psychological Association. All rights reserved.

Because these situations involve different levels of power, we address each individually but also note commonalities. As such, we provide examples of dilemmas—including laying out some of the pitfalls outside of the classroom—and ways to navigate them successfully.

FACULTY REFLECTION

Wendy's Experience

I have previously written about my social justice identity and the path I took to get to my current position (Williams, 2014). In short, I had early lessons in privilege and injustice. By accident of birth, I was healthy, but my sister, Roberta, was not. At 3 months of age, we discovered she had hydrocephalus: Cerebrospinal fluid had built up in her brain, compressing it against her skull and causing her to lapse into a coma. Although she eventually woke from the coma and lived for 28 years, the hydrocephalus resulted in brain damage and other complications. Because she was 6 years younger than me, her illness, multiple brain surgeries, numerous hospitalizations, and resulting disabilities had a profound impact on me. As a cisgender, White, heterosexual, able-bodied person without cognitive impairments, I understood that I had a great responsibility to take advantage of the opportunities I had done nothing to deserve but, nevertheless, had been given to me. My sister's life inspired me to teach and research the topics of prejudice and inequality—her experiences honed my sense of (in)justice and the need for those with privilege to act on behalf of those with less privilege.

Tyler's Experience

As a first-generation college graduate, I came to my identity as a social justice advocate through the teachings of my parents. As an only child, I grew up working-class in rural Lincoln County, West Virginia (WV)—the geographical center of Appalachia—in the house my father built. My parents were born in WV during the Great Depression with little money and large families: My mother had nine siblings and my father seven brothers. My father (1929–2015) completed the eighth grade before he was required to quit in order to work on the family farm; my mother (1931–2020) dropped out of high school at age 16 and earned her GED at age 42. I am the only college graduate of my generation among my considerable extended family, most of whom still reside in Appalachia. Although my parents' own generation, regional origin, and social formation may well have led them toward racist and xenophobic attitudes and bigotry, they both—particularly my father—taught me to value diversity and to treat all people equally, just as my grandfather (1891–1953) had taught him. Thus, despite many advantages as a cisgender, heterosexual male, my parents' teachings, along with my own experiences with classism and prejudice based on my Appalachian background, have helped me see the ways I can use my other privileges to advocate for those who have less privilege.

Helping Individual Students

Professors are a predominant source of mentorship for students (Strada–Gallup, 2018). Despite evidence that shows the importance of mentoring (Campbell & Campbell, 1997), faculty rarely get formal training in mentorship. As a result, faculty may be unprepared for dealing with the difficult (let alone traumatic) situations students report to them. For faculty who are justice-oriented, this can present a dilemma about whether to act on behalf of the student or not. Specifically, because faculty are typically more experienced in navigating university systems, they have important knowledge to impart to students. Faculty should, nevertheless, be careful to preserve students' sense of efficacy. At the same time, encouraging students to rectify unfair situations can put faculty at odds with their own peers or administrators who are the source of the injustice.

For example, at our institution (Berea College), all students are low-income but high-achieving. Because many cannot afford college, Berea created a unique funding model which requires students to work for the college as part of their financial aid package (see Williams, 2016, for a more detailed explanation of Berea's funding model). On occasion, students will report difficulties in their labor positions to faculty members, including being taken advantage of by their labor supervisors, such as being forced to work overtime or to endure hostile environments. Because administrators may not be aware of these workplace violations, students need to know how to navigate the system to get abuses to stop and also gain the efficacy to advocate for themselves. Specifically, I (Tyler) have worked behind the scenes on several occasions to educate students about their workplace rights, including how to report labor violations and work-related injuries, as well as to support students emotionally through that process. Faculty at other institutions without labor programs may also face helping students with workplace situations, including work study positions or as teaching/research assistants. In addition, faculty may be called on to help with other difficult situations, including challenging discrimination by staff, faculty, or fellow students, and reporting and prosecuting on-campus sexual assault. These instances often arise unexpectedly, so faculty often must decide whether, when, and how to take action, without prior notice and in a short timeframe.

Helping Groups of Students

Similar to above, faculty often get called on to help groups of students as well. Unlike one-on-one situations, with groups of students, faculty members rarely have close, mentoring relationships with all of the students involved. Moreover, the group may have official standing at the college, which makes processes and administrative oversight clearer. At other times, the group may have come together in an unofficial capacity, making the route to adjudication or resolution less clear.

For example, I (Wendy) worked with the Student Government Association (SGA) to coordinate a trip in mid-October 2011 to the Occupy Wall Street protests in New York City. The students had allocated some of their internal funding and secured external funding, but the administration froze all their accounts just days before the students planned to leave, causing students to stage a sit-in at the administrative building. Although the administration acted primarily out of concern for student safety in the wake of Occupy protesters being attacked by police in the week prior to departure (Associated Press, 2011), the administration also denied access to funding because the students had not followed all the rules tied to using college funding prior to departure. In the end, the students decided to travel to New York despite lack of administrative approval and asked me to accompany them. I agreed, but having only been at the institution for 7 weeks at that point, I had to build relationships with the students quickly in order to institute safety precautions while they were in New York. On our return, I also had to repair relationships between administrators and students that were damaged through the protest process.

The Trump Administration's removal of amnesty for undocumented students in November 2016 caused immediate concern on our campus, but because undocumented and Deferred Action for Childhood Arrivals (DACA) students are not an official student organization/club, there was no clear process nor established policies for protecting them. In addition, because the issue spanned a variety of internal entities, creation of these processes was even more complicated. For example, three separate administrative units within the college might need to be involved: (1) Student Life, if law enforcement agents showed up to resident halls; (2) faculty members, if agents showed up in classrooms; and (3) Public Safety, if agents entered any campus property. I (Tyler) worked with undocumented students and their allies to know students' rights (documented and undocumented) in relation to situations in which Immigration and Customs Enforcement (ICE) agents might access campus property (see Hill-Zuganelli & Sergent, 2018, for more details). As part of a campus taskforce, I helped students and their allies create a plan for emergency responses while also advocating to establish enduring administrative guidelines related to undocumented and DACA students generally.

Facing Personal Discrimination by Peers

Despite amassing a certain amount of privilege as a result of their educational attainment, faculty still face discrimination within academia. For instance, women, people of color, LGBTQ+ individuals, and people with disabilities encounter overt and subtle prejudice from their peers (Gutiérrez y Muhs et al., 2012; National Academies of Sciences, Engineering, and Medicine, 2018). Although Title IX statutes provide some protection, faculty must still navigate official channels from disadvantaged positions of power (e.g., untenured, bringing charges against superiors). Some discriminatory acts, moreover, may fall short of statute requirements (i.e., not severe, persistent, or pervasive) or the actions may be microaggressions that can be difficult to prove but are impactful and can cause trauma (Nadal, 2018).

For example, I (Wendy), along with two colleagues, filed a Title IX hostile work environment complaint. Although we had tried to resolve the issues on which the complaint was based informally, we believed a formal complaint was ultimately the only avenue to make the behavior stop. Because those who label negative experiences as discrimination are disliked and dismissed, even when discrimination has clearly taken place (Kaiser & Miller, 2001), each new incident required that we decide anew whether to report or not—and to whom—as well as to consider the effect reporting would have on our reputations. Ultimately, our Title IX complaint was found to have merit, and the offenders were disciplined for their actions, but the process was traumatic, took years to adjudicate internally, and external litigation is ongoing.

Supporting Peers Facing Injustice

Similar to the situations described above, faculty may encounter situations in which they are called on to assist their peers, either because of discrimination against the peer or other unjust outcomes the peer is facing. Those who point out discrimination on behalf of others are also derogated, and this effect is larger for members of the group facing discrimination than for members of privileged groups. For example, women pointing out discrimination on behalf of other women are liked less compared with men who exhibit the same behavior (Eliezer & Major, 2012). Thus, although the costs to faculty providing assistance may be less severe, there is still a cost.

I (Tyler) was faced with this situation, in part, because I am married to Wendy. Throughout her Title IX case and the aftermath, I had to determine how to best support her. As both a confidant and a social justice ally, I had to balance my outrage over the circumstances she was facing with actions that did not take agency away from her. I could not fight the Title IX case for her. At the same time, people would be more likely to listen to and consider information presented by me (as a man). Yet, consistent with the research described above, if Wendy (as a woman) presented the same information, she would be liked less for it. Specifically, the SGA was considering giving an award to one of the opposing individuals involved in Wendy's complaint during the time that colleague was facing termination proceedings. I was serving as one of two elected SGA faculty advisors at the time. Rather than asking Wendy to personally disclose painful and confidential information about the Title IX case—actions for which she may have been derogated—I instead provided student leaders in the SGA with factual information pertinent to their deliberations in my formal role as their advisor, trusting that they might consider these facts carefully and without bias, thus averting additional injustice to Wendy and her colleagues. In the end, the faculty member under disciplinary review did not receive the award.

Administrators' or Institutions' Unjust Policies

There are times when the institution itself is the perpetrator of injustice, either through purposeful actions or as a result of unforeseen consequences—or both. At these moments, faculty may feel more reluctant to speak out because identifying institutional flaws could endanger their livelihoods. At the same time, because of their content expertise, faculty who teach diversity topics are often better situated than administrators to elucidate the nature and consequences of unjust policies when they arise.

Specifically, I (Wendy) chose to speak up in the wake of a massive administrative change in the college health insurance policy. In this instance, administrators unveiled a plan that exponentially increased out-of-pocket health care costs for many on campus (i.e., lowering premiums but forcing faculty and staff into high-deductible plans). Although many institutions have implemented high deductible plans with the assumption that this would encourage better triage of illness (i.e., only going to the doctor when absolutely necessary and thus eliminating expensive but unnecessary or inappropriate tests, hospitalizations, or prescriptions when they may not be needed), research does not support these assumptions. Specifically, the main effect of higher deductible plans is that people stop seeking services, regardless of whether services are necessary or appropriate (Brook et al., 2006). Although discouraging treatment when faculty and staff are sick is one way to lower plan costs, it also leads to catastrophic long-term consequences because people get treatment only when their illnesses are more advanced. Moreover, these plans are likely to hit low-wage workers hardest because they are least likely to have savings on hand to pay out-of-pocket costs. Because my research analyzes social class, I was aware of the barriers to paying for healthcare among low-income people and able to understand how the numbers were stacked against certain segments of the college community under the proposed plan, including those with preexisting illnesses. As a result of my advocacy, backed by several other colleagues, the college revised the health insurance plan to include a plan without a high deductible. Although this was not a complete solution to the problem, the college also instituted a sliding scale for subsidizing premiums of low-wage employees on campus for the first time ever, which did allay some of the financial burden created by the new system.

CONSIDERATIONS OF CONTEXT AND INTERSECTIONALITY

To be effective in dealing with social justice dilemmas outside the classroom, faculty should consider the mission and policies of their institution, their own status and identities, and the historical moment in time. Specifically, being aware of how these factors provide context, as well as how their own positionality intersects with those whom they are interacting, can facilitate (or hinder) faculty success in these situations.

Institutions With Social Justice Missions or Policies

When confronting injustice outside the classroom, it is helpful to know whether the institution either implicitly or explicitly defines itself as a social justice institution. Because of the United States' history of discrimination against underrepresented groups, minority-serving institutions, coeducational founded schools (those that were never men-only), and women's colleges typically have advocated for equality or taken action to rectify injustices

(Gasman et al., 2015; Harwarth et al., 1997). When faculty are employed at institutions that explicitly value social justice, and thus assume their students, colleagues, or administration will behave with fairness, these incidents may be especially shocking (Mack, 2005). Alternatively, when faculty work at institutions that do not value equality, these incidents may be less surprising but may present a different dilemma: whether or not to act when there is no expectation the institution will provide justice. For example, in the situations provided in this chapter, we were always able to harken to the mission of the institution and to illustrate why remediation was necessary based on the college's own stated values.

Faculty Status

Faculty status can play an integral role in the degree to which faculty feel comfortable speaking on their own behalf or on behalf of others. Research shows that power differentials affect the willingness of individuals to confront discrimination (Ashburn-Nardo et al., 2014). In addition, as the trend in academia to hire part-time, non-tenure track, and short-term contractual labor continues (American Association of University Professors, 2014), many faculty face the dilemma of risking their own livelihoods if they speak out because their contracts can be easily terminated. Nevertheless, faculty—especially tenured faculty—often have more power than those being discriminated against including students and adjunct faculty. For instance, we often found ourselves taking action in the examples given in this chapter because we had more power than those experiencing injustices. Even so, several of the examples given occurred when we were not tenured ourselves. Consequently, each time we acted, we had to weigh carefully the likelihood of retaliation against us versus the costs if we failed to act.

Faculty Identities

Certain faculty are called on to do more emotional labor than others, including women (Hanasono et al., 2019) and people of color (Wood et al., 2015). In addition, we tend to trust those who are similar to ourselves (Singh et al., 2015). As a result, certain groups of faculty are more likely to face the dilemmas described in this chapter than other faculty. For example, I (Wendy) find that female students are much more likely to disclose sexual assault to me than to Tyler, even when we mentor the same student. This is supported by research that shows women are more likely to disclose harassment to other women than to men (Cortina, 2004). Often those who do not share the disadvantaged identity are, however, best positioned to file complaints because they are more likely to be liked and believed (Eliezer & Major, 2012). Thus, Tyler would be a better strategic choice to advocate for them, but I am often seen as "safer."

Historical Moment in Time

The historical moment in time should be weighed when determining the potential costs of acting or not acting. If there is growing momentum on an issue—a Zeitgeist—(e.g., sexual assault and harassment in light of the #MeToo movement), action may come with fewer consequences, but failure to act may lead to more consequences including lawsuits for failure to protect. Other times, lack of awareness on an issue may require educating others while simultaneously working to remedy the injustice (e.g., protecting DACA students in light of the revocation of protections for DREAMERs). Thus, the work is twice as hard with a lower potential for victory. Again, faculty must carefully weigh for themselves the degree to which (in)action could lead to positive or negative outcomes.

BEST PRACTICES

As described above, we have encountered a variety of unjust situations outside our classrooms throughout our careers. Nevertheless, in each we have described, we felt compelled to act. As a result, there are a number of lessons we have learned about how to be successful in these moments.

Know Your Institutional Policies

All institutions have policies to govern faculty, staff, and student behavior, including handbooks, manuals, and catalogs. They also have grievance procedures for violation of these policies. In addition, institutions must follow various local or national laws. In the United States these include, but not limited to, state and federal laws related to the Higher Education Act and Amendments (e.g., Titles II and III, which cover the Americans with Disabilities Act and disability services, Title IX, which covers harassment and sexual assault, and Title VII of the Civil Rights Act, which covers hostile work environment). In countries outside the United States, there may be other specific legislation (or no legislation), but the basic advice is the same: learn which policies govern the situation, including looking outside the institution for policy assistance or guidance. Many schools also have other guiding documents like mission or vision statements, strategic plans, founding charters, and stated commitments. Finally, knowing the history of the institution on the topic may also be helpful to illustrate when the institution has acted for (or against) an issue. Learning this information prior to action can be especially important. For example, the standards at different levels (institution, state, national) may affect which evidence is admissible, what the penalties are, and timelines for filing suit.

Moreover, we find that members of most institutions (faculty, staff, and students) are not familiar with all of these documents. Because people prefer that their own attitudes and behaviors match, and because attitude and behavior mismatches cause discomfort or cognitive dissonance (Festinger & Carlsmith, 1959), knowing the specific policies is especially important when arguing for why the institution must act. For instance, faculty can point out that action is consistent with the institutional charge or hold their institutions accountable for actions that are contrary to these documents, such as pointing out inconsistencies in institutional actions. Sometimes a lack of knowledge of these policies, even on the part of administrators themselves, allows problematic behavior to occur. In these cases, merely pointing out the relevant policies may be sufficient for corrective action. If not, following institutional policies and procedures is necessary for adjudication within the institution (i.e., institutional hearing panels) or to seek justice outside of the institution (i.e., a lawsuit or going to the press).

Seek a Values Match

As noted above, not only can it be important to point out where institutional actions (do not) match values, seeking a values match among the individuals within the conflict can also prove beneficial. Because the interpersonal relationship literature shows that we like those who are like us (Byrne & Nelson, 1965), demonstrating points of agreement can help bridge gaps between those who are being harmed and those responsible for ending the harm. Specifically, in the United States, a core foundational value is the American Dream in which fairness, opportunity, and equality are core tenants of the narrative (Hochschild, 1995). Using language that appeals to the opponent's sense of fairness or support for equal opportunity is consonant with this ideal and can be effective when raising complaints, even if the institution does not have a social justice history that can be highlighted or even if individuals otherwise do not agree. Similarly for those outside the U.S., framing issues using their own national values can be a way to seek common ground.

Know Individuals' Power and Effectiveness

Some administrators wield more power and efficacy than others. Recognizing when to circumvent someone who is ineffective or who has no power to change the situation can save significant time and frustration. Sometimes this knowledge is only learned after-the-fact, as we have personally (painfully) experienced. Colleagues who have been at the institution for a length of time can often help strategize the best route based on the power and effectiveness of those involved (Case et al., 2012).

Know One's Own Limits

Although we have focused in this chapter on times we chose to act, there are many instances in which we were unable to act for a variety of reasons. Faculty members must recognize their own limits, including their own lack of power or status (i.e., not tenure-track, membership in a disadvantaged group) or the ability to add one more item without incurring burnout. As described in the chapter by Eaton and Warner (Chapter 3, this volume), not only must faculty members monitor themselves for burnout, but they must recognize that there are instances in which they cannot act because they have no more bandwidth. At the same time, either a strong belief in the righteousness of a cause or feelings of satisfaction for lending assistance may provide faculty members with the necessary boost to persevere through these difficult situations. At the core, however, faculty must have honest conversations—both with themselves and with those involved—about their ability to help. It is worse to promise action and then fail to act than to discuss honestly one's (in)capacity to help—even if refraining from action runs counter to one's identity as an advocate.

Seek Additional Allies

In moments when a clear injustice has occurred, it may feel lonely and insurmountable. Even so, we have typically found that when we share what is happening to us or to people on our campuses, others step in to help and provide support. People often want to act but do not know what is happening or how to help. Additionally, although there are times when faculty are best suited to take the lead in advocating for students and staff, there are times when other stakeholders, such as students, alumni/ae, or interested press, are actually more persuasive (Case et al., 2012). Knowing one's allies and who is likely to be most persuasive can relieve pressure from those who are (or have been) fighting injustices alone. For example, besides liking and values matches, persuasion research shows that those with particular expertise on a topic (Hovland & Weiss, 1951) and those who argue against their own interest (Eagly et al., 1978) are particularly persuasive.

Trust the Person in the Situation

Especially when trying to support those with less power, faculty should use their own access to power without impeding the self-efficacy of those less empowered. For example, it is tempting to tell students what they should do or to do things for them, but research shows that students' sense of self-efficacy is important to their continued academic success (Bandura et al., 1996). Therefore, care should be taken to avoid removing students' sense of agency. Moreover, in these situations, the student or peer has to live with the consequences of (in)action, not the faculty member. Faculty members should always seek to honor the wishes of those they are helping rather than taking the actions they think are best—and this can include sometimes not taking action even if the faculty believe action is necessary.

CONCLUSION

Both new and seasoned faculty who care about social justice may be called on to act outside of their classrooms. Many of these situations arise unexpectedly and can contain some inherent risk for the faculty member. Nevertheless, we argue that faculty have a responsibility to use their power and privilege to navigate these difficult moments toward just resolutions. To do so, though, faculty must assess the situation with clear eyes in order both to be effective in the moment and to preserve their power to fight another day.

RESOURCES

American Association of University Women. (n.d.). *Legal advocacy fund*. AAUW. https://www.aauw.org/resources/legal/laf/
    This website provides information related to assisting individuals to challenge sex discrimination in higher education and the workplace. It provides resources to inform people of their rights and connects them with finding legal help, but also provides financial and technical case support to balance the scales of justice for people working toward gender equity through the legal system.

McCrary, N. E., & Ross, E. W. (2016). *Working for social justice inside and outside the classroom: A community of students, teachers, researchers, and activists*. Peter Lang Publishing.
    This volume critically examines the relationship of education to capitalism and democracy by posing difficult questions, exposing inequities, and offering ideas for change.

National Education Association. (n.d.). *EdJustice*. NEA. https://neaedjustice.org/
   This website assists educators in advocating for social justice inside and outside their classrooms. It provides resources on a variety of topics including gender, race/ethnicity, LGBTQ, and the criminal justice system.

REFERENCES

American Association of University Professors. (2014). *Contingent appointments and the academic profession*. AAUP. https://www.aaup.org/report/contingent-appointments-and-academic-profession

Ashburn-Nardo, L., Blanchar, J. C., Petersson, J., Morris, K. A., & Goodwin, S. A. (2014). Do you say something when it's your boss? The role of perpetrator power in prejudice confrontation. *Journal of Social Issues, 70*(4), 615–636. https://doi.org/10.1111/josi.12082

Associated Press. (2011, October 9). *NYPD to investigate pepper spraying at protest*. CBS News. https://www.cbsnews.com/news/nypd-to-investigate-pepper-spraying-at-protest/

Bandura, A., Barbaranelli, C., Caprara, G. V., & Pastorelli, C. (1996). Multifaceted impact of self-efficacy beliefs on academic functioning. *Child Development, 67*, 1206–1222. https://doi.org/10.2307/1131888

Brook, R. H., Keeler, E. N., Lohr, K. N., Newhouse, J. P., Ware, J. E., Rogers, W. H., Davies, A. R., Sherbourne, C. D., Goldberg, G. A., Camp, P., Kamberg, C., Leibowitz, A., Keesey, J., & Reboussin, D. (2006). *The health insurance experiment: A classic RAND study speaks to the current health care reform debate*. RAND Corporation. https://www.rand.org/pubs/research_briefs/RB9174.html

Byrne, D., & Nelson, D. (1965). Attraction as a linear function of proportion of positive reinforcements. *Journal of Personality and Social Psychology, 1*(6), 659–663. https://doi.org/10.1037/h0022073

Campbell, T. A., & Campbell, D. E. (1997). Faculty/student mentor program: Effects on academic performance and retentions. *Research in Higher Education, 38*, 727–742. https://doi.org/10.1023/A:1024911904627

Case, K., Kanenberg, H., Erich, S., & Tittsworth, J. (2012). Transgender inclusion in university non-discrimination statements: Challenging gender-conforming privilege through student activism. *Journal of Social Issues, 68*(1), 145–161. https://doi.org/10.1111/j.1540-4560.2011.01741.x

Cortina, L. M. (2004). Hispanic perspectives on sexual harassment and social support. *Personality and Social Psychology Bulletin, 30*(5), 570–584. https://doi.org/10.1177/0146167203262854

Eagly, A. H., Wood, W., & Chaiken, S. (1978). Causal inferences about communicators and their effect on opinion change. *Journal of Personality and Social Psychology, 36*(4), 424–435. https://doi.org/10.1037/0022-3514.36.4.424

Eliezer, D., & Major, B. (2012). It's not your fault: The social costs of claiming discrimination on behalf of someone else. *Group Processes & Intergroup Relations, 15*(4), 487–502. https://doi.org/10.1177/1368430211432894

Festinger, L., & Carlsmith, J. M. (1959). Cognitive consequences of forced compliance. *Journal of Abnormal and Social Psychology, 58*(2), 203–210. https://doi.org/10.1037/h0041593

Gasman, M., Nguyen, T., & Conrad, C. F. (2015). Lives intertwined: A primer on the history and emergence of minority serving institutions. *Journal of Diversity in Higher Education, 8*(2), 120–138. https://doi.org/10.1037/a0038386

Gutiérrez y Muhs, G., Niemann, Y. F., González, C. G., & Harris, A. P. (Eds.). (2012). *Presumed incompetent: The intersections of race and class for women in academia*. Utah State University Press.

Hanasono, L. K., Broido, E. M., Yacobucci, M. M., Root, K. V., Peña, S., &, D. A. (2019). Secret service: Revealing gender biases in the visibility and value of faculty service. *Journal of Diversity in Higher Education, 12*(1), 85–98. https://doi.org/10.1037/dhe0000081

Harwarth, I., Maline, M., & DeBra, E. (1997). *Women's colleges in the United States: History, issues, and challenges*. National Institute on Postsecondary Education, Libraries, and Lifelong Learning. https://files.eric.ed.gov/fulltext/ED409815.pdf

Hill-Zuganelli, D., & Sergent, F. T. (2018). Strengthening the sanctuary: Institutional policies to support DACA students. In S. E. Weissinger & D. A. Mack (Eds.), *Law enforcement in the age of Black Lives Matter: Policing Black and Brown bodies* (pp. 97–116). Rowman & Littlefield.

Hochschild, J. L. (1995). *Facing up to the American dream: Race, class, and the soul of the nation*. Princeton University Press.

Hovland, C. I., & Weiss, J. (1951). The influence of source credibility on communication effectiveness. *Public Opinion Quarterly, 15*(4), 635–650.

Kaiser, C. R., & Miller, C. T. (2001). Stop complaining! The social costs of making attributions to discrimination. *Personality and Social Psychology Bulletin, 27*(2), 254–263. https://doi.org/10.1177/0146167201272010

Mack, D. (2005). "Ain't gonna let nobody turn me around": Berea College's participation in the Selma to Montgomery March. *Ohio Valley History 5*(3), 43–62.

Nadal, K. L. (2018). *Microaggressions and traumatic stress: Theory, research, and clinical treatment*. American Psychological Association.

National Academies of Sciences, Engineering, and Medicine. (2018). *Sexual harassment of women: Climate, culture, and consequences in academic sciences, engineering, and medicine*. The National Academies Press. https://doi.org/10.17226/24994

Singh, R., Wegener, D. T., Sankaran, K., Singh, S., Lin, P. K. F., Seow, M. X., Teng, J. S. Q., & Shuli, S. (2015). On the importance of trust in interpersonal attraction from attitude similarity. *Journal of Social and Personal Relationships, 32*(6), 829–850. https://doi.org/10.1177/0265407515576993

Strada–Gallup. (2018). *Strada–Gallup alumni survey: Mentoring college students to success*. Gallup. https://news.gallup.com/reports/244031/2018-strada-gallup-alumni-survey-mentoring-college-students.aspx

Williams, W. R. (2014). No yellow tickets: The stigma of poverty in the school lunch line. In C. Collins, J. Ladd, & F. Yeskel (Eds.), *Class lives: Stories from across our economic divide* (pp. 48–52). Cornell University Press.

Williams, W. R. (2016, October). The free-tuition debate: Promises and possibilities. *The SES Indicator, 9*(3). http://www.apa.org/pi/ses/resources/indicator/2016/10/free-tuition.aspx

Wood, J. L., Hilton, A. A., & Nevarez, C. (2015). Faculty of color and White faculty: An analysis of service in colleges of education in the Arizona public university system. *Journal of the Professoriate, 8*(1), 85–109.

13
CONTEMPORARY ISSUES IN TERMINOLOGY

Using Gender-Inclusive Language to Create Affirming Spaces

AMANDA J. WYRICK

The environment of the classroom is a sacred and transformative space. It is a space of asking students to grapple with big questions, tolerate intellectual discomfort, and express their ideas in scholarly ways. But what happens when students feel as though their very identity is not included in this space? Will students find motivation and risk intellectual vulnerability when they feel disconnected from the classroom? In my roles as a professor and a Safe Zone trainer, my experiences indicate that the answer to these questions is "no." In discussing the dilemma of how to create inclusive spaces, I draw on experiences of people's gender identities as a window into the broader issue of how to create these spaces for people with complex identities of all kinds. Throughout the chapter, I most often use the term "trans" as an inclusive term for individuals who have gender identities that are different from the sex assigned at birth. While this is the term I use in the chapter, it is necessary to remember language is an ever-evolving process, and terminology usage is an intimate part of a person's identity; therefore, one should always respect the terminology used by a specific individual.

---

https://doi.org/10.1037/0000216-013
Navigating Difficult Moments in Teaching Diversity and Social Justice, M. E. Kite, K. A. Case, and W. R. Williams (Editors)
Copyright © 2021 by the American Psychological Association. All rights reserved.

The dilemma of creating inclusive spaces for trans people is part of a larger conversation about professors encountering individuals with a variety of gender identities inside and outside their classrooms. Professors may also face colleagues and administrators who push back against trans-affirming practices. It is necessary to question the individuals and structures that hinder progress and recognize that we may find ourselves in environments where change is not welcome. While this is critical to the conversation of trans inclusivity, this chapter will focus on specific changes in professors and their interactions with students. Though not focused on pushing our colleagues to change, there may be information in the current chapter about classroom spaces that can be used to conceptualize change at the institutional and collegial level.

When working with students, the question of how to create inclusive spaces exists at two levels. On the macro level, the question takes the form of creating syllabi and campus policies that affirm a range of student identities. On the micro level, this question addresses how an individual professor navigates the classroom space using best practices in lectures and student interactions. A professor may also think about maneuvering supervisory and advising roles in gender-affirming ways. Although best practices and knowledge of gender-affirming terminology may feel overwhelming at first, at the core of affirmation for trans students is respect for, and use of, the name and pronouns that match their identity (Pryor, 2015). With that being said, it is also important to consider the vulnerability and risk for professors when shifting their classrooms to trans-inclusive spaces.

In my journey as an educator, I was not always proactive about inclusive classroom design for trans students. When I obtained Safe Zone certification, I had little awareness about the variety of gender identities and the myriad of policies trans students encountered that devalued their sense of self. As is typical when we develop an awareness of an issue, I then noticed the many ways I perpetuated these systems of oppression by not pushing my thinking or challenging institutional blockades that prohibited full trans inclusivity. I still find myself searching for a balance between affirming my students' demands for inclusivity with my belief that slow, methodical movements gain the most traction with college administrators. In fact, when I sit in meetings where preferred pronouns and inclusive housing are seen as radical ideas by faculty, staff, and administrators, I can better understand why students feel that campus culture and policies are not advancing at an acceptable speed.

After several semesters of facilitating Safe Zone trainings and advocating for institutional change, I regularly hear from students and professors about campus incidents that discriminate against or exclude awareness of trans identities. For example, one student was misgendered the entire semester because she did not feel safe in correcting her professor. In another incident, a professor continued to call a trans student by their[1] dead name (i.e., the legal name given at birth that no longer matches their identity) because the professor insisted on using the legal name on college record for class and email communication. When I hear of these reports, I feel both a sense of anger and humility. I want to push professors to honor what I consider the fundamental dignity of another human, while also recognizing that I still make mistakes with pronoun usage. In those moments, I do feel vulnerable and criticize myself because I am supposed to be one of our "campus experts." I also feel the discomfort of cognitive dissonance when I espouse to advocate for trans students and yet still feel a sense of unease when I fear students will complain on course evaluations about my use of gender-inclusive content (see Boysen, Chapter 17, this volume).

In the United States, gender is often seen in essentialist terms, the belief that there is something fundamentally different between women and men (Prentice & Miller, 2006), which leaves little room for discussion of other gender identities. In turn, gender essentialism makes it difficult to then change our binary thinking and language. Even though this change can be difficult, the attention to language, policies, and classroom practices is vital to the well-being of students. In moments of error, it is helpful to find support, campus or beyond, that can normalize mistakes, affirm efforts to change, and provide resources for the constant growth that is required to support students with trans identities.

FACULTY REFLECTION

In the past, I sometimes allowed my beliefs about gender to seep into the classroom and perpetuate stereotypes, thereby negatively influencing the felt sense of belonging and emotional health of my students. Over the years, however, I've learned that trans identities can be supported in the classroom if we actively work against conscious and unconscious classroom and cultural norms that discount the core identities of trans students. These classroom and cultural norms are shaped by genderism, the stigmatization against nonbinary gender expressions rooted in the belief that sex and gender are congruent and immutable characteristics (Hill & Willoughby, 2005). The

---

[1] As per American Psychological Association Style guidelines, the use of the pronoun "their" is intentional in this instance. The student identified outside the gender binary and used "their" as the pronoun congruent with identity. In this chapter, each use of "their" to refer to a single individual reflects the student's pronoun.

following section will cover how gendered language influences the well-being of students and the role of genderism in our classrooms.

Belonging, Mental Health, and Language

Before class began on the first day, a quiet student made their way to the front of the room and asked me a mumbled question. I quickly ascertained that the student wanted me to call them by a different name than was listed on the roster. As soon as I stated that students would be able to introduce themselves to the class by the name that matches their identity, the student breathed a sigh of relief and expressed their appreciation. Only in the last few years did I realize this is an affirming practice for trans students. These small moments are reminders of the importance of language for validation of identity and a sense of belonging and connection in the classroom. Research demonstrates that trans students rate their sense of belonging on campus as lower than their peers (Dugan et al., 2012). When trans students are asked about improving their campus climate, they first and foremost list the need for faculty and staff training about issues such as terminology, pronouns, and increasing inclusivity (Goldberg et al., 2019).

Professors need to recognize that the use of affirming and congruent identity language is an essential component of the social transition process for trans youth and young adults. Research even suggests that when trans youth can use the congruent name in multiple contexts, including educational settings, rates of depressive symptoms and suicidal ideation decrease (Russell et al., 2018). This is particularly important given that in a survey of transgender adults, 40% reported making a suicide attempt, and 92% of these individuals made the attempt before the age of 25 (The Trevor Project, n.d.). It is also important to note that although educational research most often focuses on issues of identity development in traditional college-aged populations, validating an individual's true self positively impacts mental health no matter the age.

How Genderism Shapes the Classroom

If members of an institution know the benefits of inclusive language for trans persons, improving the practice of affirmation requires an understanding of why the change in language is often difficult. I believe this adaptation is as much about changing a larger mindset as it is about using language. In fact, the act of addressing contemporary issues in terminology is a process that shifts and evolves to represent the ideas and identities of the culture accurately.

For example, before I attended the Safe Zone facilitator training, I was unaware of the term *omnigender*, meaning that a person's identity encompasses all genders. Given that it may be challenging to master all terminology, a professor can commit to a mindset that opposes genderism instead of focusing exclusively on the memorization of changing terminology.

One way to combat genderism is by understanding the difference between sex and gender. Essentially, sex is the biological anatomy that traditionally leads to identification as a male, female, or intersex body. It is worth mentioning that the term *intersex*, which is meant to denote sexual characteristics that are neither strictly male nor female, can feel categorical and limiting to the acknowledgment of a continuum of sexual identity. *Gender* refers to the social construction of behaviors that are typically prescribed for only two categories (boy/man, girl/woman; Unger, 1979). Even with the knowledge of sex and gender differences, rigidity around gender can still exist. For example, I know individuals who are committed to diversity yet adhere to the belief that individuals should use the bathroom that matches their physical anatomy instead of their gender identity.

There is growing societal recognition and acceptance of gender as existing on a continuum. As such, individuals may experience more freedom in expressing gender outside of traditional norms; thereby, a professor may encounter students pushing back against the gender binary through dress, language, and advocacy for inclusive resources. For example, a professor may interact with a student who could be culturally identified as a "man" wearing feminine attire and makeup. Students may also push back against traditional gender norms that are represented in text and film or advocate for the inclusion of gender-nonconforming voices in class materials. Finally, students may feel more empowered to use language identifiers such as genderqueer, gender nonconforming, or gender fluid. When professors encounter student challenges to genderism, it is vital to remain open to hearing student feedback and meeting students from a place of unbiased acceptance of gender expression to foster greater classroom inclusivity (see Kite et al., Chapter 4, this volume).

Recently I received feedback about my use of the terms *female body* and *male body* in my effort to distinguish physical characteristics from gender identity. One student pushed back and stated they did not perceive their body as female or male. This was a pivotal moment for me in reducing my own bias. This moment helped me realize that even though I was trying to help students understand the distinction between sex and gender, I boxed students into a dichotomy of physical anatomy. It also challenged me to move beyond the idea that an individual would always use their physical characteristics for sex identification even if science uses this anatomical distinction. After discussing more with this student, I will now use language that denotes anatomical patterns that correspond to female, male, and intersex identities while acknowledging that intersex may truncate the continuum of sex identification.

CONTEXTUAL FACTORS IN THE CLASSROOM

In the context of the classroom, professors must recognize that students have varying degrees to which they believe gender-inclusive language is necessary and relevant to classroom lectures. It is our role as professors to teach to all of our students; thus we must hold student development in awareness during the navigation of the difficult, but necessary, practice of using affirming language for trans students. Within this space, understanding the utility of the transtheoretical model and motivational interviewing can be helpful in meeting educational goals of affirming trans identities and reaching all students in the course.

Transtheoretical Model and Motivational Interviewing

The transtheoretical model is helpful as a professor considers how to navigate a student's readiness for change. While this section will focus on using these strategies in a classroom, the information may also be useful for professors to think about their own readiness for change, as well as the readiness of their colleagues and institutions. As a professor prepares lectures and interacts with students in the classroom, one should remain aware that individuals progress through a series of stages when confronted with the idea that a change in action and/or belief is warranted (Prochaska et al., 1995). Individuals begin at precontemplation, where they are unaware that a problem exists. Secondly, individuals enter into contemplation, where they are aware that a problem exists but feel ambivalent about making a change. Individuals may then progress to preparation and then finally to action, where they are in the process of making the change (Prochaska et al., 1995).

As individuals progress through stages, the concept of motivational interviewing can assist professors in creating classroom dialogue and activities that match an individual's stage of change. In the context of change, "motivation is a *state* of readiness or eagerness to change, which may fluctuate from one time or situation to another. This state is one that can be influenced" (Miller & Rollnick, 1991, p. 14). Thus, the goal of motivational interviewing is to assist an individual in developing personal motivations for change instead of persuading them that change is necessary (Miller & Rollnick, 1991). At its essence, motivational interviewing is about recognizing and reducing resistance while emphasizing an individual's identified motivations for change.

When I infuse my classroom with gender-inclusive language, I inhabit the space as if students are in the precontemplation stage. Professors may find that students in this stage minimize the importance of trans inclusivity, rationalize their use of binary language, or place blame on trans individuals for not conforming to social norms. At this stage, the most effective technique to enhance readiness for change is to raise consciousness (Prochaska et al., 1995). Becoming aware of trans identities and gender-inclusive language, in a supportive relationship with a professor, increases the chance for movement beyond precontemplation. For those students who are in advanced stages, either considering or actively making changes in their language, my classroom practices are meant to act less like motivators for change and more as a means to establish myself as an ally to trans students.

When there is a more specific instructional focus on topics of diversity and gender, special attention to the creation of the classroom environment is warranted. For example, when teaching topics of diversity, professors can engage students in dialogue, have a clear focus for student change (e.g., decreasing genderism), and evoke the ideas, perspectives, and motivations for change from students (Venner & Verney, 2015). In addition, it is of utmost importance to maintain respect for student autonomy using language such as, "I invite you to consider the topics along the way and see what you make of it" (Venner & Verney, 2015, p. 119). It may initially feel counterintuitive to move with, instead of against, a student's resistance, but ultimately the perceived acceptance of the professor facilitates a student's movement toward change.

CONTEXTUAL FACTORS

One contextual factor that impacts institutional progress, in particular, is the inclusion, or lack thereof, of nondiscrimination policies that include gender identity. Institutions that hold more politically conservative beliefs and/or have a strong antitrans religious identity are least likely to offer protections for members of the trans community. In this section, I will focus most specifically on how attention needs to be paid to the intersection of religious affiliation and nondiscrimination policies.

Nondiscrimination Policies

I teach at an institution with a Christian identity. My institution does include gender identity in the nondiscrimination policy, thus giving me additional authority when speaking about the importance of affirming language. Other religious-affiliated or politically conservative institutions may offer less support for faculty and staff about gender identity inclusion or actively work against the affirmation of trans identities. It may be the case that without an antidiscrimination policy, peers at these institutions actively engage in bullying and harassment against trans students (Rockenbach & Crandall, 2016). Also, some religious institutions have Title IX exemptions that allow them to discriminate against students based on sexual orientation and gender identity. From my perspective, this makes it even more critical that classroom spaces infuse a sense of belonging by including gender-inclusive language and practices.

When students or colleagues argue antitrans religious perspectives, I consistently fall back on the institution's nondiscrimination policy. For example, during one Safe Zone training, a staff member asked me what to do about individuals who believe that nonbinary identities are against God's will. I find the most effective approach is to say that individuals are certainly allowed their beliefs; what they are not allowed to do is use language and actions to create a harassing and discriminatory environment for trans students (Warner, Chapter 16, this volume). For institutions that do not include gender identity in the nondiscrimination policy, faculty and students may choose to partner together and advocate for change. Some strategies for effective change include building campus relationships where open and honest communication can occur about the need for gender-identity inclusion, educating individuals about trans identities and myths, and creating a support network to process and stay committed to the goal of policy change (Case et al., 2012). The addition of gender identity to a nondiscrimination policy can take extensive work and may even fail; however, the use of partnerships across campus to honor the trans community is vital work.

INTERSECTIONALITY

When addressing trans inclusivity, it is important to be aware of the intersections among our identity categories, as well as the identity categories of trans students. These social identities serve to organize our experiences of the world and have emergent properties not recognized in any one identity alone (Shields, 2008). In this section, I will first address the ways my social identities influence my work as an educator and trans ally. Then I will address the identity category of ethnicity and the importance of culture-specific language.

Personal Identity

My intersectional identity categories that show up in my work are those of being cisgender, White, and agnostic. I am aware that gender-inclusive language is easier for me because I have a cisgender identity, privileging me to present information about trans identities as facts and not be perceived as a marginalized person putting forth an agenda. In addition, because I am agnostic, I have to be careful to avoid quickly rebuffing any questioning of trans identities that are rooted in a religious context. Finally, the privilege of my whiteness protects me from a full understanding of the ethnic context of trans marginalization. I can intellectually understand that ethnic identity may change one's understanding of their gender identity; however, I cannot speak to the specific experiences of individuals with marginalized ethnic identities. What I can do is ensure that my classroom lectures and presentations include diverse representations of trans identities and the complexity of inclusion. This includes being mindful of the ethnic identities of my students and culture-specific language used to describe gender identities.

Ethnic Identity

During my first Safe Zone training, an African American colleague pointed out that I did not consider the intersection of ethnicity and gender identity. Without discussions of such intersections, one could interpret that all families respond to loved one coming out as trans in similar ways. As a result of this challenge by my colleague, I committed myself to learn more. When I immersed myself in the literature, it became apparent that research on intersectionality most often focuses on "nonnormative identities" (Shields, 2008, p. 305), which in this case means non-White identities. In studies that do make whiteness overt, it is usually in the context of examining a different oppressed social identity. For example, one research article looked at the varying levels of maternal acceptance among a predominately White sample from Central Appalachia (Aaron & Rostosky, 2018). Thus, much of the research is silent on the issue of the intersection between whiteness and trans identities.

Given the nondominant conceptualization of ethnicity and intersectionality, the Human Rights Campaign offers information and resources that specifically highlight only marginalized ethnic groups. For example, one cultural consideration for some Latinx individuals as they decide to come out is the concept of *familismo*, or dedication and loyalty to family. This cultural norm may pressure Latinx individuals to conform to the hopes of their families who may not accept trans identities. Furthermore, the concept of *machismo* may dictate binary gender norms, leaving little room for gender-nonconforming identities (Human Rights Campaign, 2019a).

Beyond coming out, interconnected forms of discrimination may impact the well-being of trans individuals. For example, 90% of African American LGBTQ youth report experiencing discrimination (Human Rights Campaign, 2019b). Discriminatory policies and biases against African Americans impact their ability to fully explore and navigate their gender-nonconforming identities (Human Rights Campaign, 2019b). Conversely, it is important to recognize the resilience of trans youth of color. One study found that trans youth of color employ resilience strategies such as self-defining gender and racial identities and developing self-advocacy skills (Singh, 2013). As professors, we can commit to affirming trans identities by simultaneously working to dismantle systems of oppression while recognizing individual and cultural strengths.

Culture-Specific Language

Another cultural consideration directly relates to gender-inclusive language. Professors need to be aware that some cultures have specific language to describe trans identities. For example, some Indigenous communities use the term *two-spirit* for gender-variant individuals. Although I can present this information in Safe Zone trainings or class discussions, I acknowledge that this language is culture-specific and can be considered cultural appropriation if used by non-Indigenous people. It does not mean that one cannot use this language as an identifying descriptor of others but one should not take this label for one's own identity or even assume this is the language identifier that an Indigenous person would use. If I have more time, I can allow for additional discussion on the impact of cultural entitlement and language as a way to exert or remove power from a group of individuals. For example, I would encourage students to think about how "stealing" language elevates the dominant culture by allowing them the benefit of the language without the prejudicial views that impact nondominant cultures.

BEST PRACTICES

When considering best practices for gender-inclusive language, it is important to give thought to implementation at both the interpersonal and institutional levels. Student support at the classroom level and not the institutional level, or vice versa, is less effective at mitigating the negative consequences of trans exclusion. Depending on the institution, a professor may find it necessary to prioritize interpersonal change. As is standard advice for interactions with students of marginalized identities, I urge professors to gather individual information about their trans students, yet not use those students as authorities on gender. The following best practices are meant as starters for knowledge and implementation of ideas.

Affirming Names and Pronouns

Many professors work at an institution that embraces trans identities and allows students to have the appropriate name recorded on official documents, such as a classroom roster. Professors at other institutions need to think about how to affirm names and pronouns in their interactions. This affirmation of student identity becomes particularly important when considering college-bound LGBTQ youth. Statistics find that only 27% feel they can be themselves in school, as few as 13% report hearing positive messages about their identity from their school, and a mere 26% report feeling safe in the classroom (Kahn et al., 2018).

One way to affirm names and pronouns is to practice public self-identification. As stated above, I do not call roll on the first day of class. When students introduce themselves, I simply ask that they also use their last name in their introduction to find them on the roster. Furthermore, trans undergraduate and graduate students suggest that faculty maintain an attitude of openness and acceptance and ask for names and pronouns but suggest that asking for these in front of the class may not be the best option (Goldberg et al., 2019). A recent opinion piece from *Inside Higher Ed* suggests that this practice may inadvertently create more distress for trans students (Levin, 2018). The article suggests that asking individuals to share their pronouns in the classroom setting is essentially asking them to make a decision to either lie or come out as trans in a space where they have yet to assess their safety fully.

To communicate inclusivity, while protecting the trans student's coming-out process, I state that if a student wishes to share identity pronouns with me after class, I will make sure to note them for use that semester. Alternatively, professors may email all students in the course before the first day of class and ask for any changes that should be made to names on the official roster and ask for personal pronouns that fit the identity of the student. Finally, I include my personal pronouns on the syllabus and have a statement of inclusivity, which includes the following: "Finally, all people in this classroom have the right to be addressed and referred to in accordance with their personal identity. This means I will work to ensure you are addressed by the name and pronouns with which you identify." I feel this statement allows students to immediately know that I recognize and support gender-inclusive practices in my classroom.

Singular *They*

One of the more discussed aspects of moving beyond gendered language is the use of the singular *they*. Airton (2018) outlined how the singular *they* is already used in Standard English when the speaker does not know the gender identity of a person (e.g., "Someone left a note on my door, but I don't know who they are"). Therefore, the leap to using the singular they only happens when referring to someone who is known to us. Although some individuals feel *he or she* is the most grammatically correct option for a singular, genderless antecedent, historical text suggests that the singular *they* has been used pervasively as a third-person singular pronoun (LaScotte, 2016).

Scholars advocate that the use of the singular *they* respects and honors all genders, is less cumbersome than *he or she*, and avoids the sexism associated with the generic masculine *he* (LaScotte, 2016). The most recent edition of the *Publication Manual of the American Psychological Association* (American Psychological Association, 2020) recommends using the "singular 'they' to refer to a person who uses 'they' as their pronoun" (p. 120). Additionally, the manual states the singular "they" is used when the gender of a person is unknown or not relevant to the current context. The *MLA Handbook* (Modern Language Association, 2016) and *The Chicago Manual of Style* (University of Chicago Press, 2017) do not yet fully support the use of the singular *they*. As professors, it is important to engage in critical conversations about language, identity, and grammar. Although the MLA and Chicago manuals may change with more acceptance of the singular *they*, each manual currently offers alternatives to the practice to be used for classroom assignments and for honoring personal pronouns. In addition, professors may refer to *The Associated Press Stylebook* (Associated Press, 2019) as a reference for including the singular they in formal writing.

Teaching the Concept of Genderism in Research

My identity of being cisgender gives me a significant amount of privilege when I walk into my classroom. For many semesters of teaching, this privilege meant it never occurred to me that the majority of research I cited in course lectures exclusively used gender binary terms of male/female, boy/girl, or men/women. Although research in many fields works to include more diverse samples, it is often the case that studies which do not focus exclusively on trans identities either do not report information on these identities or the sample size is too small to account for significant differences. I currently incorporate a mini-educational lesson on gender identity at the beginning of the semester to inform students that when I present results on men and women, I am using research that most often does not collect gender identity data beyond asking people to choose male or female. Given this practice, we often do not know the percentage of trans participants, but we can safely assume it would be a small number; therefore, most research results are talking about individuals who are cisgender. I explain the concept of cisgender and inform the students that when research includes a diverse representation of gender identities, I will include that information. This lesson typically takes no more than 5 minutes and is not course-specific.

Using Gender-Inclusive Language in Lecture

Professors can affirm trans identities largely through an awareness of the ways genderism is perpetuated through everyday language. For example, instead of saying "husband" or "wife" use the terms "spouses" or "partners." Also, the word "children" can be used to replace "boys and girls" and "siblings" instead of "brothers and sisters." With relatively small changes such as these, the professor moves beyond the assumption of gender binaries. In my Introductory Psychology course, I recognized I was using gendered language when teaching about "maternal" health and risk factors. Upon reflection of this practice, I made an inherent assumption that the individual carrying the child has a gender identity of "woman." Now I simply talk about health factors related to the "individual" carrying or birthing the child and discuss briefly with my class why I use this language.

Reducing Genderism in Communication

Another place to consider genderism is in classroom and institutional communications. Some common practices that assume the gender binary when the individual is unknown to us are to address emails as "Dear Sir or Madam" or including pronouns when giving directions such as "the student should upload his or her _____." Instead, an individual could address an email to "Dear Colleagues" or "Dear members of _____." Additional practices include dropping the pronouns when they are not necessary, such as "Please upload the _____" or using the singular they "the student should upload their _____." Writing in the plural also reduces genderism in communication. When an individual's name is known, it is common practice to use Mr., Ms., or Mrs. to communicate formality. One alternative is to use the gender-neutral title Mx. although this term is not recommended as common usage unless it is indeed the title selected by the individual (Airton, 2018).

Another option is to drop the pronoun once again and address the correspondence using the individual's first and last name (chosen name is used if known or available via institutional databases) such as "Dear Amanda Wyrick."

Creating Inclusive Surveys

When collecting data, professors and administrators can also consider whether sexual orientation and gender identity are relevant to data collection. For example, employers and researchers should think about the rationale for asking the question; employers should consider how the questions relate to diversity goals of the institution and finally how that data will be stored and protected (Human Rights Campaign, 2016). If the researcher or employer decides to collect the information, then it is necessary to be inclusive in category descriptions. Furthermore, the survey should clearly delineate between sexual orientation (i.e., to whom one is sexually attracted) and gender identity (i.e., an individual's psychological understanding of their identity) given that these are two separate identity components. Every survey designer may choose to include different terminology; however, it is better to use "prefer to self-describe" as the open category descriptor rather than using the term "other" (Human Rights Campaign, 2016).

RESOURCES

Campus Pride. https://www.campuspride.org/tpc/
   This website is an invaluable resource for professors who want to make a change at the institutional level. The site provides resources for topics such as advocacy and activism, athletics, leadership, and religion. Each topic area addresses trans identities as part of the larger LGBT umbrella. In addition, readers can find specific trans policies for colleges and universities.

GLSEN. https://www.glsen.org
   This website is primarily dedicated to K–12 education, but it can provide college professors with informative articles on topics such as pronouns, curriculum, and news stories. This is particularly useful for professors in education departments.

Guidelines for Psychological Practice With Transgender and Gender Nonconforming People (American Psychological Association [APA], 2015). https://www.apa.org/practice/guidelines/transgender.pdf
   In 2015, the APA revised practice guidelines for Transgender and Gender Nonconforming clients. These guidelines provide information for professors who teach or practice in the clinical field. In addition, the guidelines include information on research and educational practices.

Human Rights Campaign. https://www.hrc.org/resources/topic/transgender
   This website offers up-to-date legislative news regarding LBGTQ communities. For professors, the most relevant part of the website is "Resources." Within this section of the website, there are tips for allies and college campuses that include information on trans identities. Professors can also navigate to specific trans resources.

Safe Zone Train-the-Trainer Toolkit. https://thesafezoneproject.com/ttt
   The Safe Zone project hosts workshops and allows for the download of curriculum and activities to create programming.
University of Louisville LGBTQ Center. http://louisville.edu/lgbt/trans-uofl
   This center strives to create an inclusive and welcoming campus and provides resources to students and staff. The center is an example of institutional support that earned the University of Louisville a five-star rating from Campus Pride. Specific information about trans policies are also included.

REFERENCES

Aaron, A., & Rostosky, S. S. (2018). Transgender individuals' perceptions of maternal support in Central Appalachia. *Journal of GLBT Families, 15*(1), 1–21.

Airton, L. (2018). *Gender: Your guide. A gender-friendly primer on what to know, what to say, and what to do in the new gender culture.* Adams Media.

American Psychological Association. (2015). Guidelines for psychological practice with transgender and gender nonconforming people. *American Psychologist, 70,* 832–864. https://doi.org/10.1037/a0039906

American Psychological Association. (2020). *Publication manual of the American Psychological Association* (7th ed.).

Associated Press. (2019). *The Associated Press stylebook.* Basic Books.

Case, K. A., Kanenberg, H., Erich, S. A., & Tittsworth, J. (2012). Transgender inclusion in university nondiscrimination statements: Challenging gender-conforming privilege through student activism. *Journal of Social Issues, 68*(1), 145–161. https://doi.org/10.1111/j.1540-4560.2011.01741.x

Dugan, J. P., Kusel, M. L., & Simounet, D. M. (2012). Transgender college students: An exploratory study of perceptions, engagement, and educational outcomes. *Journal of College Student Development, 53*(5), 719–736. https://doi.org/10.1353/csd.2012.0067

Goldberg, A. E., Beemyn, G., & Smith, J. Z. (2019). What is needed, what is valued: Trans students' perspectives on trans-inclusive policies and practices in higher education. *Journal of Educational & Psychological Consultation, 29*(1), 27–67. https://doi.org/10.1080/10474412.2018.1480376

Hill, D. B., & Willoughby, B. L. B. (2005). The development and validation of the genderism and transphobia scale. *Sex Roles, 53*(7–8), 531–544. https://doi.org/10.1007/s11199-005-7140-x

Human Rights Campaign. (2016). *Collecting transgender-inclusive gender data in workplace and other surveys.* https://www.hrc.org/resources/collecting-transgender-inclusive-gender-data-in-workplace-and-other-surveys

Human Rights Campaign. (2019a). *Black and African American youth report.* https://www.hrc.org/resources/black-and-african-american-lgbtq-youth-report

Human Rights Campaign. (2019b). *Coming out: Living authentically as LGBTQ Latinx Americans.* https://www.hrc.org/resources/coming-out-living-authentically-as-lgbtq-latinx-americans

Kahn, E., Johnson, A., Lee, M., & Miranda, L. (2018). *2018 LGBTQ youth report.* Human Rights Campaign. https://www.hrc.org/resources/2018-lgbtq-youth-report

LaScotte, D. K. (2016). Singular they: An empirical study of generic pronoun use. *American Speech, 91*(1), 62–80. https://doi.org/10.1215/00031283-3509469

Levin, R. (2018, September 19). *The problem with pronouns*. Inside Higher Ed. https://www.insidehighered.com/views/2018/09/19/why-asking-students-their-preferred-pronoun-not-good-idea-opinion

Miller, W. R., & Rollnick, S. (1991). *Motivational interviewing: Preparing people to change addictive behavior*. The Guilford Press.

Modern Language Association. (2016). *MLA handbook for writers of research papers* (8th ed.).

Prentice, D. A., & Miller, D. T. (2006). Essentializing differences between women and men. *Psychological Science, 17*(2), 129–135. https://doi.org/10.1111/j.1467-9280.2006.01675.x

Prochaska, J. O., Norcross, J. C., & Diclemente, C. C. (1995). *Changing for good: A revolutionary six-stage program for overcoming bad habits and moving your life positively forward*. Avon Books.

Pryor, J. T. (2015). Out in the classroom: Transgender students experiences at a large public university. *Journal of College Student Development, 56*(5), 440–455. https://doi.org/10.1353/csd.2015.0044

Rockenbach, A. N., & Crandall, R. E. (2016). Faith and LGBTQ inclusion: Navigating the complexities of the campus spiritual climate in Christian higher education. *Christian Higher Education, 15*(1–2), 62–71. https://doi.org/10.1080/15363759.2015.1106355

Russell, S. T., Pollitt, A. M., Li, G., & Grossman, A. H. (2018). Chosen name use is linked to reduced depressive symptoms, suicidal ideation, and suicidal behavior among transgender youth. *The Journal of Adolescent Health, 63*(4), 503–505. https://doi.org/10.1016/j.jadohealth.2018.02.003

Shields, S. (2008). Gender: An intersectionality perspective. *Sex Roles, 59*(5), 301–311. https://doi.org/10.1007/s11199-008-9501-8

Singh, A. A. (2013). Transgender youth of color and resilience: Negotiating oppression and finding support. *Sex Roles, 68*(11–12), 690–702. https://doi.org/10.1007/s11199-012-0149-z

The Trevor Project. (n.d.). *Facts about suicide*. https://www.thetrevorproject.org/resources/preventing-suicide/facts-about-suicide/#sm.0000mqc753vl5d91w222nk21jpuri/

Unger, R. K. (1979). Toward a redefinition of sex and gender. *American Psychologist, 34*(11), 1085–1094. https://doi.org/10.1037/0003-066X.34.11.1085

University of Chicago Press. (2017). *The Chicago manual of style* (17th ed.).

Venner, K. L., & Verney, S. P. (2015). Motivational interviewing: Reduce student reluctance and increase engagement in learning multicultural concepts. *Professional Psychology, Research and Practice, 46*(2), 116–123. https://doi.org/10.1037/a0038856

14

AGING AS AN ELEMENT OF DIVERSITY

Best Practices for Challenging Classroom Conversations and Avoiding Ageism

LISA S. WAGNER, TANA M. LUGER, AND MATTHEW CALAMIA

Age represents a unique social/demographic category for educators to tackle. An inevitability of aging is that every person will progressively change membership into different age groups throughout their lifespan (e.g., childhood, adolescence, young adulthood, middle-aged, older adult). Yet, in spite of this shared experience, negative stereotypes of older people are very prevalent and become increasingly negative the older and frailer a person becomes (Hummert et al., 1994). It does not make logical sense that people are biased against a group that they will eventually join, yet ageism, or systemic prejudice against people due to their advanced age (Butler, 1969), is ubiquitous. The effects of ageism can be seen in employment, housing, health care decisions, and media and entertainment (Pasupathi & Löckenhoff, 2002).

    As instructors who teach courses related to aging, we vary in our experience addressing issues of ageism. Matthew is a clinical neuropsychologist whose research focuses on the assessment of cognitive functioning and neuropsychiatric symptoms in those with dementia or other neurocognitive disorders. He teaches a broad introduction to psychology course and more advanced courses on clinical assessment. Tana is a health psychologist

https://doi.org/10.1037/0000216-014
Navigating Difficult Moments in Teaching Diversity and Social Justice, M. E. Kite, K. A. Case, and W. R. Williams (Editors)
Copyright © 2021 by the American Psychological Association. All rights reserved.

whose research works to improve health care for special veteran populations, including older adults. Her teaching centers on health disparities across different elements of diversity. Lisa is a social psychologist whose research focuses on ageism, specifically stereotypes about older adults and how these affect people as they age. She teaches a range of traditional undergraduate psychology courses (e.g., social psychology) as well as courses related to aging and to prejudice. As coauthors of this chapter, we offer dilemmas that have arisen in our classrooms to illustrate our different perspectives and experiences in addressing ageism in social justice courses.

As a new professor, Matthew was focused on presenting course-related content in accurate and engaging ways. As his focus now turns to consider the nuances of his teaching, he recognizes that aging-related material in his courses is almost always connected to problems that can occur with age, sometimes labeled the "Devastating Ds" (i.e., death, dying, disease, disability, dementia, decline, and dependence; McGuire, 2017). He worries that presenting aging material as only related to these issues may reinforce students' stereotypes about aging. For example, after a special movie presentation of a popular film about Alzheimer's disease, undergraduate majors in psychology and allied health fields were given the opportunity to ask questions to a faculty panel. "Doesn't everyone get dementia eventually?" one student asked as others nodded in agreement. As evidenced by this example, Matthew has become increasingly concerned about whether including content about dementia in his courses inadvertently reinforces aging-related stereotypes, perhaps to the point that students begin to think that every older adult is cognitively impaired. Similarly, given the nature of his research, undergraduate students taking Matthew's research practicum course may primarily spend their time in settings where they encounter older adults who are experiencing some degree of memory or other cognitive impairment. This can also lead them to a distorted view of aging. Matthew at times finds it difficult to determine ways to teach accurate information about diseases related to aging while avoiding overgeneralizing negative aging-related course knowledge.

As a health psychologist, Tana's courses often spotlight ways to improve health and health care for everyone, including older adults, through various psychological, medical, and technological interventions. Her teaching focuses on health disparities related to various elements of diversity (e.g., race/ethnicity, sexual orientation, gender identity) across the lifespan and often draws students from the social sciences, public health, and medicine. To foster a respectful and inclusive classroom environment, Tana communicates her expectation that students support their assertions with evidence from the texts and their own experiences managing their health. Yet, even with careful preparation, ageist comments have occurred. Determining how and when to respond to these comments can be challenging. For example, through an academic-community partnership with local senior services, three older adults participated alongside traditional college-aged undergraduate students in Tana's seminar on health disparities. In the context of a discussion on gender identity, a younger student commented that "old people are set in their ways and not interested in updating their ideas about others." Glancing at the older adults in the room, the student's eyes grew wide upon realizing the ageist assumptions just made. "Well, not ALL older people . . ." the student sheepishly conceded. In this case, Tana felt fortunate that the student had the self-awareness to recognize the misstep and apologize (which the older adult students readily and gracefully accepted), but Tana wondered how she should have addressed the comment if the student had not been so self-aware or if there had not been older adults in the room to nudge the student toward greater reflection. Tana also wonders how she will navigate these challenges in the years ahead as she ages and the college-age students begin to see her as an older adult. Thus, Tana struggles to find effective strategies to address ageist comments from students in both mixed and age-segregated settings in ways that will promote age-healthy attitudes for everyone.

In Generation-to-Generation, Lisa's intergenerational discussion class, sets of two traditional college-aged and two retired older adults sit in small groups to discuss topical articles. Stereotypes about both older and younger people can arise, sometimes because a student's behavior unintentionally confirms a negative stereotype about their own age group (e.g., a younger adult who keeps checking a cell phone or an older adult who makes a prejudiced comment). When discussing an article on issues faced by people who are LGBT, an older adult commented, "There's nothing wrong with being homosexual, but I don't see why they have to be so blatant about it. I don't discuss my private life with other people, so I don't know why they should be so public with private issues." Younger students later reacted in private journal entries about how prejudiced they found the older adult's statement, but none of them said anything in person. In responding to these journal entries, Lisa asked the college-age students why they did not say anything to the older adult. Their response was that it would have been disrespectful to challenge an elder in that way. Given the complexities of attitudes toward older adults (e.g., we negatively stereotype them and yet also feel that we must respect them), Lisa struggles with helping students of all ages navigate challenging prejudiced comments while still respecting each other.

Aging is a process shared by all humans, yet it is not commonly discussed when examining difficult moments in teaching diversity and social justice.

We have expertise in aging-related issues, and yet all three of us are still challenged to present aging concepts and facilitate classroom interactions in ways that do not reinforce ageism. Given that instructors work within a society where ageism is prevalent as they themselves are aging, determining ways to address ageism in the classroom is an important tool for instructors to extend social justice to all age groups.

FACULTY REFLECTION

Although the American Psychological Association (2013) clearly identifies age as an element of diversity that should be a part of every undergraduate psychology curriculum, research on ageism is relatively rare compared with research on racism and sexism (Whitbourne & Montepare, 2017), and relatively few diversity-related or social justice–oriented courses incorporate aging as a factor for discussion. For example, the Teaching Tolerance (2018) website does not list aging or ageism among its nine diversity-related topics. It does have one aging-related activity, but one would need to search for "ageism" to find it. As a result, instructors may be less prepared to facilitate nuanced in-class discussions about aging and older adults.

Given the relative avoidance of aging as an element of diversity, instructors of social justice- and diversity-related issues may have limited knowledge about aging, may have ageist attitudes themselves, and may be uncomfortable facing their own aging. As instructors shift from being a young faculty member to being older, the difference between their age and their students' ages widens. Aware of negative stereotypes about aging, instructors may themselves face age-related stereotype threat as they worry that they could confirm stereotypes about older people (see Rios et al., Chapter 5, this volume). Instructors may also inadvertently promote ageism if they focus only on the negative aspects of the aging process or if they attribute their own missteps to age (e.g., "senior moments"). Additionally, most colleges and universities tend to be age-isolated; although some faculty and "nontraditional" students are older, the vast majority of the student population is comprised of younger adults and perhaps older community members auditing classes (Whitbourne & Montepare, 2017).

The lack of older adult representation and intergenerational communication on most campuses can be seen as a missed opportunity for higher education, given the number of positive effects of contact between generations. For younger adults who are able to connect with older people, intergenerational interactions such as service-learning programs have been found to promote a greater understanding of course concepts, reduce misconceptions about the aging process, improve attitudes toward older people, and increase interest in a career in elder services, a field which is facing significant workforce shortages (Roodin et al., 2013). For older adults, intergenerational contact has been found to positively affect physical and mental well-being, including a general higher quality of life. In the classroom, interacting with few older adults can create a situation where instructors and students inadvertently perpetuate ageism as outlined in our classroom scenarios. Yet, instructors also have the opportunity to use age as an exemplar social category to illustrate concepts of prejudice in a less "hot-button" topic than race/ethnicity or sex/gender (see Best Practices below).

CONSIDERATIONS OF CONTEXT AND INTERSECTIONALITY

In Lisa's intergenerational class, most older adults are White, and two thirds of younger adults are students of color. This can lead the younger students to think that the older students have all lived privileged lives and have no experience with prejudice. When Lisa pointed out that some of her oldest students have concentration camp tattoos from the Holocaust, the younger students were shocked and reflected on the obvious, yet important, lesson not to judge a book by its cover. Similarly, Matthew grew up in Louisiana and teaches at a university where nearly 70% of the undergraduate students identify as White and over 80% are from the state of Louisiana. When discussing his own state, he noticed that some students do not at first appreciate the influence of factors such as racial segregation on an older adult's life experience. These examples highlight the importance of intersectionality when considering age and prejudice. Perhaps one reason that ageism is not commonly included in courses on prejudice is because people tend to stereotype older adults as being White and wealthy. We work to address this stereotype by considering that (a) not all older adults are White, (b) intergenerational relationships are not the same across cultural groups, and (c) using a resilience framework is key.

Not All Older Adults Are White

When asked to picture a "senior citizen," many people visualize an older White man (Kite, 1996), yet older people in the United States reflect the full diversity of the population. Although the current U.S. older adult population is less racially diverse than the younger adult population, 25% of people over age 60 are members of an ethnic minority group (Mather et al., 2015). By 2060, this percentage will grow to almost half (45%) of the older adult population (Mather et al., 2015). Educating both students and faculty/staff about the diversity of the older adult population is an important step in countering ageism.

Intergenerational Relationships Are Not the Same Across Cultural Groups

Cross-cultural differences in the relationships between younger and older adults have been documented. Although Western (e.g., North American and Western European) adults may feel some responsibility for caring for their aging parents (e.g., opting to live close by or help with expenses), "filial piety" dictates that Asian adults also respect their parents' wishes, express gratitude, and bring them honor in the community (Kim et al., 2015). Although filial behaviors like living with a parent or showing obedience have declined in recent decades, there is still a strong expectation and endorsement of filial values within Asian and Asian American communities (Löckenhoff et al., 2015). Hispanic or Latinx cultures often have the same value of respecting elders through the commitment to *familismo* or intergenerational solidarity and obligation (Mehrotra & Wagner, 2018). In many indigenous cultures, respect for elders is also ingrained. For example, many Native Hawaiian and Pacific Islander cultures value intergenerational connections and relationships, including honoring the tradition of serving one's parents (Braun et al., 2004). Similarly, in many American Indian and Alaska Native cultures, the term "elder" does not just connote advanced age, but it also refers to a position of leadership (Hendrix, 2000). Of importance to classroom instruction, filial beliefs can affect intergenerational communication, with young adults from Asian cultures being less interested and comfortable conversing with older adults than Western young adults (Löckenhoff et al., 2015). It may be important for instructors to provide guidelines for intergenerational interactions in the classroom in order to support active participation from all students.

Other facets of identity, such as sexual orientation or gender identity, can also influence the experience of aging. LGBT older adults are more likely to live alone and less likely to have children than their heterosexual counterparts (Houghton, 2018). As a result, older LGBT community members often rely on a "chosen family" of friends or neighbors in addition to (or in place of) biological family contact. Students of all ages may take for granted having consistent social ties on which to call upon while aging. Class discussions might center upon the domains in which people help others across the lifespan (i.e., tangible, informational, and emotional supports), adaptation and resilience in aging, reasons for a lack of family support, and possible behaviors to prevent social isolation. LGBT older adults also face discrimination in elder housing (e.g., assisted living and nursing homes) and health care; this is especially the case for transgender seniors (Houghton, 2018). The National Resource Center on LGBT Aging (https://www.lgbtagingcenter.org) produces and hosts publications and multimedia which can be used to prompt discussion on these and similar topics; for example, *Gen Silent* (2011) is a 90-minute documentary that follows six LGBT older adults as they make decisions about their long-term care and health (see Resources).

Using a Resilience Framework Is Key

Finally, the resilience of older people must be an integral part of education about aging. There is a tendency in coursework to focus on problems in aging, like illness, disability, or dementia, which ignores the fact that many older adults demonstrate tremendous strength and resilience as they age (Pipher, 2019; Pruchno & Carr, 2017). Including a resilience perspective gives students a more nuanced view of aging. This is especially important for communities that have experienced lifelong, systematic inequalities yet persevere, such as older Black women (Baker et al., 2015) or LGBT older adults (Houghton, 2018).

BEST PRACTICES

As few students are exposed to aging as an element of diversity during their education, it may seem an immense task to introduce aging in a way that will present an accurate and nuanced portrayal of older adults and avoid ageism. Resources for instructors interested in incorporating such content do exist. In our experiences as instructors, we have developed and uncovered practices and activities to facilitate this goal.

Include Age as an Element of Diversity

In classes where there is no older adult representation, instructors can use the category of age to illustrate different concepts within prejudice, such as by having students identify examples of stereotypes and discrimination of older adults. Because there usually are no older adults in the room, students are often more comfortable talking about these examples than they may be about race/

ethnicity or sex/gender. A structured in-class activity could involve students completing an assessment of implicit or explicit ageism (see Resources) to gain additional insight into their own beliefs and prejudices toward aging. After fully examining the prejudice concepts using age, instructors can turn the discussion to the unique aspects of age, having students identify some possible effects of having prejudice toward a group that they will all become part of. Using age as a social category can help illustrate prejudicial concepts and allow students to consider how their own ageism may affect their treatment of their families and even themselves as they age. Including age in a social justice curriculum is an important step to counteract ageism.

Provide a Balanced View of Aging

Content related to aging is given minimal attention in textbooks in a number of fields and is often treated as a separate topic rather than fully integrated with other course material (e.g., Tompkins et al., 2006). The limited content can be heavily focused on pathology (e.g., Wellman et al., 2004), which may reflect biases in aging research that highlight disease and decline (e.g., cognitive decline in Alzheimer's disease; Whitbourne & Montepare, 2017). Providing a more balanced perspective involves going beyond the "Devastating Ds" of aging (McGuire, 2017). For example, Matthew makes a point in his classes of discussing ways in which cognitive and emotional functioning can change in positive ways as we age (e.g., continued increases in vocabulary knowledge and greater pursuit of emotion-related goals that can improve well-being). To provide a more accurate perspective, instructors should carefully select appropriate texts or find supplementary readings and resources. Instructors have an opportunity to correct myths and misperceptions; in fact, accurate knowledge of aging is associated with less ageism (e.g., Cherry et al., 2016). Discussion of both real-world examples and media portrayals of stereotypical and counter-stereotypical aging can avoid reinforcing the preexisting beliefs of some students that aging is the process of "falling apart," but balance is key. The tendency to highlight "super seniors" or those older adults who are extraordinarily active and engaged (like Senior Olympics competitors; Sweetland et al., 2017) can create a contrast between the abilities of "extraordinary" older adults and everyone else. This may lead people to believe that they or others are not aging well or successfully. It also erroneously suggests that personal choice (e.g., to exercise or take medications) is the sole determinant of aging well. In her classes, Tana encourages discussion of the broader social environment which facilitates health in order to reduce a sole emphasis on individual behavior, which can lessen blame for those whose abilities have declined.

Focus on Within-Group Variability

We recommend that instructors emphasize the significant variability and diversity of the older adult population in order to begin to dispel ageist stereotypes and beliefs in the classroom. Course content should highlight multiple aspects of aging, such as biological, cognitive, emotional, and social processes, to encourage students to view aging as a complex process with multiple trajectories (Association for Gerontology in Higher Education, 2014). Visual media and assignments that expose students to the myriad ways that older adults live, grow, and contribute to society can help achieve this goal. Tana introduces the topic of aging to her classes by presenting a photograph of a nonagenarian woman and describing her life and interests. Although the initial facts about the older adult are more in line with aging stereotypes ("She lives in a retirement community" and "She has multiple health conditions"), the students are often surprised to hear that she also "online dates" and takes ballroom dance lessons.

It is also important that instructors remind students not to make assumptions based on appearance or biological age. Tana's students are often also surprised when reminded that many judges and elected politicians are currently of advanced age and serve the public into their 80s (Katznelson, 2017). To introduce such topics as work, retirement, and political activism, a class activity could examine the biographies of a number of elected officials to place their actions in a lifespan context. As an example, Representatives John Lewis and Nancy Pelosi and Senators Dianne Feinstein, Orrin Hatch, and Chuck Grassley have all served multiple terms in Congress and represent a variety of political interests. Discussions around social norms for work and retirement can be inspired by encouraging students to consider the age at which public servants begin their political careers, term limits, and even the mental and physical capacity to serve. As previously mentioned, in Lisa's intergenerational class, younger students often make assumptions about the older students based on appearance (predominantly White). Yet ongoing discussions about life experiences and beliefs reveal that some older students are Jewish immigrants who survived the Holocaust, others are LGBT older adults who fought for civil rights in the 1960s, and still others were some of the first computer programmers (who are all women). Highlighting within-group variability helps students view older adults in a more nuanced and accurate way.

Do Advance Preparation for Intergenerational Discussions

In mixed-age classrooms, prejudiced statements may be made by both groups. Older adults may make prejudiced statements, as did the older adult who wanted people who are LGBT to hide their sexuality expressed in Lisa's classroom, or younger adults may make ageist comments as the student did in Tana's class. Responding to these situations can feel tricky as, despite ageism in society, there is also the value to respect elders. As with any type of prejudiced remarks, addressing the comment is important because silence may be viewed as agreement (Czopp et al., 2006). Some older adults may be unaware of contemporary terminology, inadvertently using terms that might be offensive to many groups. Similarly, younger adults may not be aware of how recently language convention has changed and may assume that the older person is being deliberately insulting. In Lisa's intergenerational discussion class, the issue of changing terms is discussed openly as it is eye-opening for all age groups to consider the ways that terms for some social categories have changed in the past 70 years. This often leads students to be more understanding when someone inadvertently uses an older term that has fallen into disfavor. Instructors will want to prepare an intergenerational class for discussions about these issues early so that students do not unintentionally use terms that are offensive to many. For example, the term "homosexual" was preferred for a while, was then avoided, and is now returning to favor among some groups. Similarly, it is important for younger adults to know that some of their preferred terms such as "queer," are often viewed negatively by older adults, even those who are LGBT.

Even with advanced preparation, students may make prejudicial comments about other age groups, as occurred in Tana's classroom. Coaching all students to appropriately challenge the negative behavior while valuing the person is important. Soliciting discussion "ground rules" from younger and older students during the first course sessions can bring an awareness of the concerns and values of the different age groups and encourage students of all ages to take responsibility for their contributions (see Goldstein, Chapter 2, this volume). The ultimate goal is to have both age groups engage in effective ally behavior toward each other.

Promote Meaningful, Nonstereotypical Intergenerational Contact

To decrease ageism, we do not need to reinvent the wheel but instead can consider strategies developed to decrease prejudice. Decades of research (see Pettigrew & Tropp, 2011) have suggested that optimal contact between two groups of people is required; optimal contact involves situational characteristics such as (a) equal status of the group members, (b) mutual interdependence of the members in the interaction, (c) acquaintance potential so that it is possible for ongoing relationships to develop, and (d) institutional support for the interactions. Many programs designed to promote intergenerational connections do not meet these conditions as they often have older adults serve as mentors to younger people or younger adults provide assistance to older adults. In this context, the two age groups do not have equal status within the interactions amid the context of existing societal power structures (e.g., certain age groups need to be helped). To combat ageism, we recommend programs developed for optimal contact, such as the intergenerational discussion class mentioned earlier. In this class, a topical news article is read weekly and discussed in small, mixed-aged groups. The groups also take two field trips outside of class together. Both older and younger adults reflect that the course changed their attitudes toward the other generation and gave them hope in the future. For example, in Lisa's class a young student who is lesbian expressed concern about sharing her sexual orientation with the older adults in her small group and was amazed to find that one of the older adults in her small group was gay and the other accepted her as well. Meaningful connections between the generations develop as the stereotypes decrease. Similarly, creating intergenerational interactions that highlight the strengths and challenges faced by both age groups may facilitate more nuanced understanding of the generations and of aging processes. For example, an intergenerational cooking class might highlight the expertise of older adults sharing familial food while recognizing the challenge in reading small print from a cookbook.

Instructors should model the aging process and how older people should be treated. If discussions of aging always focus on frailty and dependence, students will internalize these ideas. A more balanced approach toward aging and older people can be taught by including discussions of the resilience, strength, and life satisfaction that older adults demonstrate. With such careful instruction, younger people will have a more appropriate perspective regarding aging to bring to their careers, their families, and their own aging experience.

STRUCTURAL IMPLICATIONS

Although industrialized societies are aging rapidly, there has been a decline in the number of gerontology and geriatrics programs in U.S. higher education since 2000 (Pelham et al., 2012). While no definitive reason for this trend has been revealed, some sources hypothesize that the difficulty in attracting students to gerontology and geriatrics (whether due to a lack of interest in the population or prestige of the specialty) combined with shrinking university budgets has resulted in the closing of many programs (Glenn, 2010; Hafner, 2016). Similarly, other professional disciplines such as social work or nursing may cover some (but not exclusively) similar content, leading to the belief that a gerontology program duplicates already available instruction (Pelham et al., 2012). However, this shuttering of programs has resulted in fewer opportunities for students to obtain specific degrees and certifications (from associate to graduate) and minors or concentrations in aging. Similarly, this leaves students with few courses that incorporate aging as a factor for discussion. As mentioned previously, brief units on aging (such as the dementia film screening from Matthew's class described earlier) often focus on biological and cognitive decline, which can paint a stereotypical profile of older adults and ignore the significant variability in the aging process both within and between groups of people. Limited access to coursework and certifications in gerontology has implications for social health and well-being across the lifespan. Internalizing common negative stereotypes of aging can affect a person's self-perception, which, in turn, affects both physical and emotional functioning in later life (Levy, 2017).

The decreased availability of aging-related programs occurs at the same time that diversity-related courses do not include aging as an element of diversity. People interested in promoting social justice often do not consider the situation of older people as relevant to social justice issues. For example, in the fall 2018 election, an advertisement was created using older spokespersons to scare younger adults into voting by portraying older adults as selfish and uncaring about pressing issues such as climate change and school shootings (NAIL Communications, 2018). To see people who work on social justice issues respond to this ageist video with "Love it!!" on social media illustrates a failure to see the downsides of demonizing older people. Failing to recognize age and its intersections (e.g., race/ethnicity, gender, socioeconomic status) as an element of diversity and ageism as a pervasive social problem illuminates a significant blind spot in social justice work. Instructors can help to combat societal ageism by committing to challenging negative stereotypes of older adults and including nuanced aging content in their courses.

RESOURCES

Breytspraak, L., & Badura, L. (2015). *Facts on aging quiz*. http://info.umkc.edu/aging/quiz/

Implicit Association Test of Aging: https://implicit.harvard.edu/implicit/Study?tid=-1

    Instructors can use measures of implicit ageism (e.g., Implicit Association Test) or explicit ageism (e.g., Facts on Aging Quiz; see Breytspraak & Badura, 2015) as part of a structured in-class activity to gain additional insight into their and students' own beliefs and prejudices toward aging.

Goldstein, S. (2008). Activity 4.8: Culture and perceptions of growing old. In *Cross-cultural explorations: Activities in culture and psychology* (2nd ed., pp. 137–140). Pearson.

    Goldstein's learning activity examines different cultural perceptions about aging and growing old.

McGuire, S. L. (2017). Aging education: A worldwide imperative. *Creative Education, 8*(12), 1878–1891. https://doi.org/10.4236/ce.2017.812128

McGuire describes the need for aging education and the importance of fighting ageism. The article also provides excellent educational resources.

National Resource Center on LGBT Aging: http://www.lgbtagingcenter.org

The National Resource Center on LGBT Aging provides materials and media that can be used to prompt discussions on issues for older people who are LGBT. For example, the film *Gen Silent* (2011) mentioned earlier is available through this center.

REFERENCES

American Psychological Association. (2013). *APA guidelines for the undergraduate psychology major: Version 2.0.* http://www.apa.org/ed/precollege/undergrad/index.aspx

Association for Gerontology in Higher Education. (2014). *Gerontology competencies for undergraduate and graduate education.* https://www.aghe.org/images/aghe/competencies/gerontology_competencies.pdf

Baker, T. A., Buchanan, N. T., Mingo, C. A., Roker, R., & Brown, C. S. (2015). Reconceptualizing successful aging among Black women and the relevance of the strong Black woman archetype. *The Gerontologist, 55*(1), 51–57. https://doi.org/10.1093/geront/gnu105

Braun, K. L., Yee, B. W. K., Browne, C. V., & Mokuau, N. (2004). Native Hawaiian and Pacific Islander elders. In K. E. Whitfield (Ed.), *Closing the gap: Improving the health of minority elders in the new millennium* (pp. 55–67). The Gerontological Society of America.

Butler, R. N. (1969). Age-ism: Another form of bigotry. *The Gerontologist, 9*(4), 243–246. https://doi.org/10.1093/geront/9.4_Part_1.243

Cherry, K. E., Brigman, S., Lyon, B. A., Blanchard, B., Walker, E. J., & Smitherman, E. A. (2016). Self-reported ageism across the lifespan: Role of aging knowledge. *International Journal of Aging & Human Development, 83*(4), 366–380. https://doi.org/10.1177/0091415016657562

Czopp, A. M., Monteith, M. J., & Mark, A. Y. (2006). Standing up for a change: Reducing bias through interpersonal confrontation. *Journal of Personality and Social Psychology, 90*(5), 784–803. https://doi.org/10.1037/0022-3514.90.5.784

Glenn, D. (2010, November 21). Despite an aging population in U.S., fewer programs are training gerontologists. *The Chronicle of Higher Education.* https://www.chronicle.com/article/Despite-an-Aging-US/125461

Hafner, K. (2016, January 25). As population ages, where are the geriatricians? *New York Times.* https://www.nytimes.com/2016/01/26/health/where-are-the-geriatricians.html

Hendrix, L. (2000). Health and health care for American Indian/Alaska Native elders. In G. Yeo (Ed.), *Core curriculum in ethnogeriatrics* (2nd ed., pp. 1–57). Stanford Geriatric Education Center.

Houghton, A. (2018). *Maintaining dignity: Understanding and responding to the challenges facing older LGBT Americans.* AARP Research. https://doi.org/10.26419/res.00217.001

Hummert, M. L., Garstka, T. A., Shaner, J. L., & Strahm, S. (1994). Stereotypes of the elderly held by young, middle-aged, and elderly adults. *Journal of Gerontology, 49*(5), 240–249. https://doi.org/10.1093/geronj/49.5.P240

Katznelson, G. (2017, November 28). Reflecting on dementia and democracy: America's aging judges and politicians. *Bill of Health*. http://blog.petrieflom.law.harvard.edu/2017/11/28/reflecting-on-dementia-and-democracy-americas-aging-judges-and-politicians/

Kim, K., Cheng, Y. P., Zarit, S. H., & Fingerman, K. L. (2015). Relationships between adults and parents in Asia. In S. Cheng, I. Chi, H. H. Fung, L. W. Li, & J. Woo (Eds.), *Successful aging* (pp. 101–122). Springer Dordrecht.

Kite, M. E. (1996). Age, gender, and occupational label: A test of social role theory. *Psychology of Women Quarterly, 20*(3), 361–374. https://doi.org/10.1111/j.1471-6402.1996.tb00305.x

Levy, B. (2017). Age-stereotype paradox. *The Gerontologist, 57*(Suppl. 2), S118–S126. https://doi.org/10.1093/geront/gnx059

Löckenhoff, C. E., Lee, D. S., Buckner, K. M., Moreira, R. O., Martinez, S. J., & Sun, M. Q. (2015). Cross-cultural differences in attitudes about aging: Moving beyond the East–West dichotomy. In S. Cheng, I. Chi, H. H. Fung, L. W. Li, & J. Woo (Eds.), *Successful aging* (pp. 321–337). Springer Dordrecht.

Mather, M., Jacobsen, L., & Pollard, K. (2015). Aging in the United States. *Population Bulletin, 70*(2), 1–19. https://www.prb.org/wp-content/uploads/2016/01/aging-us-population-bulletin-1.pdf

McGuire, S. L. (2017). Aging education: A worldwide imperative. *Creative Education, 8*(12), 1878–1891. https://doi.org/10.4236/ce.2017.812128

Mehrotra, C. M., & Wagner, L. S. (2018). *Aging and diversity: An active learning experience* (3rd ed.). Routledge. https://doi.org/10.4324/9781315628097

NAIL Communications. (2018, September 24). *Dear young people, don't vote* [Video]. YouTube. https://www.youtube.com/watch?time_continue=2&v=t0e9guhV35o

Pasupathi, M., & Löckenhoff, C. E. (2002). Ageist behavior. In T. D. Nelson (Ed.), *Ageism: Stereotyping and prejudice against older persons* (pp. 201–246). MIT Press.

Pelham, A., Schafer, D., Abbott, P., & Estes, C. (2012). Professionalizing gerontology: Why AGHE must accredit gerontology programs. *Geriatrics Education, 33*(1), 6–19. https://doi.org/10.1080/02701960.2012.638348

Pettigrew, T. F., & Tropp, L. R. (2011). *When groups meet: The dynamics of intergroup contact*. Psychology Press.

Pipher, M. B. (2019). *Women rowing north: Navigating life's currents and flourishing as we age*. Bloomsbury.

Pruchno, R., & Carr, D. (2017). Successful aging 2.0: Resilience and beyond. *The Journals of Gerontology: Series B, 72*(2), 201–203. https://doi.org/10.1093/geronb/gbw214

Roodin, P., Brown, L. H., & Shedlock, D. (2013). Intergenerational service-learning: A review of recent literature and directions for the future. *Gerontology & Geriatrics Education, 34*(1), 3–25. https://doi.org/10.1080/02701960.2012.755624

Sweetland, J., Volmert, A., & O'Neil, M. (2017). *Finding the frame: An empirical approach to reframing aging and ageism*. FrameWorks Institute. http://frameworksinstitute.org/assets/files/aging_elder_abuse/aging_research_report_final_2017.pdf

Teaching Tolerance. (2018). *Topics*. The Southern Poverty Law Center. https://www.tolerance.org/topics

Tompkins, C. J., Rosen, A. L., & Larkin, H. (2006). Guest editorial: An analysis of social work textbooks for aging content: How well do social work foundation texts prepare students for our aging society? *Journal of Social Work Education, 42*(1), 3–23. https://doi.org/10.5175/JSWE.2006.042110001

Wellman, N. S., Kondracki, N. L., Johnson, P., & Himburg, S. P. (2004). Aging in introductory and life cycle nutrition textbooks. *Gerontology & Geriatrics Education, 24*(3), 67–86. https://doi.org/10.1300/J021v24n03_06

Whitbourne, S. K., & Montepare, J. M. (2017). What's holding us back? Ageism in higher education. In T. D. Nelson (Ed.), *Ageism: Stereotyping and prejudice against older persons* (pp. 263–289). MIT Press.

15

OUTSIDERS TEACHING INSIDERS

How Instructors From Privileged Groups Can Effectively Teach About Diversity

SUSAN B. GOLDSTEIN

During the past semester, I have found myself explaining the term *Latinx* to students who identify as Hispanic, teaching about the risk and protective factors of immigrants' mental health to the children of immigrants, and discussing the logic of the Cherokee Nation's statement on Senator Elizabeth Warren's DNA ancestry test in a class with several Native American students in attendance. For each of these topics, I am an outsider teaching to insiders. I wonder, how do I best acknowledge and value the lived experiences of my students and at the same time contribute my own, more academic knowledge—particularly when I am doing so through a privileged lens?

FACULTY REFLECTION

In instances such as those just described, I am often reminded of an episode of the PBS *Nova* series entitled "Anthropology on Trial." In one segment, a Belgian anthropology professor is haltingly teaching from note cards on the

---

https://doi.org/10.1037/0000216-015
Navigating Difficult Moments in Teaching Diversity and Social Justice, M. E. Kite, K. A. Case, and W. R. Williams (Editors)
Copyright © 2021 by the American Psychological Association. All rights reserved.

topic of Melanesian kinship systems to a class of Melanesians. Afterward, the students explain that this situation places them in the bizarre position of acting as outsiders relative to their own society—posing questions about Melanesians to the professor, writing papers based on published sources that don't ring true to them—when they are in fact insiders with valuable experiences and knowledge. I sometimes wonder if I am taking a role similar to that professor and question my own qualifications for teaching about groups of which I am not a member. Even more concerning, I wonder if I am placing my students in the position of outsiders and failing to appreciate the perspectives they bring to the discussion.

There is much controversy over what Mayberry (1996) termed "teaching what you're not" in a book by the same name. This situation becomes particularly sensitive when the instructor identifies with a privileged group, such as when White faculty teach African diaspora studies, male faculty teach women's studies, or heterosexual/cisgender faculty teach courses on LGBTQ+ issues. Such instances have been the subject of vigorous debate among scholars and in some cases have spurred student protests (Fowler, 2003). This is a complex matter. Is it appropriate for me as a White, Jewish, middle-class, heterosexual, cisgender, disabled woman to teach about the topics mentioned in the above dilemma? Is it even appropriate for me as a physically disabled woman to teach about other aspects of disability that I have never personally experienced, such as Deaf Culture?

Certainly, disciplinary training enables all faculty, regardless of social identity, to offer students rich information on validated models with which to frame their experiences and observations. For example, with knowledge of the cognitive processes involved in stereotyping, students can identify common sources and consequences of categorization across social groups. Still there is great value in having personal experience that relates to the content of our courses. bell hooks (1994) stated, "I share with the class my conviction that if my knowledge is limited, and if someone else brings a combination of facts and experience, then I humble myself and respectfully learn from those who bring this great gift" (p. 89). Even though research shows little difference in how diverse scholars envision the mission of their academic disciplines, personal experiences may influence how faculty engage with text, develop research questions, and are perceived by and relate to students (Rojas & Byrd, 2012; Thompson, 2000).

Students from marginalized groups often voice a desire for instructors whose identity aligns with the subject matter (Morgan Consoli & Marin, 2016), and these preferences create pressures that have had a positive impact on efforts to recruit and hire diverse faculty (Fowler, 2003). Yet placing responsibility for diversity courses on faculty from nondominant groups creates an unfair burden. In addition to assuming a high level of insider knowledge as a function of group membership and potentially limiting teaching opportunities (Tuitt et al., 2009), this practice puts those who "teach what they are" at greater risk for difficult classroom dynamics and harsher student evaluations (Brooms & Brice, 2017; Schueths et al., 2013) because they may be perceived as having an agenda or teaching out of self-interest rather than scholarship (Barnett, 2013; Messner, 2000).

In some respects, teaching beyond one's identity is a matter of degree. It would be nearly impossible to only address content dealing with one's own race/ethnicity, gender, sexual orientation, social class, and so on. In fact, historically, the tendency to do just that has resulted in significant limitations in academic disciplines, such as a lack of diversity among research participants, scholars, and topics of study (Medin, 2017) and the focus on "WEIRD" (Western, Educated, Industrialized, Rich, and Democratic; Henrich et al., 2010) societies in psychology. As student populations are increasingly diverse and instructors strive for greater inclusivity and allyship in their courses, teaching as outsiders becomes an imperative. Yet the complexity of doing so is amplified when the instructor is teaching from a position of privilege, which can shape course content, pedagogy, and classroom dynamics, or when members of the class are insiders (Case, 2013). For me, this results in considerable apprehension about being an outsider teaching insiders, but also an excitement about the ways that doing so can contribute to the inclusivity and diversity of my courses.

CONSIDERATIONS OF CONTEXT AND INTERSECTIONALITY

For faculty seeking to effectively teach about diversity as outsiders, it is important to consider the impact of their own unique and multiple identities and that of their students. The social identities of faculty outsiders may dictate the manner in which they share their expertise. The social identities of student insiders may shape the nature and presentation of course content.

The Outsiders

As Davis et al. (2015) explain, "*who* we are has an impact on *what* we teach and *how* we teach it" (p. 303). For example, Gregory Fowler (2003), a Black male scholar, describes how he and Marjorie Podolsky, a White female scholar, structure their African American literature classes differently based on their own racial identification. Whereas Fowler states that he finds himself refraining from "any desire to assert [his] authority based on personal experience" (p. 254), Podolsky, as an outsider, downplays her role as an expert and instead relies heavily on text, film, and other insider voices.

Furthermore, among outsiders, how to approach teaching from privilege may depend in part on one's own intersectional positionality and the forms of privilege one possesses (Wise & Case, 2013). For example, it is often recommended that instructors be transparent in class about their own challenges with coming to understand the implications of their social power (see Best Practices later in the chapter). Yet students may appraise such behaviors more favorably when enacted by White male faculty, who are often assumed to be competent unless proven otherwise, whereas those with marginalized identities may be at greater risk of having their expertise challenged as a result of disclosing instances of bias (Brooms & Brice, 2017; Messner, 2000). Intersectional identities such as older age and disability, for example, may negate the assumption of competence that accompanies white privilege (Fiske, 2012). For these faculty, it may be best to wait until a relationship has been established with students and to relate stories of emerging awareness of privilege with an emphasis on competence gained rather than personal failings.

The Insiders

The degree to which the identities of student insiders are represented in both the classroom and the larger society may have implications for how course topics that involve those identities might be discussed. For insider identities with limited representation, it is often helpful to adopt an intersectional lens and emphasize within-group diversity in presenting content concerning members of those groups. This may reduce insiders' concerns about being stereotyped and may also lessen their classmates' tendency to engage in stereotypic thinking. This is particularly critical when insiders are members of groups about whom most classmates have inaccurate perceptions and with whom few classmates have had close relationships, as is often the case with Native American students (McInnes, 2017). Instructors might also note that insider status is frequently ambiguous and that some insiders may be invisible in the classroom, such as those experiencing mental illness or homelessness. A more respectful pedagogical approach may emerge from acting as though there are always student insiders in the classroom, whether or not that is in fact the case.

BEST PRACTICES

Best practices for outsiders teaching insiders from a position of privilege focus on making this dynamic explicit. This involves interrogating one's own positionality and privilege as well as welcoming the voices of insiders into the classroom. These approaches require the instructor to be both vigilant and self-reflective.

Interrogating One's Own Positionality and Privilege

Despite the growing literature on the importance of teaching *about* privilege and oppression, there are few studies investigating strategies for teaching *from* a position of privilege (Davis et al., 2015), particularly on issues other than race/ethnicity. Effective teaching from a position of privilege requires an ongoing process of self-education and personal reflection, including an understanding of both the conscious and unconscious ways identity and power shape attitudes, beliefs, and behaviors (Smith et al., 2017). Spanierman et al. (2017) frame the relationship between expertise and self-reflection in terms of *cultural humility*. Although recently incorporated into models for the research, practice, and training of psychologists (Hook et al., 2013), Tervalon and Murray-García (1998) first coined this term in conjunction with the multicultural training of medical practitioners to emphasize the need to move beyond knowledge of multicultural content areas to incorporate a process oriented engagement with diversity. According to these authors, cultural humility involves a commitment to (a) ongoing self-evaluation and critique, acknowledging when additional resources are needed to interact effectively across cultures; (b) address power imbalances in interpersonal and intercultural interactions; and (c) develop partnerships with individuals and communities who advocate for the promotion of social justice systemically.

In this vein, several authors have advocated that instructors discuss their own intersectional identities with their classes and describe the challenges they have faced in recognizing their own forms of privilege. This can be done by acknowledging instances where assumptions were made based on a limited worldview and by relating personal stories of gaining awareness of and addressing unearned privilege (Davis et al., 2015, p. 305; Messner, 2011). Smith et al. (2017) characterize this process as "attempt[ing] to infuse our teaching with snapshots from our own development" (p. 661). For students, this act of self-disclosure models how they might interrogate their own positionality in a nondefensive manner and may allay concerns about negative reactions on the part of the instructor or classmates should the students choose to acknowledge their own social power (Davis et al., 2015; Sue et al., 2009; Wise & Case, 2013).

Interrogating one's own positionality and privilege also involves examining decisions about course content and pedagogy in that the selection of course materials, and topics may reflect experiences with power and oppression. For example, after I taught a unit on family configurations in my cross-cultural psychology course, a transgender student pointed out that I failed to include families of choice in the discussion. In doing so, I may have inadvertently sent a message to students about which identities are valid and valued (Davis et al., 2015).

Welcoming the Voices of Insiders

Instructors who are outsiders may struggle with how to be inclusive without speaking for or about others with experiences unlike their own (Peterson, 1996). One key strategy is to invite insider voices into the discussion. Certainly, students whose identity aligns with the course content should feel comfortable speaking about their experiences. Faculty can encourage all students to share their knowledge and experience as part of the collective learning process. Yet, it is critical that students not be placed in the position of spokespersons for a specific identity group in that such actions minimize ingroup variability, assume specific group knowledge, and create a situation in which students—often from nondominant groups—have the added burden of educating their classmates in addition to working toward their own academic success. In welcoming insider voices, faculty should also indicate that anecdotal information is viewed differently from and does not replace factual sources. Kite (2013) suggested informing students that while personal experiences can be used to illustrate a principle, they do not themselves serve as evidence.

Students of all backgrounds can be asked to identify insider perspectives as part of course assignments. Faculty should note, however, that it is somewhat contradictory to suggest to students that an academic literature is limited in terms of diversity and then require students to use that literature exclusively as a source for their research. Students can be encouraged to investigate sources across academic disciplines and then evaluate them based on such criteria as authors' qualifications and organizational affiliation, presence of valid and verifiable evidence for claims made, and presence of ideological or personal biases on the part of the author or sponsoring institution (see, for example, Blakeslee, 2004). Addressing this situation can be a good way to introduce issues of institutional and structural forms of privilege, such as the historical role of academic gatekeepers.

In addition to relying on student experiences and assignments for insider perspectives, these views can come from readings, films, guest speakers, and coteachers (Yoon et al., 2014). Even in these cases, however, it is important to emphasize to students that these may be single voices and should not be generalized to all members of an identity group. Insider perspectives can also emerge from classroom demonstrations and simulations. For example, Williams and Melchiori (2013) described a series of assignments and activities designed to teach social class privilege, regardless of the student's economic status. Much caution should be taken, however, with experiential learning activities that seek to convey an insider perspective by simulating some form of oppression or marginalization. For example, research has found that activities in which students undertake such tasks as navigating campus in a wheelchair or using a blindfold to simulate vision loss can produce fear, apprehension, and pity toward individuals with disabilities rather than empathy or understanding (Nario-Redmond et al., 2017).

Finally, insider voices may emerge from community engagement and service learning. Norvilitis (2010), for example, developed an action teaching project as part of a cultural psychology course in which student groups learn about the perspectives of diverse refugees by providing education about the U.S. financial system to local refugee families. Faculty can also build time into the class session for students to make announcements for relevant campus and community events and volunteer activities (Winkler, 1996). Williams and Melchiori (2013) emphasized the need for guided reflection in experiential learning so that students are able to frame their activities in terms of community action toward social justice rather than as charity toward individuals unable to help themselves.

STRUCTURAL IMPLICATIONS

The often-severe *emotional labor* experienced by those teaching diversity courses, particularly by faculty of nondominant groups, has been well documented (Miller et al., 2019; see also Rios et al., Chapter 5, this volume). Miller et al. (2019) defined emotional labor in an academic setting as "attending to students' needs beyond course content, both inside and out of the classroom, as well as addressing one's own emotional management and displays as a faculty member" (p. 493). Along with greater infusion of diversity across the curriculum and more widespread participation of faculty in teaching such courses, attention must be given to strategies for effective teaching from positions of privilege. Smith et al. (2017) coined the term *multicultural impostor syndrome* to refer to the anxiety and self-doubt that accompanies teaching about issues of privilege while still in the process of interrogating one's own privilege (see Warner, Chapter 16, this volume). These authors explained that for faculty in this situation, "the feeling of inevitability that surrounds [missteps in the multicultural classroom] can be paralyzing, even when we understand on an intellectual level that all individuals have biases to work through on a continuing basis" (p. 656). As part of providing support to faculty teaching courses on diversity and social justice, programs such as faculty development workshops, mentoring opportunities, and teaching circles that explicitly address issues of privilege should be designed (Barnett, 2013; Davis et al., 2015). Institutions can also support faculty efforts to bring diverse voices into the classroom by funding films, speakers, coteaching opportunities, and community connections. They can also provide travel funding to national and international conferences on diversity-related topics. With support and self-reflection, outsiders can effectively and respectfully teach about diversity and play a key role as social justice allies.

RESOURCES

Action Teaching. https://www.actionteaching.org/
These free classroom activities, field experiences, student assignments, and web-based resources are all recipients of the Social Psychology Network Action Teaching Award, which recognizes teaching materials that contribute to "peace, social justice, and sustainable living."

Davis, A., Mirick, R., & McQueen, B. (2015). Teaching from privilege: Reflections from White female instructors. *Journal of Women and Social Work*, *30*, 302–313. https://doi.org/10.1177/0886109914560742
The authors of this article, all White female social work instructors, reflect on their growing awareness of how privilege affects how and what they teach. They detail their practice of telling privilege stories in the classroom as a vehicle for modelling how students can explore their own relationships to social power.

Kite, M. E. (2013). Teaching about race and ethnicity. In D. S. Dunn, R. A. R. Gurung, K. Z. Naufel, & J. H. Wilson (Eds.), *Controversy in the psychology classroom: Using hot topics to foster critical thinking* (pp. 169–184). American Psychological Association.
This chapter makes recommendations for both content and pedagogical strategies in teaching about race and ethnicity. Kite first describes several concepts fundamental to an understanding of race and racism. She then details possible student reactions to this material and specific strategies for productive and reflective student engagement with issues of social justice.

Smith, L., Kashubeck-West, S., Payton, G., & Adams, E. (2017). White professors teaching about racism: Challenges and rewards. *The Counseling Psychologist, 45*, 651–668. https://doi.org/10.1177/0011000017717705
This article addresses personal and professional challenges faced by White faculty teaching social justice courses. Smith and colleagues discuss how these faculty can strive to develop a White antiracist identity despite dealing with self-doubt, student resistance, or a lack of colleague or administrative support.

Teaching Tolerance. https://www.tolerance.org/
A project of the Southern Poverty Law Center, Teaching Tolerance provides free classroom resources for antibias and social justice education. Although aimed at K–12 teachers, much of the material may be adapted for postsecondary use.

Teaching While White. https://teachingwhilewhite.org/being-an-ally
This site was designed to help teachers and students become racially literate and better understand the role of race and privilege in the classroom. It includes podcasts, student and teacher blog posts, and an extensive list of links to print resources.

REFERENCES

Barnett, P. E. (2013, Summer). Unpacking teachers' invisible knapsacks: Social identity and privilege in higher education. *Liberal Education*, *99*(3), 30–37. https://www.aacu.org/publications-research/periodicals/unpacking-teachers-invisible-knapsacks-social-identity-and

Blakeslee, S. (2004). The CRAAP Test. *LOEX Quarterly*, *31*(3), 6–7. https://commons.emich.edu/loexquarterly/vol31/iss3/4

Brooms, D. R., & Brice, D. A. (2017). Bring the noise: Black men teaching (race and) White privilege. *Race and Justice*, *7*(2), 144–159. https://doi.org/10.1177/2153368716689490

Case, K. A. (2013). Beyond diversity and Whiteness: Developing a transformative and intersectional model of privilege studied pedagogy. In K. A. Case (Ed.), *Deconstructing privilege: Teaching and learning as allies in the classroom* (pp. 1–14). Routledge. https://doi.org/10.4324/9780203081877

Davis, A., Mirick, R., & McQueen, B. (2015). Teaching from privilege: Reflections from White female instructors. *Journal of Women and Social Work*, *30*(3), 302–313. https://doi.org/10.1177/0886109914560742

Fiske, S. T. (2012). Managing ambivalent prejudices: The smart-but-cold, and the warm-but-dumb stereotypes. *The Annals of the American Academy of Political and Social Science*, *639*(1), 33–48. https://doi.org/10.1177/0002716211418444

Fowler, G. (2003). Racial dynamics in the classroom: A White female and a Black male discuss how race affects teaching and learning in an African American literature class. *American Studies*, *48*(2), 249–259. https://www.jstor.org/stable/41157826

Henrich, J., Heine, S. J., & Norenzayan, A. (2010). The weirdest people in the world? *Behavioral and Brain Sciences*, *33*(2–3), 61–83. https://doi.org/10.1017/S0140525X0999152X

Hook, J. N., Davis, D. E., Owen, J., Worthington, E. L., Jr., & Utsey, S. O. (2013). Cultural humility: Measuring openness to culturally diverse clients. *Journal of Counseling Psychology*, *60*(3), 353–366. https://doi.org/10.1037/a0032595

hooks, b. (1994). *Teaching to transgress: Education as the practice of freedom*. Routledge.

Kite, M. E. (2013). Teaching about race and ethnicity. In D. S. Dunn, R. A. R. Gurung, K. Z. Naufel, & J. H. Wilson (Eds.), *Controversy in the psychology classroom: Using hot topics to foster critical thinking* (pp. 169–184). American Psychological Association. https://doi.org/10.1037/14038-011

Mayberry, K. J. (Ed.). (1996). *Teaching what you're not: Identity politics in higher education*. New York University Press.

McInnes, B. D. (2017). Preparing teachers as allies in Indigenous education: Benefits of an American Indian content and pedagogy course. *Teaching Education*, *28*(2), 145–161. https://doi.org/10.1080/10476210.2016.1224831

Medin, D. L. (2017). Psychological science as a complex system: Report card. *Perspectives on Psychological Science, 12*(4), 669–674. https://doi.org/10.1177/1745691616687746

Messner, M. A. (2000). White guy habitus in the classroom. *Men and Masculinities, 2*(4), 457–469. https://doi.org/10.1177/1097184X00002004005

Messner, M. A. (2011). The privilege of teaching about privilege. *Sociological Perspectives, 54*(1), 3–13. https://doi.org/10.1525/sop.2011.54.1.3

Miller, R. A., Struve, L. E., & Howell, C. D. (2019). "Constantly, excessively, and all the time": The emotional labor of teaching diversity courses. *International Journal on Teaching and Learning in Higher Education, 31*(3), 491–502. https://www.researchgate.net/publication/334654510_Constantly_Excessively_and_All_the_Time_The_Emotional_Labor_of_Teaching_Diversity_Courses

Morgan Consoli, M. L., & Marin, P. (2016). Teaching diversity in the graduate classroom: The instructor, the students, the classroom, or all of the above? *Journal of Diversity in Higher Education, 9*(2), 143–157. https://doi.org/10.1037/a0039716

Nario-Redmond, M. R., Gospodinov, D., & Cobb, A. (2017). Crip for a day: The unintended negative consequences of disability simulations. *Rehabilitation Psychology, 62*(3), 324–333. https://doi.org/10.1037/rep0000127

Norvilitis, J. M. (2010). Financial education for refugees. *Action Teaching*. https://www.actionteaching.org/award/refugees

Peterson, N. J. (1996). Redefining America: Literature, multiculturalism, and pedagogy. In K. J. Mayberry (Ed.), *Teaching what you're not: Identity politics in higher education* (pp. 23–46). New York University Press.

Rojas, F., & Byrd, W. C. (2012). Intellectual change in Black studies: Evidence from a cohort analysis. *Journal of African American Studies, 16*, 550–573. https://doi.org/10.1007/s12111-011-9209-7

Schueths, A. M., Gladney, T., Crawford, D. M., Bass, K. L., & Moore, H. A. (2013). Passionate pedagogy and emotional labor: Students' responses to learning diversity from diverse instructors. *Journal of Qualitative Studies in Education, 26*(10), 1259–1276. https://doi.org/10.1080/09518398.2012.731532

Smith, L., Kashubeck-West, S., Payton, G., & Adams, E. (2017). White professors teaching about racism: Challenges and rewards. *The Counseling Psychologist, 45*(5), 651–668. https://doi.org/10.1177/0011000017717705

Spanierman, L. B., Poteat, V. P., Whittaker, V. A., Schlosser, L. Z., & Arévalo Avalos, M. R. (2017). Allies for life? Lessons from White scholars of multicultural psychology. *The Counseling Psychologist, 45*(5), 618–650. https://doi.org/10.1177/0011000017719459

Sue, D. W., Torino, G. C., Capodilupo, C. M., Rivera, D. P., & Lin, A. I. (2009). How white faculty perceive and react to difficult dialogues on race: Implications for education and training. *The Counseling Psychologist, 37*(8), 1090–1115. https://doi.org/10.1177/0011000009340443

Tervalon, M., & Murray-García, J. (1998). Cultural humility versus cultural competence: A critical distinction in defining physician training outcomes in multicultural education. *Journal of Health Care for the Poor and Underserved, 9*(2), 117–125. https://doi.org/10.1353/hpu.2010.0233

Thompson, D. A. (2000). Teaching what I'm not: Embodiment, race, and theological conversation in the classroom. *Teaching Theology and Religion, 3*(3), 164–169. https://doi.org/10.1111/1467-9647.00082

Tuitt, F., Hanna, M., Martínez, L. M., Salazar, M. D. C., & Griffin, R. (2009, Fall). Teaching in the line of fire: Faculty of color in the academy. *Thought & Action, 25*, 65–74. http://www.nea.org/assets/docs/HE/TA09LineofFire.pdf

Williams, W. R., & Melchiori, K. J. (2013). Class action: Using experiential learning to raise awareness of social class privilege. In K. A. Case (Ed.), *Deconstructing privilege: Teaching and learning as allies in the classroom* (pp. 169–187). Routledge.

Winkler, B. S. (1996). Straight teacher/queer classroom: Teaching as an ally. In K. J. Mayberry (Ed.), *Teaching what you're not: Identity politics in higher education* (pp. 47–69). NYU Press.

Wise, T., & Case, K. A. (2013). Pedagogy for the privileged: Addressing inequality and injustice without shame or blame. In K. A. Case (Ed.), *Deconstructing privilege: Teaching and learning as allies in the classroom* (pp. 17–33). Routledge.

Yoon, E., Jérémie-Brink, G., & Kordesh, K. (2014). Critical issues in teaching a multicultural counseling course. *International Journal for the Advancement of Counseling, 36*(4), 359–371. https://doi.org/10.1007/s10447-014-9212-5

16

WHEN STUDENTS FRAME PREJUDICIAL SPEECH AS "FREEDOM OF SPEECH"

Classroom and Institutional Implications

LEAH R. WARNER

In an introduction to social issues class, during a debate on transgender individuals' access to public bathrooms, a cisgender student (a person whose gender corresponds with sex assigned at birth), whom I will call "Bill," made a comment rejecting the legitimacy of transgender identities by saying, "This whole transgender thing is fake. You can't just ignore your sexual parts and claim you're a different gender just because you want to." Another cisgender student challenged the statement by saying that biological parts do not determine gender identity. A few other students muttered under their breaths, expressing surprise that Bill made the comment. Eyes also darted towards the sole out genderqueer student in the class, whom I will call "Sam." Sam remained silent throughout this discussion. Bill then said, "It's my right to free speech to say this. This class only allows liberal points of view." The debate ended with a situation in which other conservative students in the class shut down and Sam was visibly upset.

As an instructor, I faced a number of challenges in this dilemma. As part of this debate assignment, I instructed students to moderate the discussion with little to no intervention from me. My intention was to encourage students to take ownership over their learning; however, in this case, I realized that

https://doi.org/10.1037/0000216-016
Navigating Difficult Moments in Teaching Diversity and Social Justice, M. E. Kite, K. A. Case, and W. R. Williams (Editors)
Copyright © 2021 by the American Psychological Association. All rights reserved.

223

perhaps I should have intervened. I worried that these classroom dynamics could replicate patterns of oppression rather than fulfill my pedagogical goal of students learning to think critically about systemic oppression. Public bathrooms, predominately constructed in accordance with the gender binary, necessarily impact all who identify outside this binary. It pained me to see the impact of this debate on Sam. For other students in the class, the debate was an abstract exercise. But the debate personally impacted Sam's life, and, as I learned in a subsequent conversation, Bill's comment made Sam feel alone and rejected. Although Sam, who uses they/them pronouns, does not identify as transgender, they fall within the broader category of *gender variant*. Gender variant is an umbrella term that includes transgender, genderqueer, as well as additional labels for those who identify outside the binary of male or female sex assigned at birth (BrckaLorenz et al., 2017). I use this term because it refers to many identities at once; however, appropriate terms for transgender and nonbinary individuals vary over time and circumstance, and thus instructors should refer to updated resources for their own language choices (van Anders et al., 2019; see Wyrick, Chapter 13, this volume).

In addition to the negative impact on Sam, I worried that socially conservative students would close themselves off during the remainder of this class session. And, given that this incident occurred only a month into the semester, I wondered if they would resist engaging with the material for the rest of the semester. I felt a precarious balance in this class between allowing space for multiple perspectives, alongside my steadfast rejection of societal oppression. Once Bill declared that my classroom commitment to reject societal oppression "restricted his freedom of speech," I found that, rather than opening their minds to social justice, Bill and a few other students resisted the lessons in course readings and discussions during the remainder of the semester.

FACULTY REFLECTION

This dilemma highlights several challenges. First, issues of freedom of speech can arise in classroom discussions on controversial social issues. Second, the dilemma highlights the experiences of marginalized students when individuals use "free speech" to justify prejudicial comments. I use the term *marginalized* to convey that in college and university settings, systemic practices create underrepresentation and subordination of certain social groups; examples include People of Color, first-generation college students, immigrant students, and lesbian, gay, bisexual, transgender, and queer (LGBTQ) students. Third, the dilemma demonstrates the heightened consequences that students experience when inhabiting a solo status in the classroom. I begin by reflecting on these challenges and consider how context and intersectionality informs them. I then propose best practices for resolving the dilemma, which involves techniques within the classroom but also requires structural changes to institutions of higher education, particularly in the United States context where this dilemma occurred.

Understanding Students' "Freedom of Speech" Statements

Bill's claim about freedom of speech reflects two common reasons for using this phrase. First, Bill's invocation of "freedom of speech" reflects the American value of liberty, but perhaps without an understanding of the legal context of this concept. Students often do not understand the nature of constitutional protections, particularly when they mistakenly believe that the right not to be censored by the government also means that no one is allowed to morally condemn the speech acts of other people (Manne & Stanley, 2015). In addition, even if students do understand constitutional protections, colleges and universities' speech regulations sometimes operate differently from these protections (Chemerinsky & Gillman, 2017). Colleges and universities in the United States, especially those that are private, are often considered special-purpose institutions. This means that colleges and universities can design speech regulations to fit with the aims of the learning environment. Often, these institutions rely on student handbook codes of conduct, many of which contain antidiscrimination statements that restrict prejudiced speech. Note, however, that lawsuits and state legislative bills have recently challenged this reliance on student handbooks (Chemerinsky & Gillman, 2017). In contrast to institutions that contain antidiscrimination statements, some institutions, most often religiously affiliated, integrate explicitly anti-LGBTQ policies and statements, such as Biola University's Statement of Biblical Principles. Thus, speech environments vary from institution to institution.

A second way to interpret Bill's comment was that he used it to mask and justify prejudice against gender-variant individuals. Because people associate prejudice with irrationality and view it as socially undesirable in some contexts, a speaker may attempt to use a seemingly rational argument to appear nonprejudiced. For example, White and Crandall (2017) found explicit racial prejudice reliably predicted invocation of "freedom of speech" to endorse racist expressions. Notably, endorsement of freedom of speech did not occur for equivalent discriminatory statements toward other groups, such as police officers. Thus, although a person may convey "freedom of speech" as an expression of principle, at times prejudice drives the use of the phrase.

Considerations for Responding to "Freedom of Speech" Statements

In navigating ways to address "freedom of speech" statements, some paths appear clearer than others. When someone uses explicit bias to harm, such as a slur used against a social group, clear strategies exist, including reaffirming discussion ground rules (see Goldstein, Chapter 2, this volume). Strategies seem less clear for this dilemma where a student expresses an uninformed perspective that may result from prejudice. One common view contends that students need to express uninformed perspectives because the classroom allows them to workshop their ideas and productively engage with those who can help guide them to a more critical understanding (Boysen, 2012; Chemerinsky & Gillman, 2017). Consistent with this view, confronting ignorant speech does result in effectively lowering stereotypic responses and prejudiced attitudes of those who make the comment (e.g., Czopp et al., 2006).

A contrasting view emphasizes the importance of some speech regulations because the burden of free speech does not rest equally on all shoulders (e.g., Case, 2017; Manne & Stanley, 2015). I think about the additional burden that Sam experienced in the classroom. The assumption driving a "fight hate speech with better speech" approach implies that all people possess equal status as they discuss controversial ideas. Yet when the speech in question undermines the legitimacy of an entire marginalized group, such as perceiving transgender people as delusional, that marginalized group does not receive equal status to contribute to the discussion. In other words, when people perceive marginalized people as lacking the capacity to reason, even when they offer marginalized people the chance to speak, they ignore them. In this case, those who considered Sam's identity as illegitimate might have seen Sam as unable to be rational and logical in their responses to the debate.

Thus, even though other students in the classroom recognized gender-variant identities, Sam disproportionally received the emotional toll of others questioning their core identity, particularly as the only out gender-variant student in the class. Research on marginalized students confirms this dynamic that played out in my classroom. In a study on the effects of difficult dialogues on marginalized students, Students of Color reported strong disruptive emotions and depletion of psychic energy that affected their learning process (e.g., Sue et al., 2009). These negative consequences resulted from repeated hostile classroom dynamics. For example, students reported experiencing tokenism (Kanter, 1977), meaning that other students and faculty singled them out in discussions and asked them to speak on behalf of their entire racial group.

Additionally, unsupportive campus environments for marginalized students often accompany these classroom dynamics. For example, gender-variant students experience disproportionally higher rates of harassment relative to cisgender men and women, and even more so for gender-variant Students of Color (Rankin et al., 2010). This harassment most likely occurs in institutions without explicit policies to protect gender-variant individuals, given that approximately 3% of accredited U.S. institutions of higher education offer protective policies for gender identity and expression. Adding to these effects, college-age gender-variant students often experience identity development stages (e.g., coming out) that are particularly sensitive to campus climate (BrckaLorenz et al., 2017).

In sum, approaches to resolving this dilemma must take several factors into consideration at once. First, approaches must consider the student's "freedom of speech" claim, which requires the instructor to understand how constitutional protections apply to their institutions and also how individuals use "freedom of speech" to mask and justify prejudice. Second, approaches must acknowledge that marginalized students experience hostile dynamics often with solo status in the classroom and lack institutional support outside the classroom. Solutions need to successfully allow all students to engage critically with the course content on discrimination towards gender-variant and other marginalized individuals, while minimizing the negative consequences for these students within the classroom.

CONSIDERATIONS OF CONTEXT AND INTERSECTIONALITY

This dilemma occurred during a flashpoint moment in United States' discord over social issues: The election of Donald J. Trump as president of the United States. This pivotal moment, coupled with the intersections of identities for both individuals within my college and myself, created a particularly difficult set of circumstances for navigating this dilemma.

Post-Trump United States

Societal views about social issues change, and instructors need to place their course discussions within this wider context. In the United States, conflicts over free speech on college campuses have existed for generations (Chemerinsky & Gillman, 2017); however, these conflicts vary in form and in salience. The present dilemma occurred at a predominately White, liberal arts college in the northeastern United States during Donald J. Trump's presidential campaign. Within this context, issues related to speech restrictions gained nationwide attention. Individuals opposed to regulating "offensive" speech, for example, were more likely to support Trump (Conway et al., 2017). Postelection, White-majority Americans perceived an increased acceptability of prejudice toward social groups the Trump campaign targeted, such as Mexicans and people with disabilities (Crandall et al., 2018). Thus, this national context both increased the likelihood that students expressed explicitly prejudicial language in the classroom and resisted pedagogical techniques that challenge the use of this language (Nolan-Ferrell, 2017).

Instructor Identities

In addition to the national context, as a White female professor who identifies as queer, my identities affected the dynamics of the classroom. On the first day of class, I made my identities explicit while administering Circles of My Multicultural Self (Gorski, n.d.), a commonly used exercise in diversity courses to encourage students to reflect on their identities and to model openness to discussing social issues. Given that professors outing themselves can improve the climate for LGBTQ students (Rankin et al., 2010), knowledge of my queer identity potentially increased the comfort that my genderqueer student experienced in the classroom. At the same time, revealing one's sexual orientation should not by itself be equated with positively affecting climate for gender-variant individuals, given antitrans prejudice within queer communities (Weiss, 2004). Gender-variant students need additional support (e.g., BrckaLorenz et al., 2017).

Interaction Between Post-Trump U.S. and Instructor Identities

The openness that I expressed also affected classroom dynamics in less positive ways. Sharing my identity on day one led a student's parent to complain that I "should have kept my sexual orientation to myself." Notably, disclosing one's sexual identity can increase the risk of harassment of LGBTQ+ professors (Rankin et al., 2010). Also, professors from stigmatized groups experience the misconception that they act "biased" in favor of their ingroups (e.g., for People of Color; Littleford et al., 2010). Perceiving me as biased potentially contributed to students feeling like I restricted their speech, although my Whiteness potentially led (White) students to perceive me as more objective, at least with respect to race.

BEST PRACTICES

Although they formed a positive connection with me, Sam ended up leaving the college, in part due to interactions with other students such as those in our class. Incidentally, Bill also left the college after his first year. Although I do not believe this class debate contributed specifically to either of their exits, I took their exits as a sign that I needed to change how I taught this class. To that end, this dilemma strongly influenced my subsequent pedagogical approach, particularly in terms of my commitment to minimizing the harms for marginalized students and maximizing socially conservative students' engagement. Below I list some steps I have implemented to address the complexities within this dilemma.

Distinguishing Between Freedom of Speech and Civil Discourse

After the semester in which this dilemma took place, I changed my course to focus more squarely on civil discourse by spending an entire class session discussing readings on this topic (e.g., Linker, 2015). I now challenge students to think about the relationship between liberty and justice as values in the United States, and I observe that students find these discussions moving, particularly as they realize that they value both at the same time. Indeed, evidence from a college-aged sample in the United States suggested that students valued both freedom of speech and equal protections from harm (Cowan et al., 2002). In a separate study, students rejected hate speech without rejecting other types of objectionable speech, demonstrating that rejecting hate speech does not necessarily threaten freedom of speech in general (Harell, 2010). Several successful models exist for separating wounding comments from respectful disagreement in the classroom (see Lewis, 2017; Nolan-Ferrell, 2017).

Requiring Students to Rely on Evidence

Another way to address questions about "freedom of speech" is to ask students to support their arguments with evidence. They can say what they like, but they need to support their arguments with scientific research. In a classroom where students express concern about their freedom of speech, especially within a national context that normalizes prejudicial speech, instructors should encourage students to rely on empirical evidence for their arguments. Requiring students to utilize scientific evidence encourages critical reflection by determining whether or not arguments about diversity simply reinforce one's values (Landis et al., 2015). This requirement puts the onus on the students making the prejudicial statements to support their points, rather than on the targets of prejudicial statements to defend themselves. To be effective as a strategy, however, reliance on empirical evidence requires students to be trained in information literacy and to possess a trust in science. Faculty may need to first teach students how to find quality sources, and, given that political orientation determines trust in science (Gauchat, 2012), address that trust prior to engaging in controversial debates.

The Role of Instructor Intervention

When reflecting back on this dilemma, I question my lack of intervention. The structure of debate required the students leading the debate to respond to arguments, so I refrained from saying anything right away. But I believe I should have spoken after Bill made the comment about transgender people. Across studies, ignoring the statement or cutting off dialogue were the *least* effective techniques for responding to prejudicial statements (e.g., Boysen, 2012; Sue et al., 2009). Ignoring the comment only maintained the comfort of the biased student (Boysen, 2012), which is unproductive because student discomfort can lead to bias reduction (Czopp et al., 2006). Sue et al. (2009) cautioned professors against taking a passive approach and letting students take over the discussion. Studies on racial conflict in the classroom (Pasque et al., 2013; Sue et al., 2009) indicate that an active approach to managing the discussion produces better outcomes. This approach involves taking a series of steps, such as normalizing the conflict in the context of an inequitable society and acknowledging emotional reactions and potential biases of both students and instructors (Pasque et al., 2013). Taking these steps can prevent backlash that can occur from responding too harshly to a student who makes an ignorant comment (see Kite et al., Chapter 4, this volume).

Increasing Empathy and Recognizing Humanity

Our class discussion on that day lacked sense of care and respect for other students, and if I could go back in time and address the dilemma differently, I would have better integrated those elements into the class. In particular, I would have increased empathy (Linker, 2015) and awareness of the human impact of the discussion topic (for a model, see Nolan-Ferrell, 2017). To increase empathy and awareness of human impact, instructors can introduce students to marginalized people's personal narratives, such as through films or invited panels (Singh & Hughes, 2017). In addition, instructors can introduce students to marginalized groups' social justice actions and their resilience in the face of oppression. Exploring these strengths can counter problematic narratives, such as portrayals of gender-variant people as weak or damaged (Singh & Hughes, 2017). Lastly, instructors can facilitate students' recognition of others' humanity by counteracting dehumanization. Later that semester, when a student referred to immigrants as "illegal aliens," I directly addressed that comment. I wrote a list of labels for immigrants on the board and asked, "How are these different from each other?" The class emphasized that "alien" dehumanizes more than terms such as "migrant," and reflected back to previous class sessions on the consequences of dehumanization. We then thought about the terms for immigrants we heard in the news and in social media. This technique led fewer students to challenge or resist the lesson because I turned the comment into a general discussion for group reflection.

STRUCTURAL IMPLICATIONS

Even with best pedagogical practices in the classroom, elimination of consequences for marginalized groups is unlikely. Discussions on diversity will continue to disproportionately affect those who face systematic inequality. Further, best practices do not change the fact that gender-variant students, for example, often find themselves in the extreme minority in the classroom, nor do these practices address the hostile climate outside the classroom. Additionally, faculty who teach about controversial social issues need institutional support, especially if faculty themselves possess marginalized identities.

Institutional-Level Practices to Support Marginalized Students

Institutions of higher education should adopt best practices for marginalized students so that students' encounters with difficult discussions occur within a supportive environment. Research-supported comprehensive recommendations exist for supporting marginalized students (Hurtado et al., 2012) and for gender-variant students in particular (e.g., BrckaLorenz et al., 2017).

Institutional-Level Practices on Civil Discourse

Colleges can support discussions of civil discourse in the classroom by engaging in campus-wide efforts to address controversies over freedom of speech. Colleges can create clearer norms that free speech should not be a cover for hate speech. Recently, some colleges and universities developed speech environments that promote social justice (e.g., Morris, 2017). For example, democratic speech environments (Tinson & Benavente, 2017) promote justice-seeking conversations. These environments reframe claims of free speech by communicating that speaking on behalf of oneself is not the only purpose of speech. Instead, speech allows us also to engage across differences, demonstrate accountability for others, recognize how social inequality affects dialogue, promote solidarity, and effect change.

RESOURCES

Landis, K., Jenkins, P., & Roderick, L. (2015). *Start talking: A handbook for engaging difficult dialogues in higher education*. University of Alaska Anchorage.
   This comprehensive resource for instructors and institutions provides both individual classroom activities and institutional plans for facilitating civil discourse.

Lewis, L. C. (2017, November–December). Creating a civil classroom in an era of incivility. *Academe, 103*(6), 27–29. https://www.aaup.org/article/creating-civil-classroom-era-incivility#.XiSpundFw2w
   This author reflects on debates over freedom of speech and provides resources for teaching in a politically charged classroom.

Linker, M. (2015). *Intellectual empathy: Critical thinking for social justice*. University of Michigan Press.
   This resource provides students with many tools for discussing controversial social issues, with particular attention to respecting systemically marginalized groups.

Morris, L. V. (2017, September 2). Moving beyond critical thinking to critical dialogue. *Innovative Higher Education, 42*, 377–378. https://doi.org/10.1007/s10755-017-9413-z
   This author offers techniques to facilitate critical dialogue during difficult discussions.

Nolan-Ferrell, C. (2017, November–December). Balancing classroom civility and free speech. *Academe, 103*(6), 21–26. https://www.aaup.org/article/balancing-classroom-civility-and-free-speech#.XC5FaWl7mM8
   This author reflects on drawing the line between free speech and disruptive behavior.

REFERENCES

Boysen, G. A. (2012). Teachers' responses to bias in the classroom: How response type and situational factors affect student perceptions. *Journal of Applied Social Psychology, 42*(2), 506–534. https://doi.org/10.1111/j.1559-1816.2011.00784.x

BrckaLorenz, A., Garvey, J. C., Hurtado, S. S., & Latopolski, K. (2017). High-impact practices and student–faculty interactions for gender-variant students. *Journal of Diversity in Higher Education, 10*(4), 350–365. https://doi.org/10.1037/dhe0000065

Case, K. A. (2017). Toward an intersectional pedagogy model: Engaged learning for social justice. In K. A. Case (Ed.), *Intersectional pedagogy: Complicating identity and social justice* (pp. 1–24). Routledge.

Chemerinsky, E., & Gillman, H. (2017). *Free speech on campus*. Yale University Press.

Conway, L. G., Repke, M. A., & Houck, S. C. (2017). Donald Trump as a cultural revolt against perceived communication restriction: Priming political correctness norms causes more Trump support. *Journal of Social and Political Psychology, 5*(1), 244–259. https://doi.org/10.5964/jspp.v5i1.732

Cowan, G., Resendez, M., Marshall, E., & Quist, R. (2002). Hate speech and constitutional protection: Priming values of equality and freedom. *Journal of Social Issues, 58*(2), 247–263. https://doi.org/10.1111/1540-4560.00259

Crandall, C. S., Miller, J. M., & White, M. H., II. (2018). Changing norms following the 2016 U.S. presidential election: The Trump effect on prejudice. *Social Psychological & Personality Science, 9*(2), 186–192. https://doi.org/10.1177/1948550617750735

Czopp, A. M., Monteith, M. J., & Mark, A. Y. (2006). Standing up for a change: Reducing bias through interpersonal confrontation. *Journal of Personality and Social Psychology, 90*(5), 784–803. https://doi.org/10.1037/0022-3514.90.5.784

Gauchat, G. (2012). Politicization of science in the public sphere: A study of public trust in the United States, 1974 to 2010. *American Sociological Review, 77*(2), 167–187. https://doi.org/10.1177/0003122412438225

Gorski, P. C. (n.d.). *Circles of my multicultural self*. Critical Multicultural Pavilion. http://www.edchange.org/multicultural/activities/circlesofself.html

Harell, A. (2010). Political tolerance, racist speech, and the influence of social networks. *Social Science Quarterly, 91*(3), 724–740. https://doi.org/10.1111/j.1540-6237.2010.00716.x

Hurtado, S., Alvarez, C. L., Guillermo-Wann, C., Cuellar, M., & Arellano, L. (2012). A model for diverse learning environments. In J. C. Smart & M. B. Paulsen (Eds.), *Higher education: Handbook of theory and research* (pp. 41–122). Springer. https://doi.org/10.1007/978-94-007-2950-6_2

Kanter, R. M. (1977). Some effects of proportions on group life: Skewed sex ratios and responses to token women. *American Journal of Sociology, 82*(5), 965–990. https://doi.org/10.1086/226425

Landis, K., Jenkins, P., & Roderick, L. (2015). *Start talking: A handbook for engaging difficult dialogues in higher education*. University of Alaska Anchorage.

Lewis, L. C. (2017, November–December). Creating a civil classroom in an era of incivility. *Academe, 103*(6), 27–29. https://www.aaup.org/article/creating-civil-classroom-era-incivility#.XiSpundFw2w

Linker, M. (2015). *Intellectual empathy: Critical thinking for social justice*. University of Michigan Press.

Littleford, L. N., Ong, K. S., Tseng, A., Milliken, J. C., & Humy, S. (2010). Perceptions of European American and African American Instructors teaching race-focused courses. *Journal of Diversity in Higher Education, 3*(4), 230–244. https://doi.org/10.1037/a0020950

Manne, K., & Stanley, J. (2015, November 13). When free speech becomes a political weapon. *The Chronicle of Higher Education*. https://www.chronicle.com/article/When-Free-Speech-Becomes-a/234207

Morris, L. V. (2017, September 2). Moving beyond critical thinking to critical dialogue. *Innovative Higher Education, 42*, 377–378. https://doi.org/10.1007/s10755-017-9413-z

Nolan-Ferrell, C. (2017, November–December). Balancing classroom civility and free speech. *Academe, 103*(6), 21–26. https://www.aaup.org/article/balancing-classroom-civility-and-free-speech#.XC5FaWl7mM8

Pasque, P. A., Chesler, M. A., Charbeneau, J., & Carlson, C. (2013). Pedagogical approaches to student racial conflict in the classroom. *Journal of Diversity in Higher Education, 6*(1), 1–16. https://doi.org/10.1037/a0031695

Rankin, S., Weber, G., Blumenfeld, W., & Frazer, S. (2010). *State of higher education for LGBT people*. Campus Pride.

Singh, A. A., & Hughes, K. M. (2017). Integrating resilience and social justice pedagogical strategies when teaching about sexual orientation and gender diversity. In T. H. Burnes & J. L. Stanley (Eds.), *Teaching LGBTQ psychology: Queering innovative pedagogy and practice* (pp. 85–102). American Psychological Association. https://doi.org/10.1037/0000015-005

Sue, D. W., Lin, A. I., Torino, G. C., Capodilupo, C. M., & Rivera, D. P. (2009). Racial microaggressions and difficult dialogues on race in the classroom. *Cultural Diversity & Ethnic Minority Psychology, 15*(2), 183–190. https://doi.org/10.1037/a0014191

Tinson, C. M., & Benavente, J. (2017). Toward a democratic speech environment. *Diversity & Democracy, 20*(2/3). https://www.aacu.org/diversitydemocracy/2017/spring-summer/tinson

van Anders, S. M., Galupo, M. P., Irwin, J., Twist, M. L. C., & Reynolds, C. J. (2019). Talking about transgender experiences, identities, and existences at conferences. https://docs.google.com/document/d/1iHodSA16oP0itTjZPkB5tslBjMHOiMdy9lt9zmTPKPs/edit?usp=sharing

Weiss, J. T. (2004). The archaeology of biphobia and transphobia within the U.S. gay and lesbian community. *Journal of Bisexuality, 3*(3–4), 25–55. https://doi.org/10.1300/J159v03n03_02

White, M. H., & Crandall, C. S. (2017). Freedom of racist speech: Ego and expressive threats. *Journal of Personality and Social Psychology, 113*(3), 413–429. https://doi.org/10.1037/pspi0000095

17
STUDENT EVALUATIONS OF TEACHING

Can Teaching Social Justice Negatively Affect One's Career?

GUY A. BOYSEN

Students can be brutal in their evaluations of teachers. Consider this verbatim comment that a student posted publicly on RateMyProfessors.com: "the worst prof and class i have ever had. could have been interesting material but taught from very biased angles on his interests and beliefs. i got an A but the class was a complete waste of time!" To punctuate these comments, the student assigned a rating of 2 out of 5 for overall teaching quality. What, if anything, does such an evaluation indicate about the effectiveness of the teacher?

Decisions about teaching effectiveness are always difficult, but in this case, there is added complexity because the student was evaluating Dr. Stanley Sue, an Asian American psychologist who is well known for promoting social justice and multiculturalism. With that in mind, can the student's claims of "worst prof ever" and "biased angles" be trusted? Perhaps the underlying message was "I don't like your race," "My beliefs shouldn't be challenged," or "I am not comfortable with what you teach." All faculty who teach social justice risk negative evaluations from misguided or disgruntled students. Thus, they should work to ensure that student feedback plays an appropriate

---

https://doi.org/10.1037/0000216-017
Navigating Difficult Moments in Teaching Diversity and Social Justice, M. E. Kite, K. A. Case, and W. R. Williams (Editors)
Copyright © 2021 by the American Psychological Association. All rights reserved.

role in the evaluation and improvement of their teaching. To do so, teachers need to interpret official student evaluations within the bounds of their validity, solicit other types of performance feedback, and follow through with goals for improvement.

Student evaluations of teaching have been a source of conflict in the academic literature for decades. The most prominent and long-standing concern about student evaluations is that they are biased. Student evaluations can be considered biased if "a student, teacher, or course characteristic affects the evaluations made, either positively or negatively, but is unrelated to any criteria of good teaching, such as increased student learning" (Marsh, 2007, p. 350). Teachers worry that biasing factors outside of their control—such as course content, student interest, or demographics—might lead to low evaluations. Bias in student evaluations can be detrimental to academic careers because it is difficult to improve teaching using feedback that is not valid. Furthermore, student evaluations inform administrative judgments about hiring, tenure, and promotion (Beran et al., 2005; Miller & Seldin, 2014), and low evaluations, no matter the cause, could make it difficult to find and maintain a faculty position.

Although the possibility of bias in student evaluations should be concerning to everyone in higher education, those who teach about social justice, and diversity more broadly, have extra reason to be aware of potential bias. To begin, students often experience discomfort when talking about diversity and social justice issues, especially if the material presented challenges their worldview (see Kite et al., Chapter 4, this volume); this dissatisfaction could influence student evaluations. Furthermore, social justice topics are likely to be taught by members of underrepresented groups that face prejudice and discrimination, and students' biases may influence their evaluations. Alternatively, when majority group members teach about diversity topics, students may see them as underqualified (Littleford et al., 2010). Students are not the only concern, however. Bias may also influence the faculty and administrators responsible for interpreting evaluation results.

On a more visceral level, student feedback can be painful. I am a tenured full professor with years of experience teaching the same courses in the same department; I also have the privilege associated with being a White, heterosexual, cisgender male. Nonetheless, my heart races each semester as I review my evaluations. Teachers can take negativity in student evaluations personally and the feedback is occasionally cruel (Lindahl & Unger, 2010). Negative evaluations may be especially discouraging for instructors of social justice topics when students overtly or covertly reject the teachers' qualifications, discipline, or identity. How do teachers bring themselves to use student evaluations as a pedagogical tool when they feel so unfair?

FACULTY REFLECTION

Teachers who expose students to challenging social justice lessons may perceive that low student evaluations are one consequence of their efforts. For these teachers, the student evaluations pose dilemmas that are reminiscent of microaggressions. Sue and colleagues (2007) defined racial microaggressions as "brief and commonplace daily verbal, behavioral, and environmental indignities, whether intentional or unintentional, that communicate hostile, derogatory, or negative racial slights and insults" (p. 273). Although being the target of microaggressions and receiving low student evaluations are not equivalent, reactions to them parallel each other in specific ways. Thus, the concept of microaggressions can help faculty members understand their experiences with student evaluations.

One dilemma posed by microaggressions is their invisibility (Nadal, 2013; Sue et al., 2007). Microaggressions are often subtle and unintentional, and proving their occurrence can be difficult. When teaching social justice content, the effect on student evaluations may also be ambiguous. Short of explicit student comments, negative evaluations are impossible to trace back to social justice content. As such, teachers are left to wonder about the true motivations behind student dissatisfaction. In addition, administrators' interpretations of low student evaluations may be motivated by genuine concern about teaching quality or by ambivalence about social justice content.

People's perception of microaggressions as minimally harmful is another dilemma (Harwood et al., 2015; Sue et al., 2007). Because microaggressions are subtle, people often dismiss them as being too minor to cause real harm. Yet, such dismissals ignore the cumulative effect of repeated slights across a lifespan. To some faculty and administrators, receiving low evaluations due to social justice coverage may seem like a minor inconvenience or obstacle. In contrast, to teachers who have repeatedly faced resistance to social justice in their classes, in their departments, at their colleges, and in their communities, the additive effect of receiving low evaluations is more impactful than might be expected from an outside perspective.

Finally, microaggressions pose a catch-22; both responding to them and ignoring them have negative consequences (Sue et al., 2007). Ignoring microaggressions results in internal conflict, but confronting microaggressions results in external conflict. The parallel with student evaluations occurs with the dilemma of whether to publicly attribute low evaluations to social justice content. On one side, some faculty and administrators might view teachers who attribute low evaluations to bias negatively if they see it as making excuses for poor teaching. Nevertheless, if the bias explanation is not used, faculty and administrators may judge teachers of social justice content as having poor pedagogical skills. It is a catch-22 with no ideal solutions, but the best practices section contains suggestions on how to deal with these and other dilemmas.

CONSIDERATIONS OF CONTEXT AND INTERSECTIONALITY

Complex interactions can occur between student and teacher demographics (Basow & Martin, 2012). Students may reject social justice lessons taught by members of underrepresented groups because they believe the instructor's motives are self-serving (Major & Sawyer, 2009; Rasinski & Czopp, 2010), or students may reject lessons taught by majority group members because they believe these instructors are not knowledgeable (Littleford et al., 2010). There may also be interactions between students' identities and their evaluations of social justice instruction.

Many possible factors could affect students' evaluations of social justice lessons, but I believe that the demographic makeup of the classroom stands out as most important. Teachers would not expect to give a lesson on race the same way to a classroom of all White students as they would to a classroom of all Black students, and it is probably not reasonable to expect evaluations of such lessons to be similar in light of those, and other, demographic differences.

Institutional context should also be considered. Colleges and departments with a strong commitment to diversity may see student negativity in reaction to being challenged by social justice lessons not as an instructional failure but as an unavoidable by-product of difficult but essential learning experiences. In such a context, teachers should find support and acceptance in the face of student dissatisfaction with social justice content. In the context of an institution where diversity is not a priority, teachers may have to put extra effort into demonstrating their teaching competence and arguing for mitigating factors.

Institutional emphasis on teaching and research may also be a contextual factor. At institutions that emphasize research over teaching, a productive record of scholarship will outweigh reductions in student evaluations as long as course enrollment remains high. At institutions that emphasize teaching over research, faculty and administrators may expect teachers to work toward improving student evaluations regardless of course content.

Finally, institutional trust and investment in student evaluations is part of context. When institutions invest significant resources in administering and interpreting valid student evaluation surveys, the data are likely to affect decisions. If faculty and administrators believe that student evaluation data are meaningful, then they will expect teachers to use that feedback to inform their teaching. After all, that is the purpose of student evaluations. In other contexts, faculty and administrators might believe student evaluations are meaningless, and sometimes they even bring this belief to fruition by implementing student evaluation measures of questionable validity. Teachers in this context face the conundrum of not knowing if interpretations of student evaluations can be trusted, and they should be careful to document their teaching competency using as many methods as possible.

BEST PRACTICES FOR ENSURING VALIDITY

The purpose of student evaluations is to allow for the evaluation and improvement of teaching. Yet, evaluations are useless if their validity is suspect or if teachers misinterpret or ignore feedback. Student evaluations are tools. Poorly constructed or improperly handled tools will cause damage when used for serious work. Teaching is serious work, so faculty and administrators should ensure that student evaluation tools are constructed and implemented in ways that allow for valid and useful feedback.

Use Valid Measures

The first step in ensuring the usefulness of student evaluations is to administer measures that are reliable and valid (Boysen, 2016; Penny & Coe, 2004). Unvalidated, homemade student evaluation surveys may or may not produce results that can meaningfully inform teaching. When an official measure has unknown validity, teachers can administer a different, validated measure in paper format or using course management software (for validated survey options, see Spooren et al., 2013). When administering a supplementary student evaluation, teachers should strategically choose one that will both highlight instructional strengths and provide information about areas to improve.

Use Valid Analytic Techniques

Once data are collected, teachers should use valid methods of analysis to understand trends (Abrami, 2001; Boysen, 2016; Franklin, 2001; Lewis, 2001a). For items with rating scales, use inferential statistics to test for significant differences among courses, teaching skills, and comparison groups (Abrami, 2001). Remember, even valid measures can be rendered useless if analyzed incorrectly. Consult with teaching experts, especially those who have social justice knowledge, for help with interpretation as needed.

More than any other technique, I have used statistics to ensure that student evaluations that are lower than average did not harm my career. Interpretive tools such as statistical tests and measures of dispersion often show that means initially perceived as "low" are not meaningfully different from average. I always highlight these nondifferences in professional materials submitted for evaluation to reduce the overinterpretation of small differences.

For open-ended comments, use qualitative methods of analysis to discern trends rather than trying to informally glean patterns (Lewis, 2001a; McCarthy, 2012). When presenting comments in professional materials, I never allow raw data to prevail. Rather, I arrange comments based on those that are affirmative of my teaching and those that suggest improvements. Then, I synthesize themes in the comments and count the number of students making comments about each theme. When looking at raw data, a few negative comments about social justice may unduly stand out. In contrast, properly analyzed comments may reveal more instances of comments such as "Content was interesting" than "Content was too focused on diversity."

Use Formative Evaluations

Although end-of-semester feedback is important for official evaluations of teaching effectiveness, formative feedback is more important for teaching improvement and ensuring that students are satisfied with educational experiences. Formative evaluations simply move student surveys to an earlier point in the semester so that teachers can respond to student concerns and make any necessary pedagogical changes. Formative evaluations can occur in any format that is useful to the teacher, but they work best when teachers keep the feedback anonymous and explain that its only purpose is course improvement (Lewis, 2001b). After soliciting feedback, teachers should summarize the results for students and explain why they are or are not making changes. Irrespective of format, conducting formative evaluations sends a clear message to students that the instructor cares about teaching (Lewis, 2001b). Also, using formative evaluations increases end-of-semester evaluations (Penny & Coe, 2004).

Throughout my career, formative feedback has been more useful than any other form of student evaluation. My typical method is to wait until about 3 weeks into each semester, then I ask students to anonymously write down what I am doing as the teacher that is helping and not helping them learn, as well as what they are doing as students that is helping and not helping them learn. I analyze the results, consider them carefully, and go over them with students.

To illustrate, in my classes some students invariably express dislike of collaborative learning activities; however, an equal or larger number of students single out those same activities as helping them learn, and a large proportion of students make no mention of the activities at all. Having this feedback allows me to point out that most students have positive or neutral opinions about collaborative learning. Also, going over the feedback provides an opportunity to reemphasize the centrality of collaboration to the course design and the evidence for its effectiveness. As a result, I demonstrate that I am both open and reasonable.

BEST PRACTICES FOR DEALING WITH LOW EVALUATIONS

Teachers sometimes face low student evaluations, and they can lead to frustration, woe, and doubt. These reactions to student evaluations are amplified when the feedback seems unfair. Nonetheless, inaction is not a solution, and when faced with low evaluations, teachers can implement the following strategies.

Find Support

Speak with administrators who make decisions about teaching effectiveness and ask them, "Can I have your support as I try to cover this important but difficult content, even if it means a dip in my student evaluations?" In addition, identify mentors who have successfully overcome similar issues. They will be a source of solutions, moral support, and professional advocacy.

Collect Multiple Forms of Evidence for Teaching Effectiveness

Student evaluations are just one way to demonstrate instructional effectiveness (Berk, 2005). Counteract low evaluations by emphasizing other evidence such as peer observations, student learning outcomes, student focus groups, alumni surveys, video analysis, and teaching portfolios. Give all forms of evidence equal weight when arguing for teaching effectiveness in professional materials submitted for evaluation and take pride in areas of excellence.

Note Mitigating Factors

There may be many factors outside of a teacher's control that affect student evaluations. So, set the context for understanding student evaluations when summarizing them in professional materials (Franklin, 2001). If bias needs to be considered when interpreting student evaluation results, communicate that mitigating factor to individuals in charge of evaluating teaching effectiveness.

Focus on Improvement

Sometimes students are right to give a low evaluation because they have identified a weakness in instruction or content. If valid measures and analytic procedures suggest a weakness, then there are best practices for using student evaluations to improve that weaknesses (Malouff et al., 2015; Penny & Coe, 2004). After collecting data, consult with a trusted teaching expert. Instructors of social justice topics will want to select someone who understands the challenges of teaching such content. With the assistance of the consultant, create specific, attainable goals and a plan for change. Once the goals are set, it is up to the teacher to follow the plan. Also, set a specific date to readminister student evaluations and meet with the consultant to assess if goals have been met. To clearly establish a reputation for openness to feedback and dedication to pedagogical development, share these efforts to adapt and improve with students, colleagues, and administrators.

STRUCTURAL IMPLICATIONS

Teachers generally see student feedback as pedagogically helpful, but use of student feedback for performance evaluation is more controversial. Like any other means of assessing performance, student evaluations of teaching can be misused, and this might be particularly dangerous to teachers of controversial subjects such as social justice. Without a preestablished procedure for using student evaluations, they can be something of a Rorschach test onto which faculty and administrators project preestablished judgments about a teacher (Franklin, 2001). For example, ratings and comments that are accepted as unavoidable for teachers of a difficult topic like statistics might be seen as evidence poor pedagogy when they arise for teachers of social justice topics, which are difficult for political, rather than mathematical, reasons. Thus, it is essential to ensure that institutions have fair and valid policies for the use of student evaluations when assessing the merit and performance of teachers.

Institutional policies for the use of student evaluations break down into rules for their administration and interpretation and rules for their implementation in decision making. The first, and most essential, rule is to select and administer student evaluation surveys that are valid and thus produce meaningful results (Benton & Young, 2018; Berk, 2013; Franklin, 2001). It is impossible to consistently make sound decisions using unsound data. Research shows that students have a limited understanding of the purpose of teaching evaluations (Kite et al., 2015). Thus, institutions should determine what students are told about the evaluation process before they complete the measures. This can include an explanation of how students' ratings are used by individual instructors and at the institutional level.

Random fluctuations in data prevent even valid measures from being perfectly reliable. As such, decisions should not be made using single items from individual courses. In addition, not all differences in means are statistically significant nor are all statistically significant differences large enough to be practically meaningful. Thus, two additional rules are to aggregate means across multiple observations and use statistical analysis for the identification of meaningful trends (Abrami, 2001; Benton & Young, 2018; Franklin, 2001). Faculty and administrators tend to ignore statistics and overinterpret student evaluation means, often treating differences as small as a few tenths of point as meaningful (Boysen, 2015). Class sizes and response rates also need to be considered when assessing the reliability of data. Therefore, there should be institutional rules to hold decision-makers accountable for their interpretations of student evaluations and to provide procedures for the correction of misinterpretations.

There are established guidelines for the interpretation of empirical data, but there are no guidelines for how to implement those interpretations when making decisions about teaching performance. For example, receiving an evaluation mean of 4.0 could be considered acceptable because it represents a response of *good* on the rating scale or it may be considered unacceptable if the college-wide average is 4.4. There are many justifiable policies for decision-making, but the rules must be transparent and equitable (Abrami, 2001; Berk, 2013; Franklin, 2001). As part of any policy, faculty and administrators should consider context such as course subject and student motivation (Benton & Young, 2018; Franklin, 2001). Finally, faculty and administrators should take multiple types of evidence into account when making decisions about teachers (Benton & Young, 2018; Berk, 2013; Franklin, 2001). Even the most strident supporters of student evaluations believe that they are just one of many indicators of teaching effectiveness.

CONCLUSION

Can teaching social justice negatively affect one's career? A direct answer to this question goes beyond established knowledge in the student evaluation literature. Can the use of feedback from students improve one's career? The answer to this question is an unequivocal "Yes." Although teaching social justice can lead to difficult student reactions, they do not have to derail careers. Consider the "worst prof ever" from the start of this chapter. Despite that one student's overall rating of 2, the teacher's average rating was 4.20, which is considerably higher than the average of 3.75 among other teachers at his university. Furthermore, consider that the professor in question, clinical psychologist Dr. Stanley Sue, managed to spend 3 decades teaching about diversity and significantly impacted social justice both inside and outside of the academy—a successful career by anyone's standards. Although few teachers will achieve the influence of Dr. Sue, everyone can use student feedback to at least ensure that they are reaching as many students as possible.

RESOURCES

Benton, S. L., & Ryalls, K. R. (2016). *IDEA paper #58: Challenging misconceptions about student ratings of instruction.* https://www.ideaedu.org/Portals/0/Uploads/Documents/IDEA%20Papers/IDEA%20Papers/PaperIDEA_58.pdf

    This review addresses the most common criticisms of student evaluations. The authors review research and analyze which criticisms are supported by data and which are not.

Boysen, G. A. (2016). Using student evaluations to improve teaching: Evidence-based recommendations. *Scholarship of Teaching and Learning in Psychology, 2*(4), 273–284. https://doi.org/10.1037/stl0000069

    This review offers a brief introduction to the use of student evaluations in a scientifically valid manner. The review outlines instrument selection, survey administration, interpretation of results, and use for improvement.

Franklin, J. (2001). Interpreting the numbers: Using a narrative to help others read student evaluations of your teaching accurately. *New Directions for Teaching and Learning, 2001*(87), 59–87. https://doi.org/10.1002/tl.10001

    This article provides an essential guide to analyzing and presenting student evaluation results. The review will help teachers understand their results and effectively convey those results in professional materials.

Richmond, A. S., Boysen, G. A., Gurung, R. A., Tazeau, Y. N., Meyers, S. A., & Sciutto, M. J. (2014). Aspirational model teaching criteria for psychology. *Teaching of Psychology, 41*(4), 281–295. https://doi.org/10.1177/0098628314549699

    This article presents the model teaching criteria endorsed by the American Psychological Association. The model teaching criteria represent a comprehensive method for defining teaching competency that relies on a range of evidence, not just student evaluations.

Spooren, P., Brockx, B., & Mortelmans, D. (2013). On the validity of student evaluation of teaching: The state of the art. *Review of Educational Research, 83*(4), 598–642. https://doi.org/10.3102/0034654313496870

    This article consists of a review and critical analysis of research on the validity and utility of student evaluations. The article is a useful introduction to the vast student evaluation literature.

REFERENCES

Abrami, P. C. (2001). Improving judgments about teaching effectiveness using teacher rating forms. *New Directions for Institutional Research, 2001*(109), 59–87. https://doi.org/10.1002/ir.4

Basow, S. A., & Martin, J. L. (2012). Bias in student evaluations. In M. E. Kite (Ed.), *Effective evaluation of teaching: A guide for faculty and administrators* (pp. 40–49). Society for the Teaching of Psychology. http://teachpsych.org/ebooks/evals2012/index.php

Benton, S. L., & Young, S. (2018). *IDEA paper #69: Best practice in the evaluation of teaching.* www.ideaedu.org/Portals/0/Uploads/Documents/IDEA%20Papers/IDEA%20Papers/IDEA_Paper_69.pdf

Beran, T., Violato, C., Kline, D., & Frideres, J. (2005). The utility of student ratings of instruction for students, faculty, and administrators: A "consequential validity" study. *Canadian Journal of Higher Education, 35*(1), 49–70.

Berk, R. A. (2005). Survey of 12 strategies to measure teaching effectiveness. *International Journal on Teaching and Learning in Higher Education, 17*(1), 48–62.

Berk, R. A. (2013). Top five flashpoints in the assessment of teaching effectiveness. *Medical Teacher, 35*(1), 15–26. https://doi.org/10.3109/0142159X.2012.732247

Boysen, G. A. (2015). Significant interpretation of small mean differences in student evaluations of teaching despite explicit warning to avoid overinterpretation. *Scholarship of Teaching and Learning in Psychology, 1*(2), 150–162. https://doi.org/10.1037/stl0000017

Boysen, G. A. (2016). Using student evaluations to improve teaching: Evidence-based recommendations. *Scholarship of Teaching and Learning in Psychology, 2*(4), 273–284. https://doi.org/10.1037/stl0000069

Franklin, J. (2001). Interpreting the numbers: Using a narrative to help others read student evaluations of your teaching accurately. *New Directions for Teaching and Learning, 2001*(87), 85–100. https://doi.org/10.1002/tl.10001

Harwood, S. A., Choi, S., Orozco, M., Huntt, M. B., & Mendenhall, R. (2015). *Racial microaggressions at the University of Illinois at Champaign–Urbana: Voices of students of color in the classroom.* University of Illinois. http://www.racialmicroaggressions.illinois.edu

Kite, M. E., Subedi, P. C., & Bryant-Lees, K. B. (2015). Students' perceptions of the teaching evaluation process. *Teaching of Psychology, 42*(4), 307–314. https://doi.org/10.1177/0098628315603062

Lewis, K. G. (2001a). Making sense of student written comments. *New Directions for Teaching and Learning, 2001*(87), 25–32. https://doi.org/10.1002/tl.25

Lewis, K. G. (2001b). Using midsemester student feedback and responding to it. *New Directions for Teaching and Learning, 2001*(87), 33–44. https://doi.org/10.1002/tl.26

Lindahl, M. W., & Unger, M. L. (2010). Cruelty in student teaching evaluations. *College Teaching, 58*(3), 71–76. https://doi.org/10.1080/87567550903253643

Littleford, L. N., Ong, K. S., Tseng, A., Milliken, J. C., & Humy, S. L. (2010). Perceptions of European American and African American instructors teaching race-focused courses. *Journal of Diversity in Higher Education, 3*(4), 230–244. https://doi.org/10.1037/a0020950

Major, B., & Sawyer, P. (2009). Attributions to discrimination: Antecedents and consequences. In T. D. Nelson (Ed.), *Handbook of prejudice, stereotyping, and discrimination* (pp. 89–110). Psychology Press.

Malouff, J. M., Reid, J., Wilkes, J., & Emmerton, A. J. (2015). Using the results of teaching evaluations to improve teaching: A case study of a new systematic process. *College Teaching, 63*(1), 3–7. https://doi.org/10.1080/87567555.2014.956681

Marsh, H. W. (2007). Students' evaluations of university teaching: Dimensionality, reliability, validity, potential biases and usefulness. In R. P. Perry & J. C. Smart (Eds.), *The scholarship of teaching and learning in higher education: An evidence-based perspective* (pp. 319–383). Springer. https://doi.org/10.1007/1-4020-5742-3_9

McCarthy, M. A. (2012). Using student feedback as *one* measure of faculty teaching effectiveness. In M. E. Kite (Ed.), *Effective evaluation of teaching: A guide for faculty and administrators* (pp. 30–39). Society for the Teaching of Psychology. http://teachpsych.org/ebooks/evals2012/index.php

Miller, J. E., & Seldin, P. (2014). Changing practices in faculty evaluation: Can better evaluation make a difference? American Association of University Professors. http://www.aaup.org/article/changing-practices-faculty-evaluation#.VulYjE0UWpo

Nadal, K. L. (2013). *That's so gay! Microaggressions and the lesbian, gay, bisexual, and transgender community*. American Psychological Association. https://doi.org/10.1037/14093-000

Penny, A. R., & Coe, R. (2004). Effectiveness of consultation on student ratings feedback: A meta-analysis. *Review of Educational Research, 74*(2), 215–253. https://doi.org/10.3102/00346543074002215

Rasinski, H. M., & Czopp, A. M. (2010). The effect of target status on witnesses' reactions to confrontations of bias. *Basic and Applied Social Psychology, 32*(1), 8–16. https://doi.org/10.1080/01973530903539754

Spooren, P., Brockx, B., & Mortelmans, D. (2013). On the validity of student evaluation of teaching: The state of the art. *Review of Educational Research, 83*(4), 598–642. https://doi.org/10.3102/0034654313496870

Sue, D. W., Capodilupo, C. M., Torino, G. C., Bucceri, J. M., Holder, A. M. B., Nadal, K. L., & Esquilin, M. (2007). Racial microaggressions in everyday life: Implications for clinical practice. *American Psychologist, 62*(4), 271–286.

18
FLOTSAM AND JETSAM
Staying the Course While Navigating Difficult Moments in Teaching Diversity and Social Justice

WENDY R. WILLIAMS, MARY E. KITE, AND KIM A. CASE

Flotsam and jetsam are generally interpreted in everyday language as "odds and ends," but they are derived from specific nautical terms. *Flotsam* (from the word "floter") refers to floating items that were not deliberately thrown overboard but were lost due to storms, accidents, or shipwrecks. In contrast, *jetsam* (from the word "jettison") refers to items that were deliberately discarded, often to lighten the load of a ship in distress. Ship captains do not plan to discard their carefully stocked supplies, but circumstances can intervene. Teaching a class on diversity and social justice can sometimes feel like navigating a ship through stormy waters. Although journeys are carefully planned in advance and the ship is stocked with the needed supplies, storm clouds can roll in at any time. In order to stay the course, then, some items get left behind on purpose. Still others are unintentionally lost as instructors flounder to stay afloat. In either case, what is absent may be vital to the ultimate success of the course or may turn out to be unnecessary baggage that detracted from safe passage to the journey's end.

This metaphor also applies to our attempt, as editors of this volume, to provide comprehensive coverage of the challenges and rewards of teaching

https://doi.org/10.1037/0000216-018
Navigating Difficult Moments in Teaching Diversity and Social Justice, M. E. Kite, K. A. Case, and W. R. Williams (Editors)
Copyright © 2021 by the American Psychological Association. All rights reserved.

a social justice course. We (Mary, Kim, and Wendy) recognized that diversity and social justice are broad topics and ideals, but in order to get to the destination of creating this volume, we had to make hard decisions about what we included or excluded. Stopping in every port along the way was impossible. As a result, this single volume does not bring full coverage to all aspects of difficult moments in teaching diversity and social justice. Even so, we identified an excellent crew of scholars who were willing to share their experiences and learn from their mistakes. Our collaborators brought their combined strengths to the task, and the result was greater than the contribution of any one individual. At the same time, we found that, in our role as editors, harnessing their talents towards a single goal sometimes required a heavy hand ("Aye aye, Captains Kite, Case, and Williams!"). Throughout the process, however, we endeavored to clearly communicate our shared vision, and we offered encouragement along with critique—thus avoiding mutiny. We believe that, at the end of the day, this—and a touch of luck—resulted in an edited volume that is heartfelt, informative, and filled with feminist spirit.

As we bring this volume to a close, we think that a number of odds and ends are worth noting and briefly examining. In doing so, we will first highlight the common themes across the book, which we hope will help readers to stay the course. Then, we turn our attention to the topics that (intentionally or unintentionally) were left out. In some cases, these topics are important in their own right but were beyond the scope of what we were able to include. In mentioning these last items, we hope to inspire future authors to pick up the lost treasure we have left behind and join us on the journey.

PREPARING FOR THE JOURNEY

As discussed in the introductory chapter (Case et al., Chapter 1, this volume), we began from a template we hoped would provide continuity across chapters and develop a unified voice. Having faced difficult moments ourselves, and knowing that more than once we missed the mark, we sought to create a handbook that teachers could consult in advance of their journey, in the heat of the moment, and/or in reflective practice after the storm had passed. We asked all chapter authors to not only include theory and application based on specific situations but also offer considerations of context, intersectionality, structure, hands-on resources, and important reference documents. Although this format restricted the authors' individual voices in some ways, we hoped that the organizational freedoms that were lost would be counterbalanced by the ease of utility for the reader. As a final product, we believe the chapters are able to stand alone, yet build on one another when read and used together.

Although there are places where ideas are repeated, we believe that rather than detracting from the whole, this symmetry offers a convergence of "best practices" across difficult situations. Noteworthy cross-cutting themes include classroom management techniques (e.g., advance preparation, creating discussion ground rules, using person-first language, challenging false beliefs with empirical evidence, admitting mistakes); managing your own and students' emotional responses; acknowledging that one's privileged and disadvantaged intersectional social location may inform (and bias) one's perspective; recognizing the personal and professional risk involved in taking on social justice topics; and finding supportive colleagues inside or outside your institution.

Moreover, by starting with faculty who represent a variety of social identity locations, types of institutions, and career stages, we sought to shed light on the diversity of experiences faculty face. In doing so, we resisted one-size-fits-all solutions to the challenges of teaching about diversity that failed to acknowledge the intersectional complexity of positionality. Where the courses are located, in what historical moment the teaching occurs, who is doing the teaching, and who is in the classroom all matter. As a consequence, we believe the present volume is useful to faculty at all levels from graduate students to senior full professors. We also believe K–12 educators can benefit from our insights. A commonality among our authors, however, is their passion and commitment to the emotional labor of teaching diversity and social justice courses. We believe these characteristics are evident in each and every chapter, providing a port in the storm for our colleagues who join us in educating others about these topics.

At the same time, we know (all too well) that mistakes will be made. We pushed our authors to make each chapter highly personal by centering their own voices and experiences through anecdotes, individual stories, and reflective writing. We hoped that by laying bare our own blunders and misgivings, not just our successes, we could encourage a view of teaching diversity and social justice that evokes a journey rather than a destination. In doing so, we did not want to present an overly rosy view of the risks. Some of our authors shared events that were highly traumatic, and there were some events that authors disclosed to us that could not be shared in this volume because they were either still too raw to process fully or would put faculty at further risk to reveal the details. Even though these experiences do not appear on the printed page, they informed our thinking about the content that is included. We are so grateful to our authors for their courage in what they have shared (privately as well as within this collection), and we encourage readers to understand that these stories are a sampling, used to illustrate the risks, but they are not meant to be taken as the full collection.

Highlighting the risks involved in teaching diversity and social justice courses was important to us because we also wanted to speak directly to administrators, especially those who evaluate faculty or who are charged with diversity and inclusion at their institutions (e.g., department chairs, principals, deans, provosts, presidents, diversity and inclusion officers, directors of teaching and learning centers). We also want to speak to faculty who serve on committees, such as annual merit review and tenure and promotion committees that evaluate faculty success. We hope that by illustrating the commonalities across instructors, we make clear that evaluators have an important role in alleviating the risks for faculty who teach social justice courses. Moreover, administrators can have a direct impact on faculty retention and campus climate; thus, it is incumbent upon them to understand the challenges our faculty face and to realize how critical this work is for our students' development. Administrators must also understand that the challenges faculty face are linked to the social structure; their struggles are rarely about an individual instructor, but rather reflect the failure of system-level structures and processes. We have yet to find a faculty member who does not feel the weight of these factors when teaching social justice and diversity courses. Consequently, comprehensive solutions have to be supported from the top-down, not merely from the bottom-up.

Until then, we have to support each other. Whether we are assisting our peers at the same career stage, reaching back to give a hand to those coming up behind us, or reaching forward to "manage up" those ahead of us for whom we would like to provide knowledge and support, we need to resist the impulse to tear each other down through "call-out culture" or by interpreting truthfulness about missteps as signs of weakness. An explicit goal of this volume is to provide peer mentoring in book form by using pedagogical humility as a balm for pedagogical isolation (Case et al., Chapter 1, this volume).

Our most important stroke of luck, then, is that in searching for community for others, we found it for ourselves amongst these authors. Our most sincere hope is that this volume can also aid readers in finding their community of critical, but loving, support. We encourage readers to share this material with their existing communities of support, as well as to seek out new ones (e.g., by organizing reading groups, presenting their own difficult moments at teaching-focused conferences). This work is too hard—and too important—to do alone.

FLOTSAM AND JETSAM

As noted above, in creating a volume that would seek to be comprehensive, we knew we would be setting a difficult course for ourselves from the start. The best we could do was to aim for "as broad as possible." As we stocked our vessel, we had to make difficult choices about what to include. These decisions were not taken lightly or done dismissively but involved careful consideration about the topics we concluded were most needed for the largest number of faculty. In this section, we will touch on a few limitations of our approach.

The majority of authors in this volume are U.S.-based college teachers of psychology, and the theories and applications they describe are predominantly based on that discipline for U.S. classrooms. There are certainly particular situations that arise outside of the U.S. in K–12 classrooms, and in nonpsychology-based courses that deserve attention. Undoubtedly, theories from other disciplines could also effectively be used to address the difficult situations we describe. Nevertheless, many of our authors are recognized experts in diversity and inclusion—nationally, in their communities, and on their campuses. Thus, despite the limitations, we are confident that the content of this volume extends beyond psychology to be useful in all classrooms and beyond only individuals who teach social justice courses. All classrooms can benefit from reflection on these kind of difficult moments as well as incorporation of the best practices presented here. In our shrinking—but highly politically divided—global world, everyone has to navigate personal, social, and sociopolitical issues.

This awareness has become heightened within the United States since Donald J. Trump became president. Individuals with extreme, hateful, and/or unfounded prejudices have felt increasingly emboldened to publicly express their opinions (Alexander, 2020). Within academic settings, this has led to a number of difficult moments, including very public events, like racist flyers on campus property (Fuller, 2019), as well as semiprivate events like those detailed in this volume (see Brody & Bernal, Chapter 7, this volume; Wagner and Garrett-Walker, Chapter 6, this volume; Warner, Chapter 16, this volume). Although the issue of contrapower harassment was touched on by Wagner and Garrett-Walker (Chapter 6, this volume), much more could be said about how the political climate has changed the way in which current students interact with faculty.

Similarly, the needs of the current generation of students (Bips, 2010), the shift of institutions to consumer-based approaches (Kerby et al., 2014), and the omnipresence of technology within classrooms (McCoy, 2013; Stowell, 2015) have made traditional classrooms a thing of the past. Each of these individual forces could be additional chapters within this volume. For example, because of the ease of posting to social media, some faculty have found themselves at risk in ways they never anticipated (e.g., Perez-Pena, 2016). This volume does not fully address these larger political forces and societal changes; however, they are precisely the reasons (a) that have caused many of the events our authors have faced, (b) that we know solutions cannot be merely individual-focused, and (c) why we must seek out communities of support.

This highly politicized environment also has another effect on our classrooms—teachers are trying to reach multiple audiences (i.e., students coming into courses with varying degrees of social justice consciousness and exposure to polarizing media). The multiple audience problem is addressed in a number of chapters, but we have not been able to fully address the combined forces of different levels of consciousness, ingroup–outgroup dynamics, privileged–stigmatized identities, and lack of information literacy that lead to student outbursts as well as student burnout. Although this undoubtedly has been true for many other historical moments (e.g., classrooms during the U.S. civil rights movement), what is likely different today is the pervasiveness of the enmity and situations in which students feel they must demonstrate their "wokeness." Now, more than ever, faculty need to sharpen their pedagogical skills so that they can effectively address controversial issues that are central to today's classrooms (e.g., Dunn et al., 2013). We invite instructors to engage their students in conversation about the issues we raised; we believe this discussion can provide a vehicle for students helping other students navigate outbursts and their own burnout.

Although Williams and Sergent (Chapter 12, this volume) address moments outside the classroom, little attention is given to how faculty can collectively organize in these situations. Yet, a new wave of teacher (and student–teacher) strikes are calling attention to the labor rights issues many teachers and contingent faculty face, from defunding pensions to being able to afford rent (Flaherty, 2020; McLaren & Kobin, 2019). Thus, collective active strategies for teachers are a potentially important area of examination beyond the scope of the present volume.

Although the role of service learning, community-based learning, and meaningful contact with outgroups was touched on in this volume (e.g., Brown, Chapter 8; Goldstein, Chapter 15; Wagner et al., Chapter 14), this coverage could be expanded. A plethora of data shows that experiential learning has a number of positive effects on students (Kuh, 2008; Schmidt & Zaremba, 2015) and that these effects extend to social justice topics (e.g., Case & Rios, 2017; Dessel & Cordivae, 2017). Because this topic has received coverage in other teaching-based resources (e.g.,

Williams & Melchiori, 2013), we chose not to include additional chapters on the rewards and pitfalls of using high-impact practices within a diversity and social justice course.

Finally, as we wrote, revised, and edited this volume, a steady stream of new information continued to be relevant to existing chapters, and we had to make swift decision about which could be included without delaying production. For example, in October 2019, the seventh edition of the *Publication Manual of the American Psychological Association* recommended using "they" as a singular pronoun for the first time, and Wyrick (Chapter 13, this volume) was able to incorporate that information. In contrast, national attention to the data about gender and race bias in teaching evaluations has been steadily growing (e.g., Basow & Martin, 2012; Doerer, 2019), but that information was not able to be included. Similarly, the COVID-19 pandemic was unfolding during the final copyediting stage of this book, and it has undoubtedly affected the teaching of social justice issues in ways that were are just beginning to understand. Unfortunately, we were unable to incorporate those implications here. As mentioned at the start, we hope that by detailing the gaps described in this section, we are opening space for other authors to explore these topics.

STAYING THE COURSE

As a final note of encouragement, it is our experience that teachers of diversity and social justice are some of their own harshest critics, while also showing amazing generosity and grace in their support of others. In raising our (and their) mistakes in this volume, we want to be clear that pedagogical humility is not synonymous with flogging. We encourage our readers to leave behind the baggage of self-doubt and to treat their own mistakes with the same generosity of spirit that they extend to their students and peers. Staying the course is about perseverance not perfection. As Vincent Van Gogh said, "Fishermen [sic] know that the sea is dangerous and the storm terrible, but they have never found these dangers sufficient reason for remaining ashore." In that spirit, we wish you "Bon Voyage."

REFERENCES

Alexander, M. (2020, January 17). Injustice on repeat. *The New York Times*. https://www.nytimes.com/2020/01/17/opinion/sunday/michelle-alexander-new-jim-crow.html

Basow, S. A., & Martin, J. L. (2012). Bias in student evaluations. In M. E. Kite (Ed.), *Effective evaluation of teaching: A guide for faculty and administrators* (pp. 40–49).

Society for the Teaching of Psychology. http://teachpsych.org/ebooks/evals2012/index.php

Bips, L. (2010, October 11). Students are different now. *The New York Times*. https://www.nytimes.com/roomfordebate/2010/10/11/have-college-freshmen-changed/students-are-different-now

Case, K. A., & Rios, D. (2017). Infusing intersectionality: Complicating the Psychology of Women course. In K. A. Case (Ed.), *Intersectional pedagogy: Complicating identity and social justice* (pp. 82–109). Routledge.

Dessel, A., & Cordivae, T. (2017). Experiential activities for engaging intersectionality in social justice pedagogy. In K. A. Case (Ed.), *Intersectional pedagogy: Complicating identity and social justice* (pp. 214–231). Routledge.

Doerer, K. (2019, January 17). *Colleges are getting smarter about student evaluations. Here's how*. https://www.chronicle.com/article/Colleges-Are-Getting-Smarter/245457

Dunn, D. S., Gurung, R. A. R., Naufel, K. Z., & Wilson, J. H. (2013). Teaching about controversial issues: An introduction. In D. S. Dunn, R. A. R. Gurung, K. Z. Naufel, & J. H. Wilson (Eds.), *Controversy in the psychology classroom: Using hot topics to foster critical thinking* (pp. 3–10). American Psychological Association.

Flaherty, C. (2020, February 11). *Striking for COLA: UC Santa Cruz grad assistants strike for a living wage in their tough rental market, but the university says its hands are tied due to union contract*. https://www.insidehighered.com/news/2020/02/11/uc-santa-cruz-gradassistants-strike-living-wage-tough-rental-market

Fuller, L. (2019, November 26). *UT Martin chancellor "disappointed and disgusted" by racist flyers found on campus*. https://www.wpsdlocal6.com/news/ut-martin-chancellor-disappointed-and-disgusted-by-racist-flyers-found/article_50e0196a-1095-11ea-8095-b3442be68508.html

Kerby, M. B., Branham, K. R., & Mallinger, G. M. (2014). Consumer-based higher education: The uncaring of learning. *Journal of Higher Education Theory and Practice*, 14(5), 42–54. http://www.na-businesspress.com/JHETP/KerbyMB_Web14_5_.pdf

Kuh, G. D. (2008). *High-impact educational practices: What they are, who has access to them, and why they matter*. Association of American Colleges & Universities. https://secure.aacu.org/imis/ItemDetail?iProductCode=E-HIGHIMP&Category=

McCoy, B. (2013). Digital distractions in the classroom: Student classroom use of digital devices for non–class related purposes. *Journal of Media Education*, 4, 5–12.

McLaren, M., & Kobin, B. (2019, February 28). *Why did Kentucky teachers call a sickout over the latest pension bill*. https://www.courier-journal.com/story/news/education/2019/02/28/kentucky-teacher-sickout-strike-due-to-pension-system-bill/3012091002/

Perez-Pena, R. (2016, February 25). *University of Missouri fires Melissa Click, who tried to block journalist at protest*. https://www.nytimes.com/2016/02/26/us/university-of-missouri-fires-melissa-click-who-tried-to-block-journalist-at-protest.html

Schmidt, M. E., & Zaremba, S. B. (2015). Service learning and psychology. In D. S. Dunn (Ed.), *The Oxford handbook of undergraduate psychology education* (pp. 173–185). Oxford University Press.

Stowell, J. R. (2015). Using technology effectively in the psychology classroom. *The Oxford handbook of undergraduate psychology education*. Oxford University Press.

Williams, W. R., & Melchiori, K. M. (2013). Class action: How experiential learning can raise awareness of social class privilege. In K. A. Case (Ed.), *Pedagogy of privilege: Teaching and learning as allies in the classroom* (pp. 169–187). Routledge.

Index

A

Able-bodied privilege, 76, 111, 124, 166
Action. *See also* Social justice action
  action teaching plan, 217, 218
  to address white privilege, 160–161
  awareness vs., 161
  change in, 184
  collective. *See* Collective action
Administrator allies, 68–69
Administrators, 13, 40, 250
  as perpetrators of injustice, 170–171
  power and effectiveness of, 175
  and stereotype threat, 67–69
  support for faculty, 85–86, 167, 175, 236–238, 241, 243
Affirming names and pronouns, 189
African Americans. *See under* Black headings
Age. *See also* Aging
  and assumed competence of teachers, 214
  as element of diversity, 198, 201–202, 206
  used as social category, 202
Ageism, 195–207
  and age as element of diversity, 198, 201–202, 206
  and balanced view of aging, 202
  best practices for avoiding, 201–205
  and ethnicity of older adults, 199–200
  faculty reflection on, 198–199
  and intergenerational relationships across cultural groups, 200–201
  and preparation for intergenerational discussions, 203–204
  promoting intergenerational contact, 204–205
  resilience framework in discussing aging, 201
  resources on, 206–207
  structural implications for, 205–206
  and student incivility/bullying toward faculty, 75, 81, 86
  and within-group variability among older adults, 203
"Agenda," accusing faculty of having, 99, 123
Aging. *See also* Older adults
  decline in educational programs focusing on, 205–206
  "Devastating Ds" of, 196, 202
  discussing process of, 197–198
  highlighting multiple aspects of, 203
  presenting balanced view of, 202
  resilience framework in discussing, 201
Ainsworth, M. D., 49
Airton, L., 190
Alaska Native people, intergenerational relationships among, 200
Allies. *See also* Peer allies/supporters
  administrator, 68–69
  in confronting campus situations, 175–176
  for marginalized faculty, 68–70
  from privileged groups, 155–156
  White heterosexual faculty as, 82
American Indian/Native American people. *See also* Native and Indigenous people
  inaccurate perceptions of, 214
  intergenerational relationships among, 200

255

American Psychological Association (APA)
  on age as element of diversity, 198
  finding allies and advisers through, 83
  Guidelines for the Undergraduate Major in Psychology, 10
  Publication Manual of, 190, 253
  on responding to diversity, 69
Amnesty International, 36
Anger, when learning about injustice, 108, 109
Anonymous threats, 76–80. *See also* Threats to faculty
"Anthropology on Trial" (TV series), 211–212
Anticipatory teaching, 94, 96
Anxiety
  about emotionally charged news, 121
  with anonymous threats to faculty, 78
  with stereotype threat, 63–64, 69
APA. *See* American Psychological Association
Applebaum, B., 160
Asian adults and Asian American people, intergenerational relationships for, 200
Assimilation, 138
  and overgeneralization of stereotypes, 140–141
  through affiliation with faculty members, 141–143
Attachment theory, 49–50
Attributional ambiguity, for members of oppressed groups, 77
Attribution bias, 48
Attribution theory, 107–108
Authenticity, for faculty from marginalized groups, 123
Awareness
  action vs., 161
  of human impact of discussions, 230–231
  of prevalence and personal costs of threats to faculty, 86–87
  of racism, 109
  sociocultural, as major learning goal, 10
  of stereotype threat for faculty, 70–71
  of threats to faculty, 77

B

Beliefs
  change in, 184
  in collective efficacy, 109
  and faculty identity, 48
  filial, 200
  sources of, 47
  stereotyped, 65. *See also* Stereotype entries
  system justifying, 121, 145
Bell, L. A., 122, 124
Belonging, sense of, 182. *See also* Gender-inclusive language
Berea College, 167
Best practices
  for addressing prejudicial speech, 228–231
  for addressing stereotype threat, 66–71
  for addressing white privilege, 159–162
  for avoiding ageism, 201–205
  for avoiding mistakes made by instructors, 51–54
  for discussion ground rules, 22–25
  for efficacy, 112–115
  for gender-inclusive language, 188–192
  for handling threats to faculty, 82–86
  for inclusion–exclusion, 99–103
  for outside-of-classroom difficulties, 173–176
  for outsiders teaching insiders, 214–217
  for overcoming ingroup stereotypes, 143–146
  for responding to emotionally charged news, 126–129
  for self-care, 36–40
  with student evaluations of teaching, 239–242
Bias(es)
  in aging research, 202
  attribution, 48
  of ethnic minority instructors, 51
  examining, 47
  implicit, 66, 69
  of instructors, in favor of their ingroups, 228
  in intergroup relations, 154
  against older adults, 195
  and responding to prejudicial speech, 230
  student accusations of, 99
  in student evaluations, 142n2, 237, 241, 253
  students' perception of, 62
  unconscious, 107
  used to harm, 226
Biola University, 225

Black faculty
  anonymous email threat against, 78
  stereotype threat and performance of, 65
Black people. *See also* People of color
  emotionally charged news relating to, 120
  stereotypes about handling of money by, 133, 135
  stereotype threat and test performance of, 64
  within-group variability among, 137
Black students, and discussions of race-related issues, 20
Black trans people, discriminatory policies/biases against, 188
Blumer, M. L. C., 53–54
Bowlby, J., 49
Brody, S., 9
Brookfield, S. D., 22
Brown, L., 6
Burnout, 31–33
  addressing. *See* Self-care
  knowing personal limits to avoid, 175
  personal and systemic factors in, 34–36
Buy-in, creating, 21, 22

C

"Call-out culture," 95, 250
Campus situations, unjust. *See* Outside-of-classroom difficulties
Capodilupo, C. M., 20
Case, K. A., 8, 161–162
Ceci, S. J., 23
Change, evaluating readiness for, 184
Chicana individuals, stereotype threat and, 60–61. *See also* Latinx individuals
Circles of My Multicultural Self, 228
Civil discourse. *See also* Discussion ground rules
  freedom of speech vs., 229
  institutional practices on, 231–232
Clair, J., 126, 127
Class design, intentional, 112
Classroom management techniques, 249. *See also* Discussion ground rules
Coalitions, in addressing white privilege, 160–161
Code of conduct, 19, 225. *See also* Discussion ground rules

Cognitive fallacies, inherent in stereotypes, 135–137
Cognitive impairment, in older adults, 196
Cole, E. R., 161
Collective action
  teachers' strategies for, 252
  teaching successful methods of, 113–114
Communication. *See also* Prejudicial speech
  intergenerational, 200
  reducing genderism in, 191–192. *See also* Gender-inclusive language
Community engagement, 217
Community support model, 5, 13–14
Confidentiality
  in discussing emotionally charged news, 123
  ground rule for, 19, 20
  and recordings by students with disabilities, 21
Conflict in news reports, 121. *See also* Emotionally charged news
Contact theory, 143
Context and intersectionality
  in addressing ageism, 199–201
  in addressing efficacy, 109–112
  in addressing emotionally charged news, 122–126
  in addressing gender-inclusive language, 184–188
  in addressing inclusion–exclusion, 97–99
  in addressing ingroup stereotypes, 139–143
  in addressing mistakes made by instructors, 50–51
  in addressing outside-of-classroom difficulties, 171–173
  in addressing outsiders teaching insiders, 213–214
  in addressing prejudicial speech, 227–228
  in addressing self-care, 34–36
  in addressing stereotype threat, 65–66, 69
  in addressing student evaluations of teaching, 238–239
  in addressing threats to faculty, 81–82
  in addressing white privilege, 158–159
  for discussion ground rules, 20–22
Contrapower harassment (CPH), 75, 76, 78, 81, 86–87

Cooks, L., 94
Corrective emotional experiences, 53
Courage, 5
Course format, discussion ground rules and, 21–22
Crandall, C. S., 225
Credibility in the classroom, 142n2
Crosby, F., 5
Cuevas, J. A., 86
Cultural differences, in intergenerational relationships, 200–201
Cultural humility, 215
Cultural norms, 21, 97, 124, 125, 181, 183, 203
Culture-specific language, 188

D

DACA (Deferred Action for Childhood Arrivals), 32, 168–169
Davis, A., 213
Defensiveness
  of faculty in discussions, 48–49
  produced by course content, 97
  of White faculty, addressing, 152–153, 156–157, 159, 160
  of White students when hearing about marginalized groups, 92, 155
Deference, gender-based, 136
Deferred Action for Child Arrivals (DACA), 32, 168–169
Dehumanization, 230–231
Dementia, 196
Demographics, student evaluations and, 238
Derek Bok Center for Teaching and Learning, 128
"Devastating Ds" of aging, 196, 202
DiAngelo, R., 156
Differentiation, 138
Difficult moments, 3–4, 247–253
Digital social action, 114
Disability
  and assumed competence of teachers, 214
  and classroom podiums, 125
  and discussion ground rules, 21
  language associated with, 24
  outside-of-classroom experience with, 166
  prejudice from peers for, 169
  and sexuality, 137
  simulating insider perspective on, 217

"Disarming" strategy, 94, 96
Discrimination. *See also* Prejudice
  "battle fatigue" from facing, 36
  against faculty by peers, 169
  faculty status in confronting, 172
  against LGBT older adults, 201
  nondiscrimination policies, 185–186, 225
  against older adults, 201–202
  outside of the classroom, 167–168
  perceptions of, 107
  pervasiveness of, 111
  power differentials in confronting, 172
  and social justice institutions, 171–172
  against those pointing out discrimination, 169–170
  against trans or gender-variant individuals, 187–188, 227
  unconscious biases in, 107
Discussion ground rules, 17–27. *See also* Civil discourse
  before addressing news events, 123
  assessment of, 25
  to avoid mistakes in responding to students, 51–52
  best practices for, 22–25
  and course format, 21–22
  faculty reflection on, 18–19
  implementation of, 23–25
  for intergenerational groups, 204
  involving students in development of, 22–23
  resources on, 26–27
  sample of, 26
  structural implications for, 25
  and student characteristics, 20–21
  students' concerns about, 17–18
Discussion skills, teaching, 24
Dissenting students, stereotype threat and, 62. *See also* Inclusion–exclusion
Distancing, 48
Diversity education
  difficult moments in, 3–4, 247–253
  pedagogical isolation in, 7–8
  rules for discussion in. *See* Discussion ground rules
  teaching dilemmas in, 11
Diversity educators. *See also* Faculty and instructors
  additional challenges for, 75–76
  negative student evaluations of, 236. *See also* Student evaluations of teaching

threats toward, 81. *See also* Threats to faculty
Documentation
  of teaching competency, 239
  of threats to faculty, 84

E

Eaton, A., 6
Education, goal of, 109
Efficacy, 105–116
  of administrators, in changing campus situations, 175
  best practices for increasing students' sense of, 112–115
  faculty reflection on, 106–109
  intentional class design for, 112
  involving students in social justice action for, 115
  laying foundation of hope for, 112–113
  mentoring students to gain, 167
  resources on, 115–116
  student dissemination of social justice information for, 114
  teaching methods of collective action for, 113–114
Efficacy paradox, 107–109
Emotional labor
  by certain groups of faculty, 172–173
  defined, 217
  in social justice activism, 35–36
  by those teaching diversity courses, 217
Emotionally charged news, 119–130
  best practices for responding to, 126–129
  faculty reflection on, 121–122
  and interaction of faculty and student identities, 125–126
  and intersectionality of personal identity, 123–125
  resources on, 129–130
  types of responses to, 126–128
Emotional responses, 249
  in divisive political climate, 97
  to engaging with white privilege, 157–160
  of faculty in class discussions, 46
  fear-based, media and political activation of, 123
  to feeling inefficacious, 108
  forewarning students about, 112
  in inclusive environment, 98
  to learning about privilege and prejudice, 105, 110–111. *See also* Efficacy
  mistakes of faculty in managing. *See* Mistakes made by instructors
  in people of color, to racism, 79, 80
  of students in class discussions, 24
  to teaching about social justice, 106
  validating, 126
  to xenophobic remarks, 94
Emotional safety, material outside students' bounds of, 47
Emotional support, for students of color in discussions, 20
Emotional vulnerability
  for faculty from marginalized groups, 123
  of faculty members, 122
  perceptions of, 125
Emotion expression, stereotypes around, 123, 124
Empathy, increasing, 230–231
Errors, acknowledging, 52. *See also* Mistakes made by instructors
Ethnic groups
  among older adults, 199–200
  bias of ethnic minority instructors, 51
Ethnic identity, gender identity and, 187–188
Events-processing response approach, 127–128
Expectations
  about "college professor" social role, 123
  about emotion in discussions, 24
  arising from stereotypes, 59–60. *See also* Stereotype threat
  for social change, 103
  of social justice classes by minorities, 94
  of students, for instructors of color, 94–95
Experiential learning, 217, 252–253

F

Faculty and instructors. *See also* Diversity educators; Social justice educators
  complaints about bias or "agenda" of, 99
  effects of group memberships and personal identities of, 139–140
  emotional responses of, 46. *See also* Anxiety; Mistakes made by instructors
  expression of vulnerability by, 122
  identities of, in facing campus dilemmas, 172–173

interaction of faculty and student demographics, 238
interaction of faculty and student identities, 125–126, 140–143
from marginalized groups, 123
and negative emotions in class, 108–109
perceived credibility of, 142n2
and personal discrimination by peers, 169
from privileged groups. *See* Outsiders teaching insiders
risks and challenges for, 250
self-compassion for, 102
self-disclosure of identities by, 228
self-images of, 47–48
status of, and confronting discrimination, 172
stereotype threat experienced by. *See* Stereotype threat
student evaluations of. *See* Student evaluations of teaching
as student mentors, 167–169
students' assimilation and affiliation with, 141–143
students' expectations for instructors of color, 94–95
support for. *See* Peer allies; Peer mentoring
supporting peers facing injustice, 169–170
teaching strategies of faculty of color, 95–97
threats to. *See* Threats to faculty
Faculty development leaders, 13
Faculty evaluations of teachers
and awareness of targets of threats, 87
and negative effects of threats, 86
and peer evaluation of teaching, 241
Faculty reflection
on ageism, 198–199
on discussion ground rules, 18–19
on efficacy, 106–109
on emotionally charged news, 121–122
on gender-inclusive language, 181–184
on inclusion–exclusion, 93–97
on ingroup stereotypes, 134–139
on mistakes made by instructors, 46–50
on outside-of-classroom difficulties, 166–171
on outsiders teaching insiders, 211–213
on prejudicial speech, 224–227
on self-care, 33–34
on stereotype threat, 63–65
on student evaluations of teaching, 237–238
on threats to faculty, 80–81
on white privilege, 154–158
Familismo, 187, 200
Fear of conflict, 48
Feinstein, D., 203
Female body (term), 183
Feminists
community building by, 13–14
stereotype threat for, 60–62, 66
Filial beliefs, 200
Filter bubbles, 23
Filz, T. E., 22
Fleming, T., 49
Flexibility, 126
Formative evaluations of teaching, 240–241
Founding charters, institutional, 174
Fowler, G., 213
Free speech/freedom of speech, 224
framing prejudicial speech as. *See* Prejudicial speech
government and institutional regulations for, 225
in implementing discussion ground rules, 23
responding to statements about, 226–227
understanding students' statements about, 225

G

"The Gambler" (song), 91
Gay men, stereotypes about, 133
Gender. *See also* Men; Women; Women in teaching
deference and respect based on, 136
defined, 183
difference between sex and, 183–184
and use of singular *they*, 190
and variety of experience, 137
Gender-conforming privilege, 53–54
Gender identity, 187
and ethnic identity, 187–188
and experience of aging, 200
and nondiscrimination policies, 186
and perception of authority, 94
and use of term "trans," 179

Gender-inclusive language, 179–193, 224
  affirming names and pronouns, 189
  best practices for, 188–192
  and culture-specific language, 188
  and ethnic identity, 187–188
  faculty reflection on, 181–184
  and inclusive surveys, 192
  intersectionality in addressing, 186–188
  and motivational interviewing, 184–185
  and nondiscrimination policies, 185–186
  and personal identity, 187
  reducing genderism in communication, 191–192
  resources on, 192–193
  singular *they*, 190
  teaching genderism in research, 190–191
  and transtheoretical model, 184
  used in lectures, 184, 191
  for validation of identity and sense of belonging, 182
Genderism
  classrooms shaped by, 182–184
  in communication, reducing, 191–192
  teaching concept of, in research, 190–191
Gender variant (term), 224
Gender variant students
  prejudice against, 228
  prejudicial speech concerning, 223–224, 226
  terminology related to. *See* Gender-inclusive language
  unsupportive campus environments for, 226–227, 231
Gen Silent (documentary), 200
Gerontology and geriatrics programs, 206
Goldstein, S., 6
Gorski, P. C., 38
Grassley, C., 203
Ground rules for discussions. *See* Discussion ground rules
Guidelines for the Undergraduate Major in Psychology (American Psychological Association), 10
Guiding documents, of institutions, 174

H

Harassment
  contrapower, 75, 76, 78, 81, 86–87
  of gender-variant students, 226–227
  of LGBTQ+ professors, 228
  of women, disclosure of, 172–173
Harmful speech
  couched as freedom of speech. *See* Prejudicial speech
  viewpoint diversity and. *See* Inclusion–exclusion
Harm minimization, with inclusion–exclusion, 99–101
Hatch, O., 203
Health disparities, 196
Heterosexual privilege, 53–54
  defensiveness of students with, 76
  and threats to faculty, 81–82
Higher Education Act and Amendments, 173
Hirabayashi, L. R., 85
Hispanic people, intergenerational relationships for, 200. *See also* Latinx individuals
Historical accounts of combating injustice/inequality, 112–113
Historical moment in time, and costs of acting/not acting, 173
Holmes, J. D., 47
Homosexuality, sources of students' beliefs about, 47, 48
hooks, b., 129, 212
Hope
  laying foundation of, 112–113
  rejecting white fragility, 160
Howell, C. D., 25
Humanity, recognizing, 230–231
Human Rights Campaign, 187
Humility, 5
  cultural, 215
  pedagogical, 8–9, 250

I

Identity(-ies)
  antiracist, 157
  effects on pedagogy and on student responses to faculty, 139–140
  ethnic, 187–188
  and experience of aging, 200
  of faculty, in confronting campus dilemmas, 172–173
  gender, 94, 179, 186–188, 200. *See also* Gender-inclusive language
  and gender-inclusive language, 187
  and inclusion–exclusion, 98–99
  instructors' self-disclosure of, 228

interaction of faculty and student identities, 125–126, 140–143
intersectionality of, 123–125, 140, 186–188
language validating, 182. *See also* Gender-inclusive language
marginalized, 35, 106. *See also* Marginalized groups
outsider and insider, 213–214
in positionality, 94, 101. *See also* Positionality
social, 18, 50–51, 186, 213–214
and stereotype threat, 65. *See also* Stereotype threat
and students' affiliation with faculty members, 141–142
and students' emotional responses, 110–111
teaching beyond your, 212–213. *See also* Outsiders teaching insiders
Implicit bias
educating administrators about, 69
and stereotype threat, 66, 69
Inclusion–exclusion, 91–103. *See also* Gender-inclusive language
best practices for, 99–103
faculty reflection on, 93–97
holistic impact and "invisible" consequences of, 97–98
institutional-level acknowledgment of professional impact on teachers, 102
intersectionality in addressing, 98–99
inviting voices of insiders into discussions, 216–217
and long view of social change, 103
and minimizing harm, 99–101
in politically divisive climate, 97
and positionality as pedagogical tool, 101–102
positionality of faculty in classroom, 94
positionality of students in classroom, 94–95
resources on, 103
self-compassion for faculty, 102
and student self-selection into courses, 62
teaching strategies of faculty of color, 95–97
Inclusive surveys, 192
Indigenous communities/cultures
gender variant term used by, 188. *See also* Native and Indigenous people
respect for elders in, 200
Individualism, motivation for, 138, 139

Individual self-care, 38
Information literacy, modeling, 110
Information processing, 125
Ingroup stereotypes/stereotyping, 133–147
addressing negative stereotypes, 145–146
best practices for overcoming, 143–146
cognitive fallacies inherent in, 135–137
faculty reflection on, 134–139
forms of, 134–135, 139
and interaction of faculty and student identities, 140–143
motivations underpinning, 136–139
overgeneralization of, 140–141, 144–145
and overlapping distributions, 136–137, 144–145
resources on, 146–147
and standard prejudice reduction techniques, 143–144
Insider perspectives, welcoming, 216–217. *See also* Outsiders teaching insiders
Institutional interventions, stereotype threat and, 67–68
Institutional policies
and identification of institution as social justice institutions, 171–172
knowledge of, 173–174
nondiscrimination, 185–186, 225
as perpetrators of injustice, 170–171
regulating speech, 225, 231–232
and stereotype threat, 67–68
and student evaluations of teaching, 238–239, 242–243
to support marginalized students, 231
and threats received by faculty, 86
Institutional power
and contrapower harassment, 75, 76, 78, 81, 86–87
structure of, 86
Institutional self-care, 39–40
Instructors. *See* Faculty and instructors
Integrative responses to events, 127
Intellectual processing of events, 127
Intelligence
ascription of, as microaggression, 63
and stereotype threat, 63, 65
Intergenerational relationships and contact
across cultural groups, 200–201
campus provisions for, 198–199

preparing for intergenerational discussions, 203–204
promoting, 204–205
Intersectionality. *See* Context and intersectionality
Intersectional theory, 66
Intersex, 183

J

Jewish people
Holocaust survivors, 46–50
murdered at Tree of Life synagogue, 119–120
Jones, V., 120

K

Kidder, L., xvii
Kite, M. E., 22–24, 216

L

Landis, K., 23
Language and terminology
coded, about emotional expressiveness, 124
culture-specific, 188
discussing and teaching skills of, 24
in discussing emotionally charged news, 125–126
gender binary terms, 190, 191
for gender identities, 224
gender-inclusive. *See* Gender-inclusive language
in intergenerational discussions, 204
racist coded, in news media, 121
in validating identities, 182
Latinx faculty
stereotype threat and performance of, 65
Latinx individuals. *See also* People of color
cultural norms for, 187–188
intergenerational relationships for, 200
and stereotype threat, 60–61
Laws
governing institutions, 173
regulating speech, 225
Lectures, using gender-inclusive language in, 184, 191
Lee, M. Y. H., 92
Lewis, J., 203

LGBTQ+ individuals
affirming identity of LGBTQ youth, 189
discrimination for LGBTQ youth, 188
experience of aging for older adults, 200
harassment of LGBTQ+ professors, 228
housing and health care discrimination against older adults, 201
instructors' self-outing and climate for LGBTQ+ students, 228
older adults' prejudice toward, 197
peer prejudice for faculty, 169
use of therm "queer" by, 23
Liberal professors
anonymous threats to, 79–80
stereotype threat for, 60–64
Lin, A. I., 20
Low-income individuals
experiences overlapping with high-income individuals' experiences, 136–137
outside-of-classroom difficulties for, 167
stereotypes about, 133

M

Maathai, W., 113
Machismo, 187–188
Male body (term), 183
Marginalized groups
allies for faculty in, 68–70
and ascription of intelligence, 63
challenges to teachers from, 214
classroom reactions of, 111–112
emotional toll for, 226
faculty from, 62–63
ingroup stereotypes endorsed by, 134
institutional practices supporting, 231
and institutional stereotype threat policy/intervention, 68
majority group feelings when hearing candid speaking by, 91
managing identity in, 106
outing or singling out members of, 125
personal experiences as members of, 123
prejudicial comments about, 224. *See also* Prejudicial speech
research on, 134
students' expectations for instructors of color, 94–95
as targets of hatred, 85
and teachers' perceived neutrality, 64
teaching by outsiders of. *See* Outsiders teaching insiders

unsupportive campus environments for, 226–227
use of term, 224
well-being in, 108
White students' positionality when hearing about, 92
Marginalized identities. *See also* Stereotype threat
managing, 106
of those doing diversity work, 35
Marsh, H. W., 237
Masculinity, perception of, 136
Mayberry, K. J., 212
McClure, F., 53
Media accounts (news)
of combating injustice/inequality, 113
emotionally charged. *See* Emotionally charged news
in intergenerational discussions, 205
in teaching, 122
Melchiori, K. J., 217
Men. *See also* White men
deference and respect for women vs., 136
gay, stereotypes about, 133
Mental health of trans students, identity language for, 182
Mentors for faculty
administrator allies as, 68
peers as. *See* Peer mentoring
Mentors for students, faculty as, 167–169
Microaggressions
addressing, 52–53
ground rules for reducing, 19. *See also* Discussion ground rules
harmfulness of, 237
inadvertent, 157
invisibility of, 237
racial, 237
and stereotype threat, 61–63
and student evaluations of teaching, 237–238
Miller, R. A., 25, 217
Mindfulness practices, 38
Minorities
ethnic, older adults as members of, 199–200
expectations of social justice classes by, 94
sexual, managing students' negative opinions about, 46–48, 50. *See also* Mistakes made by instructors

Minoritized instructors/faculty
allies for, 68–70
bias of ethnic minority instructors, 51
and institutional stereotype threat policy/intervention, 68
Mission statements, institutional, 174
Mistakes made by instructors, 45–55, 249
and acknowledgment of errors, 52
apologizing for, 102
attributed to age, 198
best practices to avoid, 51–54
faculty reflection on, 46–50
and ground rules for discussions, 51–52
and letting students respond, 53
and letting time pass before responding, 52–53
and modeling of effective responding, 53–54
resources on, 55
structural implications for, 54–55
and white privilege, 153–154, 157–158
Modeling
of aging and age-related interaction, 205
of authenticity and honest dialogue, 102
of discussion ground rules, 24–25
of effective responding to student comments, 53–54
of information literacy and scientific thinking, 110
in responding to xenophobic remarks of students, 94, 98
Morale in classroom, 98
Morris, W., 37
Motivational interviewing, in affirming trans identities, 184–185
Motivations
for change, 184–185
for engaging in social justice work, 34–35
for self-enhancement and individualism, 138
underpinning ingroup stereotyping, 136–139
Multicultural impostor syndrome, 217–218
Multiple audience problem, 252
Mumby, D. K., 121
Murray-García, J., 214

N

Nag's Heart, xvii–xix, 5–7, 9, 13–14, 31–33
Names, affirming, 189

Napier, J. L., 121
National Resource Center on LGBT Aging, 200
Native and Indigenous faculty, stereotype threat and performance of, 65
Native and Indigenous people. *See also* American Indian/Native American people; Indigenous communities/cultures
　collective action by, 113–114
　gender-variant term used by, 188
Native Hawaiian and Pacific Islander people, intergenerational relationships among, 200
Neutrality, 64
News. *See* Emotionally charged news; Media accounts
Nondiscrimination policies, 185–186, 225
Nondominant groups
　concerns about discussing diversity among, 18, 19
　and discussion ground rules, 20
Nonverbal behavior of students, faculty reactions to, 49
Norcross, J. C., 37
Norvilitis, J. M., 217

O

Obese individuals, stereotypes about, 133
Older adults. *See also* Aging
　and age as element of diversity, 198, 201–202
　discrimination against, 201–202
　in intergenerational contacts. *See* Intergenerational relationships and contact
　prejudice against, 201–204
　prejudices of, 197, 203–204
　resilience of, 201
　respect for, 197, 200, 204
　stereotypes of, 195, 199, 201–202. *See also* Ageism
　within-group variability among, 203
Omnigender, 183
Online courses, discussion ground rules for, 21–22
Oppressed groups
　attributional ambiguity for members of, 77
　likelihood of threats for members of, 82
　threats to faculty from, 81
Optimal distinctiveness theory, 138–139

Outside-of-classroom difficulties, 165–177
　administrator or institutional unjust policies, 170–171
　best practices for, 173–176
　categories of, 165
　facing personal discrimination by peers, 169
　and faculty identities, 172–173
　faculty reflection on, 166–171
　and faculty status, 172
　helping groups of students, 168–169
　and historical moment in time, 173
　in institutions with social justice missions/policies, 171–172
　and knowledge of institutional policies, 173–174
　mentoring individual students, 167–168
　resources on, 176–177
　seeking values match in addressing conflict, 174
　supporting peers facing injustice, 169–170
Outsiders teaching insiders, 211–219
　best practices for, 214–217
　faculty reflection on, 211–213
　interrogating one's own positionality and privilege, 215–216
　resources on, 218–219
　structural implications for, 217–218
　welcoming voices of insiders, 216–217

P

Palmer, P. J., 48
Parkland, Florida, 114
Pasque, P. A., 19
Pedagogical humility, 8–9, 250, 253
Pedagogical isolation, 7–8
Peer allies/supporters, 249, 250
　for responding to threats, 83–84
　and stereotype threat, 69–70
　in supporting peers facing injustice, 169–170
Peer mentoring, 10–11, 250
　chapter structure based on, 12
　community building as goal of, 13–14
　transformative power of, 6
　value of, 54–55
Pelosi, N., 203
People of color
　discrimination by peers against, 169
　emotional response to racism in, 79, 80

emotional support for, and classroom discussion, 20
emotional toll for, 226
and "freedom of speech," 226
gender-variant, 227
listeners' belief in, when speaking about racism, 155
and minimization of harm for students in discussions, 99–101
modeling professionalism in responding to xenophobic remarks about, 94, 98
and stereotype threat, 60–65, 68–69
students' expectations for instructors of color, 94–95
and surprise at systemic inequalities among highly educated immigrants, 112
in teaching, student incivility/bullying toward, 75, 76, 81, 86
teaching strategies of faculty of color, 95–97
trans youth of color, 188
visible and invisible harm to students of color, 97–98
Perceived neutrality, stereotype threat and, 64
Perception
of authority, 94, 136–137
of credibility in the classroom, 142n2
of discrimination, 107
of emotional vulnerability, 125
of instructor bias, 62
of masculinity, 136–137
of power, 136–137
of power differential, 125
of teachers' neutrality, 64
Performance
and stereotype threat, 64–65
student feedback on. *See* Student evaluations of teaching
Perry, G., 94
Personal identity, intersectionality of, 123–125
Podolsky, M., 213
Policies. *See* Institutional policies
Politically divisive climate, 97, 251, 252
Positionality, 101–102
classroom assignment on, 125
defined, 94
of faculty in classroom, 94
interrogating one's own, 215–216
intersectionality of identities and, 126
and outsiders teaching insiders, 214
as pedagogical tool, 101–102

of students in classroom, 94–95
and variation in teaching strategies, 96–97
and white privilege, 157–158
of White students, 92, 101
Positive feedback
in combating stereotype threat, 67
from student allies, 70
Posttraumatic stress disorder, 122
Power
of administrators, in changing campus situations, 175
institutional, structure of, 86
in intergenerational helping relationships, 205
knowing personal limits of, 175
perception of, 136
racial, 156. *See also* White privilege
and self-efficacy of those less empowered, 176
of white privilege in addressing racism, 154–156
Power differential. *See also* Contrapower harassment (CPH); Positionality; Status
addressing, in cultural humility, 215
for faculty in confronting discrimination, 172
perceptions of, 125
between students and instructors, 94
Prejudice, 105. *See also* Discrimination
addressing uninformed perspectives resulting from, 226
"battle fatigue" from facing, 36
in intergenerational contacts, 204–205
against older adults, 201–204
of older adults, 197, 203–204
standard reduction techniques for, 143
students' reactions to learning about, 105. *See also* Efficacy
teaching about, 106–107
using "freedom of speech" to mask or justify, 225–226
using one's privilege to speak out against, 155–156
Prejudiced responses
discouraging, 19. *See also* Discussion ground rules
mistakes in handling. *See* Mistakes made by instructors
Prejudicial speech, 223–232
best practices addressing, 228–231
and empathy/recognition of humanity, 230–231
faculty reflection on, 224–227

and freedom of speech vs. civil
    discourse, 229
institutional practices on civil discourse,
    231–232
institutional practices supporting
    marginalized students, 231
and instructor identities, 228
and instructor intervention, 230
in post-Trump United States, 227–228
requiring reliance on evidence, 229–230
resources on, 232
responding to "freedom of speech"
    statements, 226–227
structural implications for, 231–232
understanding "freedom of speech"
    statements, 225
Preskill, S., 22
Privilege, 105, 249. *See also* Outsiders
    teaching insiders; White privilege
able-bodied, 76, 166
defensiveness of students with, 75–76
and experience of threats, 82
and exposure to hatred, 84–85
gender-conforming, 53–54
and gender-inclusive language, 187, 190
heterosexual, 53–54, 76, 81–82
interrogating one's own, 215–216
pervasiveness of, 111
in positionality, 94. *See also* Positionality
racial, 156
recognizing identities as, 124–125
students' reactions to learning about,
    105. *See also* Efficacy
and teachers' perceived neutrality, 64
teaching about, 106–107
teaching students to use, 67
used in speaking out against prejudice,
    155–156
Pronouns, affirming, 189
Public psychology, 40
Putnam, L. L., 121

R

Racial affinity, 154–155
Racial diversity, among older adults,
    199–200
Racial microaggressions, 237. *See also*
    Microaggressions
Racism
emotional responses in people of color
    to, 79, 80
heightening students' awareness of, 109
lack of belief in people of color who
    speak about, 155

perceptions of those addressing, 66
permanency of, in United States, 79
power of white privilege in addressing,
    154–156
teaching strategies to mitigate
    resistance to learning about, 95
and white privilege. *See* White privilege
White students' benefit from, 18
White students' guilt when learning
    about, 111
White students' perception of, 92
Reflection
in addressing white privilege, 160
and change, 161
to convey hope, 113
in experiential learning, 217
by faculty on topics. *See* Faculty
    reflection
on intersectional identities, 124
for navigating difficult moments, 128
on one's own positionality and privilege,
    215–216
on white privilege, moving to action
    from, 160–161
Refugees, 217
Religious institutions
and nondiscrimination policies, 185–186
speech environments of, 225
Relles, S., 101
Repetition, to convey hope, 113
Research
on ageism, 198
on aging, 202
creating inclusive surveys for, 192
teaching genderism in, 190–191
Resilience
of older people, 201
of stereotyped-group individuals, 106
of trans youth of color, 188
Resistance
produced by course content, 97
in use of language, 185
of White students when hearing about
    marginalized groups, 92
Resources
on ageism, 206–207
on discussion ground rules, 26–27
on efficacy, 115–116
on emotionally charged news, 129–130
on gender-inclusive language, 192–193
on inclusion–exclusion, 103
on ingroup stereotypes, 146–147
on mistakes made by instructors, 55
on outside-of-classroom difficulties,
    176–177

268 • Index

on outsiders teaching insiders, 218–219
on prejudicial speech, 232
on self-care, 41
on stereotype threat, 71
on student evaluations of teaching, 244
on threats to faculty, 87–88
on white privilege, 162
Respect
in discussing emotionally charged news, 123, 125
gender-based, 136
ground rule for, 19, 23, 25, 26
for older adults, 197, 200, 204
Responsiveness of instructors, 126
Rios, D., 9
Rivera, D. P., 20
Rocca, K. A., 18
Rodgers, K., 36

S

Safety
classroom environment of, 19, 23, 49, 50, 52, 96, 98, 123
emotional, material outside students' bounds of, 47
for minority students in social justice classes, 94
when receiving threats, 78, 79, 83–84
Scientific thinking, 110
Scott, R., 114
Self-awareness, 126
Self-care, 31–41
attention to your own emotional needs, 128
best practices for, 36–40
defining, 37
faculty reflection on, 33–34
individual, 38
institutional, 39–40
resources on, 41
returning to positive student feedback as, 67
within social movements, 38–39
and threats to faculty, 85
Self-compassion, for instructors, 102
Self-disclosure
after receiving threats, 84
by faculty of their mistakes made, 53
of instructor identities, 228
of intersectional identities and privilege, 215

Self-enhancement
motivation for, 138, 139
and need for assimilation, 140–141
Self-esteem, of negatively stereotyped groups, 106
Self-evaluation, in cultural humility, 215
Self-hatred theories, 137–138
Self-identification, for affirming student names, 189
Self-knowledge, 124
Self-martyrdom, of social justice workers, 36
Self-reflection
in addressing white privilege, 160
for navigating difficult moments, 128
Self-stereotyping, 136–139, 144–145
September 11th attacks, 126, 127
Service learning, 115, 198–199, 217, 252
Sex, difference between gender and, 183–184
Sexual minorities, managing students' negative opinions about, 46–48, 50. See also Mistakes made by instructors
Sexual orientation. See also LGBTQ+ individuals
anonymous threats based on, 77–80
biological vs. personal choice explanations for, 151n1
and experience of aging, 200
instructors' self-disclosure of, 228
older adult's prejudice about, 197
prejudice from peers for, 169
prejudicial speech concerning, 223–224, 226. See also Gender-inclusive language
religious institutions' discrimination against, 186
sources of students' beliefs about, 47, 48
and variety of experience, 137
Similarity–attraction effect, 23
Singular they, 190, 253
Smith, A., 113
Smith, L., 215, 217–218
Social change
long view of, 103
optimism about, 107
Social identities
and classroom dynamics, 50–51
discussion drawing attention to, 18
of faculty outsiders and student insiders, 213–214. See also Outsiders teaching insiders
and trans students, 186
Socialization, 107–108

Index • 269

Social justice action/work
  in addressing white privilege, 160–161
  involving students in, 115
  motivations for engaging in, 34–35
  partnerships with advocates for, 215
  self-care as it relates to, 37
  systemic factors affecting, 35–36
  teaching successful methods for, 113–114
Social justice education
  building community for, 13–14
  difficult moments in, 3–4, 247–253
  literature on teaching, 18n1
  pedagogical isolation in, 7–8
  rules for discussion in. *See* Discussion ground rules
  teaching dilemmas in, 7, 11
Social justice educators. *See also* Faculty and instructors
  additional challenges for, 75–76
  examples of stereotype threat for, 60–63. *See also* Stereotype threat
  marginalized students' expectations of, 94–95
  negative student evaluations of, 235, 236. *See also* Student evaluations of teaching
  threats toward, 81. *See also* Threats to faculty
Social justice information, student dissemination of, 114
Social justice institutions, 171–172
Social movements, self-care within, 38–39
Social norms, for work and retirement, 203
Sociocultural awareness, as major learning goal, 10
Spanierman, L. B., 215
Stallard, M., 120
Stated commitments, institutional, 174
Status. *See also* Power differential
  of faculty from marginalized communities, 123
  of faculty in speaking out, 172
  knowing personal limits of, 175
  in positionality, 94. *See also* Positionality
Steele, C., 65, 66
Stereotypes
  about "college professor" social role, 123
  about social identities, 121
  about young people, 133, 197
  beliefs based on, 65
  cognitive fallacies inherent in, 135–137

  cultural, 123–124
  fear-based, media and political activation of, 123
  of groups, intersections of, 124–125
  ingroup. *See* Ingroup stereotypes
  of older adults, 195, 199, 201–202. *See also* Ageism
  of teachers, among White students, 61
  well-known, addressing, 139
Stereotype threat, 59–71
  about losing control of emotions, 124
  and administrator allies, 68–69
  age-related, 198
  best practices for addressing, 66–71
  defined, 59
  faculty awareness of, 70–71
  faculty reflection on, 63–65
  and focus on fixing system, 66
  and focus on students' development, 67
  heightened anxiety with, 63–64
  and institutional interventions/policy, 67–68
  and peer allies, 69–70
  and perceived neutrality, 64
  performance impacted by, 64–65
  and positive feedback, 67
  resources on, 71
  and student allies, 70
Stereotyping
  self-, 136–139, 144–145
  standard reduction techniques for, 143
Strange-situation paradigm, 49
Strategic plans, institutional, 174
Structural factors
  in addressing negative stereotypes, 145
  and ageism, 205–206
  for discussion ground rules, 25
  and efficacy paradox, 107–108
  and mistakes made by instructors, 54–55
  and motivations for social justice work, 34–35
  for outsiders teaching insiders, 217–218
  and prejudicial speech, 231–232
  for reducing burnout, 39–40
  and student evaluations of teaching, 242–243
  and threats to faculty, 86–87
Student development, focusing on, 67
Student evaluations of teaching, 235–244
  and acknowledgment of professional impact on social justice instructors, 102
  administrators' interpretations of, 236, 237

best practices for dealing with low evaluations, 241–242
best practices for ensuring validity, 239–241
biases in, 142n2, 237, 253
conflict surrounding issue of, 236
in courses with and without diversity focus, 67
and defensiveness of privileged students, 76
and faculty mistakes in handling discussions, 54
faculty reflection on, 237–238
formative, 240–241
and intersections of group stereotypes, 124–125
resources on, 244
and stereotype threat, 60–61, 69
structural implications for, 242–243
validity and reliability of measures in, 239
validity of analytic techniques for, 239–240, 243
Sue, D. W., 20, 237
Sue, S., 235, 244
Suler, J., 21–22
Surveys, inclusive, 192
Syllabi for social justice-oriented courses, 95–96
Systemic factors
affecting social justice work, 35–36
in burnout, 34–36
in fixing stereotype threat, 66
System justification theory and system justifying beliefs, 121, 139, 145

T

Takacs, D., 101
Tatum, B., 109
Teachers. *See* Faculty and instructors
Teaching effectiveness, collecting evidence of, 241
Teaching strategies. *See also* Best practices
to address ingroup stereotyping, 144–145
in addressing white privilege, 161–162
to address negative stereotypes, 145
to defend identity threats, 142–143
discussion of current events as, 121
to minimize harm, 99–101
to mitigate resistance to new/challenging information, 95–97

from positions of privilege, 217. *See also* Outsiders teaching insiders
Terminology. *See* Language and terminology
Tervalon, M., 214
Teyber, E., 53
Therapeutic ally-ance, 161–162
They, singular, 190, 253
Threat assessment teams, 83–84
Threats to faculty, 75–88
administration's support in dealing with, 85–86
best practices for handling, 82–86
documenting, 84
examples of, 77–80
faculty reflection on, 80–81
preparing in advance for, 82–84
resources on, 87–88
returning to classroom after, 84–85
and self-care, 85
structural implications for, 86–87
Title IX protections, 169, 170
Torino, G. C., 20
Toxic disinhibition, 21–22
Trans students. *See* Gender-inclusive language
Transtheoretical model, in affirming trans identities, 184
Traumatic events, in the news. *See* Emotionally charged news
Tree of Life synagogue murders, 119–120
Trump, D. J., 251
and amnesty for undocumented students, 168–169
and DACA termination, 32, 168–169
and free speech issues, 227–228
remarks about Mexican people by, 92
Trust, 5, 176
Two-spirit, 188

U

Unconscious biases, 107
Underrepresented groups, 91. *See also* Nondominant groups
Undocumented students, 32, 168–169

V

Values match, seeking, 174
Van Gogh, V., 253
Vespia, K. M., 22
Viewpoint diversity, harmful speech and. *See* Inclusion–exclusion

Violence in news reports, 121. *See also* Emotionally charged news
Vision statements, institutional, 174

W

Wagner, L., 9
Warner, L., 9
Western adults, intergenerational relationships among, 200
White, M. H., 225
White fragility, 156–157, 160
White guilt and shame, 157, 160
White men
    assumed competence of teachers who are, 214
    feelings of persecution in, 93
    prejudice-based murders by, 119–120
    response of, to threats against faculty, 80–82
White privilege, 151–162
    and access to self-care, 31, 38
    addressing, 10, 18, 51, 114, 151, 152–153, 156–157, 159–162, 167, 214–218, 249
    and admitting mistakes, 153–154, 157–158
    assumption of competence accompanying, 214
    beliefs in collective efficacy in response to, 109
    defensiveness in students possessing, 76, 111
    faculty reflection on, 154–158
    feelings of students when exploring, 18
    moving from reflection to action in addressing, 160–161
    need for tools to address, 161–162
    process of challenging, 159–160
    resources on, 162
    and stereotype threat, 62
    teaching about, 7, 9, 62, 64, 67, 75, 82, 94, 101, 105, 109, 124, 190, 211, 212, 214
White students
    complaints against professors by, 99
    with exposure to marginalized group members, 111–112
    and learning about privilege and prejudice, 18, 105, 110–111
    and marginalized students' expectations for instructors of color, 95
    and minimization of harm in discussions, 99–101
    mitigating resistance to new/challenging information for, 95–97
    "outsider" and "insider" status of, 93
    positionality of, 92, 101
    stereotypes of teachers among, 61
White women, response of, to threats against faculty, 80
Williams, W. M., 23
Williams, W. R., 217
Women
    deference and respect for men vs., 136
    disabled, 137
    disclosure of assault/harassment by, 172–173
    prejudice from peers for, 169
    stereotypes about, 133
    stereotype threat and performance of, 64
Women in teaching
    anonymous threats to, 77–80
    and stereotype threat, 65
    stereotype threat for, 60–62, 64
    student incivility/bullying toward, 75, 76, 81, 86
Wortham, J., 37

Y

Young people
    intergenerational contact for, 198–199. *See also* Intergenerational relationships and contact
    stereotypes about, 133, 197